Money and Credit

Money and Credit

A Sociological Approach

Bruce G. Carruthers
and
Laura Ariovich

polity

First published in 2010 by Polity Press

Polity Press
65 Bridge Street
Cambridge CB2 1UR, UK

Polity Press
350 Main Street
Malden, MA 02148, USA

ISBN-13: 978-0-7456-4391-5
ISBN-13: 978-0-7456-4392-2(pb)

A catalogue record for this book is available from the British Library.

Typeset in 11 on 13 pt Sabon
by Servis Filmsetting Ltd, Stockport, Cheshire
Printed and bound by MPG Books Group, UK

For further information on Polity, visit our website: www.politybooks.com

Contents

Figures

Acknowledgments

For able assistance with the preparation of this book, we would like to thank Ana Patricia Mancini, from the University of Buenos Aires, and Jeong-Chul Kim, from Northwestern University. We also give thanks to Sarah Babb for her thoughtful reading of the manuscript, and to an anonymous reviewer for helpful comments. Finally, we appreciate the support of Erik Kjeldgaard.

1

Introduction

The events of 2007 and 2008 demonstrated that modern financial systems, built on solid foundations of credit and supported by massive amounts of capital, can nevertheless be surprisingly fragile. A number of the biggest financial institutions in leading international centers like London and New York City came perilously close to complete collapse. Some institutions simply failed (Lehman Brothers), some had to be rescued through acquisition by another institution (viz., JPMorgan Chase's purchase of Bear Stearns, or Bank of America's purchase of Merrill Lynch), some were simply nationalized (Northern Rock in Britain), and others survived because the British or U.S. governments directly injected huge sums of money (e.g., Britain's bailout of the Royal Bank of Scotland, or the case of AIG in the U.S.). Assets on balance sheets which in 2006 had been highly rated by the credit rating agencies (Moody's, and Standard & Poor's) and which seemed so solid suddenly became suspect, and even "toxic." Banks, which are in the lending business, stopped lending, even to each other. As reported in the *Wall Street Journal* (January 26, 2009, p. A1), big U.S. banks were doing *less* lending, even after they had received billions in government funding intended to encourage *more* lending. Liquidity had disappeared.

In retrospect, some of the practices that led up to today's crisis seem obviously unsound. So-called "subprime mortgages" were intended for riskier borrowers whose financial status and credit history did not qualify them for regular home mortgages. Helping people to buy their own homes is a commendable goal, but given the greater risks involved with subprime lending, a couple of adjustments might have seemed prudent: determining with certainty the borrower's income and ability to service the loan; insisting on a larger down-payment, and so on. In fact, the U.S. subprime mortgage market grew dramatically between 2000 and 2007 but was filled with strange practices like NINA loans (short for "no income, no assets") and "liar's loans" (also known as "no doc" or "low doc" loans because there was little or no documentation), where the lender simply took at face value the borrower's claims about their income. If someone said they earned $100,000 annually, then that was good enough for the lender. Subprime loans were then "securitized," that is, bundled together into large pools and then sold off to investors. Increasingly, mortgage loan originators no longer "held" the loans they originated, and with securitization, the originator would suffer little if the loans went sour. A strange variety of exotic financial instruments were then built out of these securitized mortgage loans: CDOs, CMOs, MBSs, SIVs, and so on. The classic movie *It's a Wonderful Life* (directed by Frank Capra and starring Jimmy Stewart) presented a memorable picture of mortgage lending that is largely irrelevant today: financial institutions no longer just take deposits from local customers and then lend the money locally, holding thirty-year mortgages in their portfolios until the loan is fully repaid. But if "liar's loans" are bad ideas in retrospect, at the time they were made they seemed attractive to many borrowers and lenders. How could appearances have been so deceiving? How could things have deteriorated so quickly?

People have been stunned by the severity of the crisis and the speed with which it hit the economy, but many find it hard to reconcile the fact that even as banks, investment banks, and other financial institutions were performing poorly, their top managers were being enriched personally. The discrepancy between organizational performance and CEO compensation has produced outrage among ordinary citizens whose tax dollars have been used to bail out many financial institutions. Among scholars, it has raised again the issue of corporate governance and how to ensure that management serves shareholder interests (Bebchuk and Fried 2004). During the 1990s, many economists and management consultants argued that the solution to the problem of corporate governance lay in the compensation system for CEOs: stock options and performance-based bonuses would supposedly ensure that the interests of top management were aligned with those of shareholders. Sadly, we have learned that it isn't that simple.

Today's crisis is among the worst in a recent series of impressive American financial debacles. Within recent memory, the savings-and-loan crisis of the 1980s, the collapse of Long Term Capital Management (a hedge fund whose partners included two Nobel Prize-winning financial economists), and the Enron bankruptcy would surely be among the best known. Although each episode had its own unique features, they were all very costly to taxpayers, shareholders, investors, and employees, and demonstrated that creditworthiness, the appearance of unimpeachable economic solidity, is ephemeral. Credit is a fickle thing, and economic value can seemingly turn into worthless vapor overnight.

If economic value is trickier than we thought (or at least much less stable), it does seem pretty obvious how to go about measuring it. As with other measurement problems, one begins with a unit of measure. To measure length, people use a ruler to indicate feet, inches, or meters. In this instance, we use some monetary unit to measure value: dollars and cents, pounds, euros, yen, pesos, shekels, dinars, won, francs, baht, and so on. Then, once the appropriate metric is selected (dollars in the U.S., euros in Germany, etc.), the value of something is indicated by its market price. An object is worth what it costs to purchase it, measured in money.

This simple recipe for measuring value seems straightforward, but it conceals a lot of complications. To begin, some extremely valuable things don't have a price because they are not bought or sold. Sacred objects, heirlooms, and other "priceless" objects have meaning and value that cannot be calculated in monetary terms. And if you attempt to attach such a value, someone is bound to become very, very upset (try getting a parent to say how much a child is worth, in dollars and cents).

Introduction

Sometimes the monetary sum that is attached to an object or relationship is essentially made up, negotiated, or stipulated. Although it looks like a price, it doesn't reflect an actual arm's-length market transaction. Examples of this would include the "transfer prices" that large corporations use to account for their own internal transactions, or the sum that a court of law sets as compensation in a wrongful death lawsuit, or the monetary gift that parents make to their married children to help them purchase their first home, or the *wergeld* ("blood money") paid to avoid a feud or vendetta. In today's financial crisis, it also seems that some of the monetary values attached to bank assets were "made up" in the sense that their true value is quite mysterious and that giving them a specific dollar value creates a misleading appearance of accuracy. It is these assets of indeterminate value that are now deemed so "toxic" and which weigh down bank balance sheets.

Monetary prices are sometimes seen from the perspective of "fairness": it isn't just that prices are low or high depending on "natural" market forces, for in addition they are sometimes perceived as fair or unfair. For example, employees compare themselves to their peers to see if their compensation seems fair; they also compare their raises with those of their superiors (so if a corporate CEO gets a 100% increase while employees get only 5% raises, the employees may feel that they have been treated unfairly). Certainly many taxpayers have been outraged by the large bonuses paid to American investment bankers whose firms have lost billions of dollars (and required massive public bailouts). The enrichment of incompetence seems just wrong. A retailer who takes advantage of a temporary shortage by jacking up his prices will be accused of "price gouging" and suffer from ill-will and bad publicity. Similarly, buyers who take advantage of desperate sellers by offering very low prices (so-called "fire sale prices") may also be accused of unfairness.

Finally, people put money into different categories and then treat it differently (even though it is "just money"). Behavioral economists call this process "mental accounting" (Thaler 1999). Even though $10,000 of earned income is indistinguishable from $10,000 won through a lottery, people perceive the winnings as special money and use it very differently than their ordinary earnings. Or suppose that someone's monetary compensation for work comes in two parts: salary and bonus. The bonus portion is "extra" and deemed "special," even though strictly speaking the money is indistinguishable. Money generated from an illicit activity is considered "dirty money," and people treat it in a distinctive manner. Within traditional families, money earned by wives was regarded as somehow "less valuable" than the money earned by the husband. Such differences remind us that money has symbolic as well as material value (Mickel and Barron 2008).

The uneven availability of credit and the unequal distribution of money (as income or wealth) are important political issues in the contemporary U.S. Why do some workers earn less than others? Has economic inequality increased? And so on. But money *per se* is not particularly controversial. Ordinary people treat money like a fact of nature: it just is. However, this taken-for-granted status wasn't always the case. In fact, the value of money was a very salient issue in American politics after the Civil War and before World War I. William Jennings Bryan's famous "Cross of Gold" speech, decrying the gold standard, resonated with many American voters even though he lost to William McKinley in the presidential election of 1896. For several decades after the Civil War, Americans argued over the gold standard, and whether the U.S. money supply should be based on gold, or on silver and gold, or on fiat money. Greenbackers argued with bullionists, "soft money" advocates took issue with their "hard money" opponents, and "free silver" supporters weighed in as well. The debate raged until the U.S. came down firmly on the side of the gold standard in 1900.

Money is no longer a "hot button" political issue, but credit and finance have returned to the U.S. political agenda because of the current financial crisis. And finance has remained a religious issue for some, particularly the devout adherents of the world religions that came out of the Middle East. Christianity, Judaism, and Islam all prohibited usury, or the payment of interest for a loan. Over the centuries, that prohibition has been relaxed or circumvented in Western countries, but it remains active in the Arab Middle East.

Given how much money has flowed into Islamic countries over the last several decades (because of oil exports), Islamic banking has become quite an active financial arena.

Even though ordinary people mostly take money for granted, their latent feelings can surface when money is threatened. One appreciates just how deeply people care about their own currency by recalling the controversies in Europe over the replacement of various national currencies (the beloved franc, guilder, pound, and lira) by the euro. It may have made perfect economic sense to create a single currency for Europe, but a national currency remains a powerful political symbol that some Europeans were reluctant to relinquish. It is also clear, from the historical record, that periods of hyperinflation (when the value of currency declines precipitously) can devastate a market economy and lead to political turmoil (e.g., Zimbabwe in 2008, Yugoslavia in the early 1990s, Hungary right after World War II, Germany in the early 1920s). Money isn't an apolitical matter, even though monetary politics come visibly to the surface only once in a while.

What is Money?

Money is a generalized, legitimate claim on value (Carruthers 2005: 355). This means that: (1) money *grants access* to valuable things – people can use it to acquire goods and services – money is a form of power; (2) the access that money makes possible is *legitimate* (i.e., it seems proper to acquire things by purchasing them, unlike the illegitimate ways in which people sometimes acquire things, such as theft or plunder); and (3) money is a *generalized* claim (it can be used generally to obtain all kinds of goods and services). Geoffrey Ingham, a sociologist who has studied money a good deal, simply states that money is "a social relation" (Ingham 2004: 12). In particular, money is constituted through the social relations between creditors and debtors (Ingham 2004: 72; 2008: 69, 74). Economists prefer to give a more functional definition in which money is what money does: it functions as a store of value, medium of exchange, and unit of account. Money is used to store value over time (perhaps in a vault or a mattress), it can be used in market exchange, and it is applied in various settings as a unit of measurement.

Under any of these definitions, it is clear that many things can serve as money. And indeed, across different eras and societies, many things have served as money, including pieces of paper, precious metals like gold and silver, not-so-precious metals like copper and brass, vodka, stringed beads, cigarettes, private debts, accounting entries, and so on. This is one reason why money is such an interesting topic: mostly we take it for granted as a self-evident feature of everyday life, and yet because it can vary in such weird ways, it warrants closer scrutiny. How is it possible that all these things can serve as money?

The substance of money has certainly changed over time. Early forms of money consisted of tangible objects of value: gold and silver in Western Europe, cowry shells in sub-Saharan Africa. Later on, representational forms began to function as money. Paper notes were invented first in China and later used in Western Europe (Goody 2004: 107). As fully developed by banks issuing convertible notes in a fractional reserve system, paper money represented tangible objects of value because the note holder could, in principle, go to the issuing bank and redeem the note for its equivalent in gold bullion. The paper note represented the gold in the bank vault, even if the note holder never actually took the gold out of the vault. Today, most people's money is in the form of a checking or savings account, and if they need cash, they simply visit an ATM (or if they are feeling old-fashioned, go to a bank teller). This means that rather than having any kind of physical object, whether representational or not, the money people possess mostly consists of electronic accounting entries maintained in their bank's computer system. Money has been physically reduced. Payment of $1 billion is a mighty chore if it means hauling sacks of gold, and it is still a physical challenge when moving stacks of $100 bills (over ten tons of currency), but it is trivial if all that needs to be done is to enter some key strokes on a computer. Money has become disembodied and virtual, and can now move around the globe in large amounts and at the speed of light.

Money and Credit

Ordinarily, money is used to buy things, and so money and market exchange are closely connected. But money and credit are equally close. For example, even when people don't have cash, they can still proceed with a purchase on credit. Either the seller extends credit directly to the buyer, or some third party lends money to the buyer so that they can buy the goods (as we will see in chapter 4, credit is an important marketing tool for sellers). In the first case, the seller lets the buyer take possession of the good, but the buyer promises to pay the money owed within a certain time period (perhaps thirty days, or ninety days, or a year). Deferred payment is a very common form of credit. In the second case, a lender gives a sum of money to a borrower (who promises to repay within a certain time, depending on the terms of the loan) and the borrower then uses that money to make a purchase (e.g., a bank lends money to an individual so they can buy a home). In either case, credit involves a promise. And the willingness of lenders to extend credit depends on the credibility of the borrower's promise. Does the lender trust the borrower?

One of the most interesting economic changes over the last two centuries concerns this simple question: when do lenders trust borrowers? The vitality of the economy rests on the answer because so many transactions now depend on credit. In fact, we live in a "credit economy." If lenders do not trust borrowers, then lending ceases and the wheels of commerce grind to a halt. But trust is a tricky matter because lenders who trust no-one never lend, and lenders who trust everyone lose their money. So the goal for lenders is to trust the trustworthy, and distrust the untrustworthy. And it can be very difficult to tell the difference between these two groups, especially when borrowers, whether they are trustworthy or not, try to appear trustworthy to lenders.

Lenders have evaluated the trustworthiness of borrowers in different ways. For most of history, this evaluation fundamentally depended upon networks of social relationships. People who were part of the same social circle, or who were members of the same community or kinship group, knew a lot about each other and so were better able to trust one another. They could also more easily sanction someone who betrayed that trust. Seldom did people lend to strangers. So, as we will see in later chapters, U.S. banks in the early nineteenth century often loaned money to people who were "connected" to the bank in one way or another: borrowers were friends of someone on the board of directors, or related to someone on the board, or had a similar connection. Direct knowledge of a person, or knowledge of their reputation within a community, allowed lenders to assess the personal character of the borrower and decide if that person were trustworthy enough. Historians have acknowledged the importance of social ties for access to credit in the past (Earle 1989; Hancock 1995; Lamoreaux 1994; Muldrew 1998), but today social connections still make a difference for business lending (Uzzi 1999). On the personal side, if someone today needs serious help, they are most likely to get a loan from a family member (Furnham and Argyle 1998: 190).

Starting in the middle of the nineteenth century, however, evaluations of trustworthiness began to change. The shift started in the wholesale sector and concerned trade credit. As the U.S. economy became a truly national economy, dry-goods suppliers based in New York City were increasingly shipping their wares to other parts of the country, without having much, or even any, personal knowledge of their customers. Suppliers typically shipped goods to their customers and received payment in one or two months' time, and so in effect they extended credit over that period. So suppliers had to figure out who was trustworthy. If they extended credit to everyone who wanted it, they would lose money, but if they gave credit to no-one, they wouldn't have any customers. And as trade expanded out of the immediate geographical region (in part thanks to an improving transportation system), suppliers couldn't rely on their social networks to help them. But help was on the way in the form of credit rating agencies, which gathered information about businesses all over the country, kept detailed files, constructed credit assessments, and then sold their assessments to customers who wanted to know whom they could trust.

Credit rating agencies, the precursors of today's Dun &

Bradstreet, grew rapidly and by the end of the nineteenth century were rating over a million firms nationwide. They even expanded overseas. The information they developed for assessing credit-worthiness was impressive enough to be used at the end of the nineteenth century by commercial banks, as they established their own credit departments, and insurance companies, as they estimated the risks associated with credit insurance. When the bond rating agencies (the predecessors of today's Moody's and Standard & Poor's) began to rate railway bonds, and later corporate bonds, in the early twentieth century, they adopted the same basic idea. And later in the twentieth century, firms began to issue credit scores for individual consumers (consider the now ubiquitous FICO score[1]). As anyone who has applied for credit knows, these scores are highly consequential. In fact, they are so important that some firms will help consumers "repair" their damaged credit scores (for a fee, of course). Without a high FICO score, it is more difficult and expensive for an individual to borrow. Insurance companies have even started to use FICO scores to price the products they sell to consumers (a low FICO score can mean higher automobile insurance premiums). In many different ways, creditors at all levels have shifted away from using social networks and personal connections when they assess the creditworthiness of debtors, and increasingly rely on impersonal, quantitative evaluations generated on the basis of large-scale data sets.

The methods and institutions developed in the Anglo-American world to allocate credit faced new challenges when other parts of the world adopted market economies. Guseva (2008) shows how the credit card industry has grown in post-communist Russia. A number of the techniques successfully used to encourage the widespread adoption of credit cards in the U.S. during the 1960s simply do not work, and so card companies have had to figure out other ways to determine who in the new Russia is creditworthy. Transplanting financial institutions from one country to another is not a trivial task, even when the basic problem (whom can you trust?) is essentially the same.

Another very important historical change concerns financial and monetary regulation. Governments have always played a central role in the creation of money, from issuance of gold coins at the royal mint to printing Federal Reserve bank notes. Governments often helped to establish financial markets, like stock exchanges, when they had to borrow on a large scale (Carruthers 1996; Ferguson 2001). Government has also played a changing role in the regulation of commercial banks, investment banks, credit unions, savings-and-loans, and other financial institutions, and in oversight of financial contracts (to protect borrowers from usurious or predatory lenders, to ensure that pension funds and insurance companies invest prudently, etc.). The level of public scrutiny over the financial system has waxed and waned, and hasn't gone in any one simple direction. Even when the financial sector goes through a period of sustained deregulation (such as happened in the U.S. during the 1980s and 1990s), the state still plays a role. And since economic crisis often motivates further change in regulation, it seems likely that before the U.S. has fully recovered from the current recession, there will be some federal re-regulation of the financial sector. After all, the Great Depression of the 1930s resulted in a lot of new public regulation and oversight in the form of the Securities and Exchange Commission (SEC), the Federal Deposit Insurance Corporation (FDIC), the Federal Savings and Loan Insurance Corporation (FSLIC), and the Federal Housing Administration (FHA). Many of these institutional innovations were the centerpieces of public policy intended to support particular kinds of credit. Indeed, it is important to remember that the aim of many regulatory interventions was not to extinguish or curtail market activity – quite the contrary – the aim was to encourage it. For instance, the goal of "Fannie Mae" (the Federal National Mortgage Association, founded in 1938) was to increase mortgage lending so people could purchase homes – a process that was encouraged by regulation.

Ideas about Money

One of the interesting things about money as a social institution is that because it is so old (if one starts from its original form as coinage in the seventh century B.C.), a lot of very smart people have had the chance to think about money, what it is, and what it means. Some of their ideas have been extremely influential. The philosopher Aristotle, for example, thought about money in ancient Greece but still had a huge impact during the Middle Ages when Western scholars rediscovered his writings at roughly the same time as the European economy was becoming monetarized again (Kaye 1998; Spufford 2003). Aristotle's concept of money helped to justify and bolster the Church's prohibition of usury because he deemed interest on a loan to be unnatural: "For money was intended to be used in exchange, but not to increase at interest. And this term interest, which means the birth of money from money, is applied to the breeding of money because the offspring resembles the parent. That is why of all modes of getting wealth this is the most unnatural" (Aristotle 1984: 1997). For many centuries, bankers and other lenders had to work around religious and secular rules about usury.

Adam Smith's ideas about money were pretty straightforward. For him, in the late eighteenth century, money was the "great wheel of circulation" (Smith 1976: 309) and its primary purpose was to facilitate market exchange. As the division of labor advanced, specialization allowed people to increase productivity, but they had to exchange goods with each other in order to obtain all they needed or wanted. Yet, barter doesn't work unless each person has exactly what the other one wants. So people invented money (according to Smith), and based it on a commodity that had certain attractive features: precious metal is easily divisible and retains its value. That way, instead of having to find a partner for barter, people could simply exchange their goods for money. And money's value and uniformity become even more reliable when a political authority provided a seal of approval (Smith 1976: 26–9). This meant that kings, princes, and emperors would issue from their mint standardized pieces of precious metal, stamped with a seal to certify the weight and purity (and hence value) of the coin. Unfortunately, sovereigns have often been tempted, said Smith, to dilute the purity of their coinage in order to raise their own revenues. This led to price inflation as the value of money diminished.

As to the source of value that underlay commodity money, Smith was a proponent of the "labor theory of value," according to which the value of a commodity (in this case, gold or silver) was determined by the amount of labor necessary to produce it.

Writing in the early decades of the twentieth century during the era of the international gold standard, the sociologist Max Weber put collective expectations at the center of his discussion of money. People will accept something as a medium of exchange if they believe that others will also accept it as such (Weber 1978: 75). In other words, what really sustains money's effectiveness in market exchange are people's beliefs about other people's beliefs: if everyone thinks everyone else will accept money, then everyone will accept money. These beliefs can be bolstered through legal sanctions, as when the law gives money the status of "legal tender," and makes it eligible for the payment of taxes. Beliefs can also be reinforced if the medium has independent value (because, for example, monetary tokens are made out of precious metal). But Weber's key idea is that money functions when people have congruent expectations, and that although use of gold and silver can help coordinate such expectations, they are not strictly necessary. People can form similarly congruent expectations about salt, or paper, or shells, or any of the other media that have functioned as money. One primary way to boost those expectations is for the state to allow citizens to use a particular medium to meet their tax obligations. Indeed, according to one argument (the Chartalist approach), imposing taxes is how governments create money in the first place (Wray 1998).

The consequences of using money are also clear to Weber: money enhances calculability and rationality. By attaching precise quantitative values to objects and outcomes, economic decision-making became an exercise in calculation (Weber 1978: 81, 86). And using methods like double-entry bookkeeping, firms could determine exactly how well (or poorly) their past decisions had turned out. Weber's insights about the significance of quantification have been explored further by sociologists interested in how cost–benefit analysis affects public policy decision-making (Espeland 1998; Espeland and Stevens 1998). Starting in the early twentieth century, decision-makers in two U.S. government bureaus, the Army Corps of Engineers and the Bureau of Reclamation in the Department of the Interior, began to make decisions about civil engineering projects using a formal method in which all the costs and all the benefits associated with a policy option were deliberately estimated, in dollar terms, and then options that maximized net benefits were chosen (Porter 1995). What makes cost–benefit analysis particularly challenging is the fact that many policy outcomes do not have market prices. They are frequently hard to value with any precision. In some cases, cost–benefit methods have been stymied by sacred objects whose value cannot be properly rendered in monetary terms (e.g., how to calculate the "cost" of a dam that will flood the ancestral lands of a Native American tribe). Despite such obstacles, cost–benefit analysis has become a mainstay of federal policymaking in the U.S.

Beyond cost–benefit analysis, it is clear that money adds a quantitative dimension to social life. Where money intrudes, precise calculation becomes a possibility. Sometimes that calculability is welcome, as when people sit down and construct a detailed family budget so they can cut their household spending and get through economic tough times, or see if college for their children is still affordable. But sometimes calculability is inappropriate. For example, in our society, people who purchase an item to give as a birthday gift are careful to remove the price tag, even when it is obvious that the gift was purchased; it is problematic to suggest to the recipient that, to the giver, they are "worth" exactly the cost of the gift. In other social settings, however, the explicit precision of money is tolerable, as in the "dollar dance" ritual that sometimes happens at weddings (male guests make a monetary contribution to the newly married couple by "paying" for the honor of dancing with the bride, and female guests do the same to dance with the groom). This practice is common among the Mexican and South Asian immigrant communities in the U.S. today.

One of the recurrent ideas about money is its association with social transformation. Sometimes money is considered only a symptom of change, but often it is regarded as an independent force that acts on society, and even endangers it. This fear certainly animated medieval scholars when they thought about the corrupting influence of money, and tried to reconcile an increasingly monetarized economy with the immorality of profit-seeking and usury (Kaye 1998: 39; Le Goff 1988). The introduction of money seemed to threaten to overturn existing social relations and reorder society. Many centuries later a similar idea formed part of Karl Marx's critique of capitalist society. Under capitalism, the imperative to maximize profits was so strong, and the hegemony of the marketplace so overwhelming, that human interaction became dominated by the one-dimensional "cash nexus" (Ingham 2008: 65; Marx 1978: 475). Religious sentiment, familial affection, status recognition, and feudal honor alike were swamped by individual self-interest. Weber also recognized money's central role in the rationalization of economic life. Since he regarded rationalization with considerable ambivalence, this was not altogether a good thing. This connection between money and rationalization was further explored by Georg Simmel, a contemporary of Weber, who devoted an entire volume to the study of money (Simmel 1978).

In addition to being considered by a mixture of philosophers, economists, and sociologists, the transformative potential of money has on occasion been wielded deliberately and practically. European colonial authorities in nineteenth-century sub-Saharan Africa were eager to obtain a labor force for the extractive industry they were trying to establish (e.g., gold, copper, and diamond mines). It was almost impossible to get European workers to move to the tropics for such dangerous jobs, so the authorities coerced the indigenous African population by imposing a tax payable in cash only. Subsistence farmers and nomadic people didn't have ready access to cash, and the colonial government wouldn't accept in-kind payment, so people had to earn the cash as wage laborers (Falola 1995; Shipton 1989). Money, in the form of mandatory taxes, was used to turn native Africans into mineworkers. Looking to the future, some environmental policy proposals currently under consideration involve attaching monetary values to the environmental impacts of various economic activities. The imposition of "carbon taxes," for example, would make some types of production more expensive and hence, it is argued, would discourage them, leading to a decline in overall carbon emissions.

More than other scholars, anthropologists have confronted the full variety of money. Economists and sociologists are mostly familiar with modern money, and historians have learned about money in the Western historical tradition, but anthropologists have studied societies where money looks very different. This has forced them to confront some of the assumptions we ordinarily make about money. For example, contemporary money can be used to purchase anything that is available for sale: money is generalized purchasing power. The anthropologist Paul Bohannan, by contrast, studied the Tiv, an ethno-linguistic group based in what is now Nigeria, and learned about separate "spheres of exchange" in Tiv society (Bohannan 1955). Exchanges occurred within spheres but not between them, and this kind of separation made it impossible for anything to fulfill the role of generalized money. Bohannan's finding is not just a piece of anthropological exotica, however, for it calls our attention to the way in which exchanges (and the money that facilitates them) are also restricted in contemporary society. Indeed, anthropologist Jane Guyer (1995: 2) reminds us that just as so-called "primitive money" was more complicated than people originally thought, "modern" money isn't always so modern. Although formally and legally modern money is uniform and generalized, in many ways people work to restrict and constrain its generalizability.

Recent sociological interest in money was boosted by Viviana Zelizer, whose 1994 book helped to rejuvenate the topic by challenging the image of money as an instrument of unilateral social change. In her study of nineteenth- and twentieth-century American households, she noted how much families took modern money and "socialized" it: giving money social meaning and introducing significant distinctions where legally there were none. Some of these social meanings articulated closely with gender roles within the family, so that mothers – who were not the traditional breadwinners within the family – would have their own special "pin money." In a number of different ways, people gave meaning to money by creating categories and distinctions. They turned general money into special money, and informally created their own spheres of exchange.

Institutions and Networks

To study money and credit is to explore a landscape dotted with institutions, organizations, and networks. Individual persons also inhabit this landscape, to be sure, but it would be a mistake to view money and credit as only involving individuals who made autonomous decisions. Both money and credit are deeply social. The relevant institutions and organizations include lenders (banks, credit unions, insurance companies, and pawnshops), borrowers (corporations, universities), regulators, and monetary authorities (e.g., mints, treasury departments, central banks, financial regulatory agencies); they are both formal and informal (e.g., rotating credit associations), and operate at both the national and international levels (e.g., the International Monetary Fund and World Bank). Institutions agglomerate and organize the actions of individuals, shaping what persons see and do, but also acting on their own behalf and deploying their own resources (Campbell 2004: 1). Institutions have a durability and logic of their own. The emergence and growth of the corporate form during the nineteenth century meant that modern economies have now become dominated by large, private organizations. The growth of the state similarly meant that governance and regulatory oversight involves large public organizations. For money and credit, the legal system is a uniquely important institution. Most lending and borrowing takes place through a legal contract between debtor and creditor. Creditors do not simply take debtors' verbal assurances at face value, but insist on a binding formal agreement, enforceable by law. Debt contracts stipulate the basic terms of the loan (amount, payment schedule, interest rate, penalties), but they can also attach a variety of strings (known as "covenants") to the money the lender extends to the borrower. These may specify, for example, that the loan can only be used for particular purposes, that the borrower cannot take on additional debts, that repayment of the loan will be accelerated if the borrower gets into financial trouble, or that some asset of the debtor will serve as collateral for the loan. Legal rules can also make debts "negotiable" (as in "negotiable securities"), which can give them money-like qualities. Without a reliable legal system to enforce loan contracts, many lenders would be extremely reluctant to lend. The law also matters since the "legal tender" quality bestowed on money is quite obviously a legal status. Particular pieces of paper with strange images and symbols printed on them have the status of money because the law says they do. And these pieces of paper can be used to satisfy all debts, public and private.

Networks concern the pattern of connections among individuals and institutions. People, for instance, do not live their lives as isolated monads. Rather, they are embedded in ongoing networks of relationships. Some social networks are pre-determined (e.g., people inherit a kinship network by virtue of the family they are born into), while others are formed through constrained choices (people select new friends, but their choices are shaped by where they live and work) or no choice at all (college students often become friends with the roommate the housing office assigned to them). Social networks shape what people do, how they perceive their own identities and interests, what resources and information they have access to, the obligations they are encumbered with, and so on. Among other things, MacKenzie's (2006) fascinating study of the invention and spread of option pricing models illustrates the importance of networks for the operation of modern financial markets. Sassen (2005) also reminds us that global financial markets are usually located in very small and particular places (lower Manhattan in New York City, or the City in London) and hence involve many overlapping social networks and communities.

There are many features of networks that are worth studying: density, structure, centrality (Wasserman and Faust 1994). Similarly, the character of the ties that knit together networks is also important: whether they are weak ties or strong ties, formal or informal, direct or indirect. For instance, weak ties are often most useful for gathering information, whereas strong ties frequently provide tangible resources. Some distinctive network structures have been found in a wide variety of settings (e.g., the "small worlds" networks discussed by Watts 1999). The main point to remember, however, is that networks affect lending and borrowing.

Organizations are themselves embedded in networks. Organizations transact with each other, form cooperative alliances, become members in groups, buy, sell, and merge with each other, and exchange personnel. One of the most studied organizational networks is formed by board interlocks, links between corporations that are established when an individual sits on two boards of directors (Mizruchi 1996). For example, if a bank president also sits on the board of a manufacturing firm, the bank and the firm have a board interlock. Mintz and Schwartz (1985) examined the network of board interlocks for U.S. firms in the mid-1960s and found that a small number of large banks occupied the center of the network. They concluded that, by virtue of their position in the corporate network, financial institutions played an especially important role in shaping the choices of non-financial firms. Other scholars have noted that corporate innovations diffuse through the networks that interlocks constitute (e.g., the "poison pill" defense, see Davis 1991), and that firms use their networks when deciding whom to partner with in strategic alliances (Gulati 1998). The connectedness of corporate boards, and their sensitivity to what each other is doing, may be one reason why we often witness corporate behavior that seems to reflect a "herd mentality." But what drives such behavior are social networks, not collective mental states.

The flow of personnel between organizations is yet another way in which distinctive and consequential networks are formed (Etzion and Davis 2008). Bandelj (2008) shows how social networks influenced the flow of foreign direct investment (FDI)[2] into the post-socialist countries of Eastern and Central Europe. A firm's prior experience and connections with a country often served as a foundation for additional investment, and even indirect connections had an effect. In the chapters below, we will see that organizations, institutions, and networks matter in a variety of ways. They are threads that run throughout the history and development of money and credit.

Outline of the Book

Money and credit are huge topics, and the complexities of today's monetary systems and financial crises would take volumes to analyze. So of necessity we will be selective in what we discuss. In chapter 2, we consider the history of money. Money has evolved over time in ways that give insight into its origins, limits, purposes, and consequences. Monetary history, it turns out, is also political, diplomatic, social, and economic history, and reaches from the personal level to the national and then to the international level. The "globalized" economy of the late nineteenth century, for example, was underpinned by the international gold standard, and after World War II institutions like the International Monetary Fund and the World Bank were established to help rebuild international trade and investment. But there are also examples of informal currencies that local communities devise for a variety of reasons (e.g., "Ithaca dollars"), including the failure of the state to establish a national currency (as was the case for Russia during the 1990s). In chapter 3, we discuss the social meaning of money and underscore that it is not simply an economic device used for exchange and measurement. People use money in a variety of ways that also give it social significance. These uses and meanings vary from society to society, and from group to group, but the symbolic power of money is undeniable. It is important to appreciate that sometimes money isn't just about purchasing power, it is primarily about status, or social power, or social values.

In chapter 4 we switch from money to credit, and examine credit for individuals. We live in a consumer society, and much personal consumption is done increasingly on credit: rather than save first so we can spend later, we borrow to spend now, and repay later. Credit substitutes for money as a type of purchasing power. The U.S. household saving rate has been in decline for many decades, going from about 10% in 1980 to less than 1% in 2006 (Dynan and Kohn 2007). From a nation of savers, we have become a nation of borrowers, and being in debt is no longer anything to be ashamed of (Calder 1999). As debts have grown, so has the cost of repaying them, and according to the Federal Reserve, in 2004 the median family used about 18% of its income for debt service (Bucks et al. 2006: A34). In short, U.S. families have increasingly borrowed a lot in order to support their lifestyle, and conversely someone has loaned U.S. families a lot. This high level of indebtedness has unfortunately made many Americans quite vulnerable to unexpected shocks like unemployment, divorce, or health-related expenses. Chapter 4 also examines how individuals became so deeply embedded in credit networks, and looks at the different forms of consumer debt (e.g., home mortgages, credit cards, unsecured loans). It deals with the fact that some people rely on *informal* credit institutions, rather than on banks, credit unions, or other *formal* organizations, in order to borrow.

Chapter 5 remains focused on credit but switches from individuals to firms. How much do firms need to borrow, and when they borrow, how do they raise money? Sometimes they borrow from their bank, or borrow by floating bonds, and sometimes they issue additional shares (equity). Corporations raise money in quite different ways depending on what country they are based in, and their size and maturity. As of early 2009, Microsoft had no long-term debt because it was able to raise money through retained earnings and new stock issues, whereas pre-bankruptcy General Motors, a much older (and deeply troubled) firm, had about $38 billion in long-term debt. When small businesses borrow, they may take out a loan from their local bank, depend on their suppliers to buy on credit, or even rely on the personal credit cards of the owner. We will see that firms, like individuals, seek credit in a variety of forms. And their ability to borrow depends not only on their relations to their bank, but also on what rating agencies like Moody's and Standard & Poor's say about their creditworthiness. Corporate finance is heavily regulated, especially for firms that are publicly traded (e.g., whose shares are traded on the New York Stock Exchange), and so reflects the imperatives of public policy as well as the funding needs of the business community. In securing resources in all these ways, firms are being entrusted with other people's money, and this always raises questions about corporate governance.

Overall, money and credit are topics whose complexity and social embeddedness make them ripe for sociological analysis. In examining how these work, both today and in the past, we will deploy a number of sociological concepts and use them in making sense of what is going on. In today's economic crisis, it is a good time for sociologists to be looking at the business pages of the newspaper.

2

A Brief History of Money

Money has a long history. Although it comes in many different forms (cowry shells, salt, iron bars, printed paper, barley, and precious metals), money in some fashion has been a part of human society for thousands of years. Cowry shells, which came from the Maldives Islands in the Indian Ocean, dominated trade in Africa and parts of Asia for many centuries (Vogel and Hieronymus 1993). In the West, coins date back at least to the seventh century B.C. in Lydia (now western Turkey), and in China and Mesopotamia coins date back even earlier (Powell 1996). Gold, silver, copper, and bronze coins have survived from previous centuries and can be quite revealing about the economy of the past. They is because of how money connected to the rest of social life. To give one example, money is related to political sovereignty. Within a given community (nation, empire, city-state, etc.), one of the classic prerogatives of the ruler was to issue money. And as a token of their political power, rulers often put their portraits on the coin. Old coins can therefore tell us about who ruled in a particular place at a particular time, and so the succession of coins reflects the succession of political leaders. Currency maps out political history. In addition, coins give evidence of social contact. If Byzantine currency is found in a Viking hoard in rural Denmark, it suggests that some contact occurred between Vikings and the Byzantine Empire. The movement of coinage over long distances reflects trade, tribute, and plunder, and maps out a pattern of far-flung social contacts.

In this chapter, we examine money from a historical perspective. History offers useful insights because of how money has varied over time, and because of the changing connections between money, economy, and society. In the U.S. today, absent hyperinflation or a complete meltdown of the monetary system, we take our money for granted and generally fail to appreciate what a remarkable social achievement an effective monetary system is. Contemporary U.S. currency enjoys a high degree of uniformity and homogeneity. Past experience, however, demonstrates that monetary systems can fail as well as succeed – failure forces people to revert to barter or in-kind exchange and makes it much harder to engage in the complex intertemporal transactions that are now a commonplace. Furthermore, economic exchange in the past frequently involved a range of monies and near-monies whose heterogeneity stood in marked contrast to the uniformity of modern currency.

Numismatists study old coins, and can appreciate the difference between a solidus, siglos, drachma, karshapana, dinar, denarius, sestertius, doubloon, tetradrachm, stater, daric, dirhem, pistole, and obol. Such coins came in varying denominations and were made out of copper, bronze, silver, or gold. Coins of greater value were made out of more valuable metals (gold rather than copper) or were of larger size (and so contained more precious metal). They were also marked by conventional symbols that served to identify their value and place of issue. A Roman citizen at the time of Julius Caesar would certainly have recognized a denarius, while a merchant living at the same time in the Magadha kingdom, in what later became India, knew a karshapana. Money provided a daily reminder of political sovereignty. In fact, the issuance of currency was one of the traditional prerogatives of rulership, and the right of seignorage was a valuable source of revenue (Wood 2002: 100). Military victory of one sovereign over another, or capture of new territory, was an occasion to affirm the status of the king by coining new money (Howgego 1992: 4; Spufford 1988: 12–14; Verhulst 2002: 129). Money was recognizable within political communities and made it easier for people to trade with each other. Trade between political entities was more complicated but still common, and so people were used to dealing with multiple currencies, both domestic and foreign. For example, evidence suggests that northern Italians in the ninth century were quite familiar with Arab coins because of numerous trade links across the Mediterranean (McCormick 2001: 323–6, 336).

People find money interesting not simply for practical reasons. Money has long been a recurrent topic for reflection and social analysis. Aristotle, for example, offered a complex analysis that proved to be influential long after his death, particularly when his ideas were appropriated by the Catholic Church during the Middle Ages. On the one hand, in his *Politics*, Aristotle stated that money was made out of materials possessing "intrinsic value," like gold, silver, or iron, and that its purpose was to effect exchange. The use of money to create more money, that is, lending for interest, was unnatural and therefore wrong (Aristotle 1984: 1997). In his *Ethics*, however, Aristotle also observed that money was a conventional measure of value, set by law (Aristotle 1984: 1788; Wood 2002: 71–4). Aristotle's critique of interest on loans helped to justify the Catholic Church's long-standing prohibition against usury (Hunt and Murray 1999: 70–1). Post-medieval economic and financial developments eventually made Aristotle less relevant, although one key tension in his work persisted: whether money was necessarily based on "intrinsic value" versus whether money was based on social convention or law.

Abstract ideas about money don't just come from famous philosophers. At a number of points in history, there was substantial popular commentary on money, its functions and its basis. For example, in England at the end of the seventeenth century (Valenze 2006: 27, 39), and in the U.S. after the Civil War (Carruthers and Babb 1996), many people participated in heated political debates about the nature of money and its relationship to "intrinsic worth." Both of these debates arose in situations where the existing monetary system had broken down. And even today, the growth of Islamic banking has posed anew the problem of how to reconcile modern financial institutions with a Koranic prohibition against usury (Kuran 2004; Warde 2000).

A monetary system based on precious metals worked reasonably well, although it meant that the money supply depended on the vagaries of the production and distribution of specie (Hunt and Murray 1999: 63). At times, production would be boosted by the discovery of a new source of metals, such as the silver mines in thirteenth-century Germany, which expanded the supply of silver (Wood 2002: 79). Dramatic expansion of the money supply, in turn, often led to higher prices and overall inflation. Distribution of coins, meanwhile, was subject to radical geographical shifts because of plunder, theft, or tribute, which meant that warfare could have extreme monetary consequences. The Crusades, for instance, were so expensive that they drained a large portion of the money supply out of Western Europe and into the Middle East. During the Middle Ages, moreover, the balance of long-distance trade consistently favored the East over the West: Western Europeans were eager to import textiles and spices from the Far East, but produced almost nothing for export (except slaves during the early Middle Ages; see Braudel 1979: 461–62; Verhulst 2002: 112). Thus, imports from the Far East had to be paid for in coin and so gold drained from West to East, gradually reducing the amount in European circulation (Spufford 1988: 18, 49). This was offset, however, with the discovery of new supplies of bullion in the conquest of the New World during the sixteenth century, which led to a steady flow from South America to Spain, from there to the rest of Europe, and then to the Far East. American silver and gold eventually ended up in Indian treasuries.

In the context of long-distance trade, where the problem of shipping specie was greatest, northern Italian merchants during the fifteenth century began to develop paper substitutes for coin, and their innovations spread to other parts of Western Europe. It was risky to transport precious metal over long distances (witness the ongoing predations against Spanish treasure ships traveling from the New World to Spain). Under some circumstances, bills of exchange and promissory notes[1] could function like money and, because they were written documents, were much easier to transport (Hunt and Murray 1999: 65; Spufford 1988: 255). Without intending to, the Italians who began to use these financial instruments initiated an important and long-term shift of money away from precious metal and towards paper that "represented" precious metal.

Some economic transactions were made in kind, and so didn't require either money or credit. Indeed, it was the shift from in-kind provision to payment with money that marked the growing monetarization of the ninth-century Carolingian economy (Verhulst 2002: 121). For example, the labor services that peasants owed their feudal lords were converted into cash payments, and more generally money came to mediate economic relationships. The availability of precious metal waxed and waned, but even when plentiful there was never enough hard money to accomplish all the market transactions that occurred in a society (see, e.g., Howgego [1992: 12–14] on Rome, Nightingale [1990] on medieval England, Earle [1989: 114–124] and Muldrew [2001] on early modern England, Parker [1973] and Braudel [1979: 439–440] on early modern Europe, Thorp [1991] and Priest [2001] on colonial America, and Balleisen [2001] on the antebellum U.S.). Many economic transactions necessarily relied on credit, and so money and credit were perpetually intertwined (Finn 2003; Muldrew 1998). Transactions with delayed payment meant that the seller would have to wait before receiving cash from the buyer, and in the meanwhile had to extend credit to cover the sale. Commercial agriculture in the U.S., for instance, involved an annual cycle in which, during spring, farmers would acquire seed and equipment on credit, and would repay what they owed after the fall harvest, when they were paid for their crops. Thanks to the credit that suppliers extended to farmers, very little cash needed to be exchanged. And finally, as we discuss below, when official money was too scarce, people sometimes devised their own informal monies. These did not have the sanction of the state, and strictly speaking were not legal tender, but within local regions or for small transactions, tokens or scrip could function like money (Muldrew 2001: 102).

In the early modern era, the money supply in Europe continued to depend largely on gold and silver. As noted above, the supplies of both were greatly expanded by Spanish conquests within the Americas and importation of precious metal (Vilar 1976: 76–83,

103–11). Long-distance payments, either international or domestic, were usually accomplished by use of paper instruments like bills of exchange, in-land bills of exchange, or promissory notes, but paper money did not yet operate on a large scale. Sovereigns occasionally abused their right of seignorage and reduced the amount of precious metal in the coins they minted in order to issue more coins (this was also called "debasing" the currency), but over the long term such action simply resulted in price inflation. Aside from mints, there was nothing akin to twentieth-century central banks, that is, publicly accountable institutions charged with management of the money supply. Government mints simply turned metal into coins, and banks functioned as private profit-seeking lenders: there was no conception of a "public interest" to govern the aggregate money supply or to inform public policy. Despite this lack of public accountability, money remained an institution closely linked to political sovereignty (Spruyt 1994).

Money in the U.S.

Each country has its own distinctive monetary history, but the U.S. in the early nineteenth century exemplified well some of the more important common features. To begin with, the domestic U.S. money supply was heterogeneous. There simply wasn't one uniform currency, and so English, French, and Spanish coins all circulated alongside domestic money (Martin 1977). Furthermore, even the domestic currency wasn't standardized because bank notes were issued by individual private American banks. Until 1913 there was no Federal Reserve System to issue notes, and before the Civil War only state-chartered banks had their own bank notes. Thus, although the nominal value of paper currency seemed uniform (a dollar was a dollar, after all), the real value of a bank note varied with the solvency and reputation of the issuing bank. The one-dollar note of a solvent and reputable bank would be treated as if it were really worth one dollar, whereas the notes of distant or troubled banks would be subject to a substantial discount. The supply of domestic notes was complicated even more by widespread counterfeiting (Mihm 2007). For many decades, the printing methods available to produce bank notes also made it relatively easy to counterfeit them. Sometimes it was unclear which was worth less: a high-quality counterfeit of a note issued by a solid bank, or a genuine bank note issued by a financially troubled bank. With so many different banks issuing their own notes, and with widespread counterfeiting, it was hard for ordinary people always to accept currency at "face value."

Another common feature reflected in the U.S. was the heavy reliance on credit (Mann 2002; Myers 1970: 13). Ordinary commercial transactions usually depended on "trade credit," meaning that a seller would supply goods to the buyer, and the latter would have some conventional period of time (ten, thirty, sixty days, etc.) in which to pay. For that period, the buyer was indebted to the seller. Ordinary firms needed credit to supply their working capital (Bodenhorn 2000: 94). In the rural areas of the country, farmers would obtain credit from their supplier or general store for a period of months not days, in order to accommodate the crop cycle. Trade credit was not supplied by banks, but by sellers, and so virtually all firms were embedded in a web of debtor–creditor relationships. Retailers offered credit to their regular customers, and on top of this, banks extended short-term credit to businesses (typically by accepting their IOUs, a written promise, or "I owe you"). The credit network encompassed almost all economic actors, and this meant that credit shocks starting in one location could soon be felt everywhere.

In the U.S. and many European countries, the nineteenth century was marked by the emergence of "territorial currency," that is, a distinctive and homogeneous money that would circulate within the physical boundaries of the nation-state (Helleiner 2003). In place of a mixture of currencies that flowed across national borders, a single currency would circulate within the country: pounds in England, francs in France, dollars in the U.S., and so on. Establishing territorial currencies helped to achieve a number of goals: it solidified a national identity by promulgating public symbols, it expanded and strengthened the domestic economy by reducing transaction costs and encouraging commerce, and it enhanced public revenues. Technological improvements in metal casting and paper printing made it possible to manufacture high-quality coins and notes on a mass scale. In the U.S., however, the establishment of a single currency was complicated by the fact that, although only the federal government was constitutionally empowered to coin money, much of the money supply during the ninteetnth century consisted of paper notes issued by private state-chartered banks (Hurst 1973: 134, 180). The federal structure of the American polity would frustrate efforts to standardize money.

After the Civil War, as noted above, the U.S. also went through one of those rare but telling historical episodes when money became a hot political issue. What followed the war was a widespread debate, extending over several decades, about the nature of money and value (Carruthers and Babb 1996). This national conversation was started by a crisis that unsettled antebellum monetary arrangements. At the outset of the Civil War, the Union government was forced to go off its *de facto* gold standard (officially both gold and silver served as the basis for money, but very little silver was in circulation). Until then, bank notes had been convertible into gold. In other words, private banks held gold in their vaults and issued bank notes on a fractional reserve basis. A holder of a bank note was legally entitled to go to the bank and claim the equivalent value in gold, although there wasn't enough gold to redeem all the outstanding notes (the reserve ratio of gold to notes was set by bank regulations). But so long as bank note holders were confident that they could redeem their notes whenever they wanted, they would not do so (for gold was awkward and bulky).[2] However, the outbreak of war led to a collapse in government revenues, rampant financial speculation, and hoarding (Unger 1964: 14–15). Private banks could not maintain convertibility and so they stopped exchanging notes for gold. Thereafter, the value of the U.S. dollar floated (it was no longer fixed in terms of gold), and as wartime expenses mounted and the U.S. government printed money to cover its deficit, the gold value of the dollar declined. The inconvertible dollars issued by the Union government to cover its deficit were called "greenbacks" and by statute they were legal tender (Nussbaum 1950: 45–6). This wasn't the first American experience with inconvertible money, however, since colonial-era state governments had also issued paper money to compensate for the lack of coin and specie. The earlier experience produced very mixed results, however (Priest 2001: 1311), and so whether and how to return to the gold standard became a very contentious question during the postbellum period.

As the war continued, the government raised taxes, but public revenues nevertheless failed to keep pace with expenses and so the Union government had to borrow heavily to fund its operations. It borrowed by issuing bonds, but the main problem was how to sell these. One measure involved developing new ways to retail government debt, and to sell bonds directly to individual investors (Bensel 1990: 245–57; Myers 1970: 161). Another solution was much more consequential for the money supply, and involved using newly chartered banks as a built-in market for government bonds. In his 1861 report, Treasury Secretary Salmon Chase proposed to establish a new system of nationally chartered banks that would issue paper currency backed by these bonds (Sharkey 1959: 29). At one stroke, this measure would standardize the domestic currency and create demand for government bonds (it also ensured that national banks would have a financial interest in the survival of the Union government). The National Banking Act of 1863 mandated the creation of nationally chartered banks that could issue their own bank notes up to 90% of the value of government bonds they placed on deposit with the Comptroller of the Currency. Subject to one set of chartering requirements, and backed by the same financial assets, national bank notes were much less variable in value than their antebellum predecessors, and the U.S. finally had something resembling uniform money (Friedman and Schwartz 1963: 21). To help make sure that national banks succeeded, the government also instituted a tax on the notes of state-chartered banks. The results must have gratified the architects of the National Banking System, for the number of state-chartered banks shrank from 1,579 to 261 between 1860 and 1870, while the number of national banks went from zero to 1,612 (James 1978: 25). The overall effect is apparent in figure 2.1, where the overall number and total assets of state banks dropped sharply during the Civil War and stayed low for a time afterwards.

Although national banks succeeded in bolstering Union government finances, they re-created some old problems and added a few new ones as well. In particular, they were very unevenly distributed across the country, and so the new bank notes were plentiful in some places and scarce in others. Regions in the West and South had suffered from a deficiency of paper money before the Civil War (Bodenhorn 2000: 63), and the new banking system simply reproduced that stark imbalance (Bensel 1990: 269, 274). Such disparities reinforced regional differences in interest rates (rates were lower in the Northeast than elsewhere). In addition, national banks were linked together through a network of accounts used to facilitate interbank clearances and earn interest on their reserves. Rural banks deposited their reserves with reserve city banks, and the latter deposited their reserves with central reserve city banks. Eventually, the funds "pyramided" in New York City, the nation's financial capital, where a substantial proportion were put out as "call loans" on the stock market.[3] This forged a strong connection

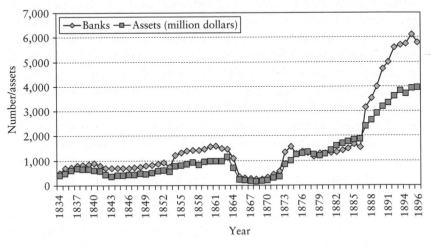

Data source: Historical Statistics of the United States, table Cj149-157

Figure 2.1 Number and assets of state-chartered banks, 1834–1896

between the banking system and the stock market, and meant that stock market crashes could cause problems throughout the entire banking system (James 1978: 37, 103).

After the end of the Civil War, the U.S. had a new banking system and a uniform currency. It also remained off the gold standard, at a time when the U.K., its chief foreign trading partner, was a fierce proponent of it, and it was being adopted by a growing number of European countries. With so much inconvertible paper money in circulation, resumption of gold convertibility would be difficult to accomplish for the simple fact that there was too much paper and too little gold. The most direct method was economically painful: retire the greenbacks (literally, take them out of circulation) and shrink the supply of paper money so that its value in relation to gold would rise and eventually return to par. Since $100 of greenbacks was worth only about $35 in gold by July 1864, there was quite a bit of ground to recover. Following passage of the Contraction Act of 1866, Treasury Secretary Hugh McCulloch pursued this for a time, but the resulting economic deflation made the policy extremely unpopular (especially among debtors) and the Act was repealed in 1868 after McCulloch had been able to retire only $48 million worth of greenbacks (Sharkey 1959: 111, 196, 241).

The failure of straightforward contraction cast serious doubts in some minds about the larger goal of returning the U.S. to gold convertibility. Was it really necessary to "back" money with gold or silver in order to have a functioning monetary system? After all, the Northern economy had functioned well enough during wartime even though it was clearly off the gold standard, and its bank notes had functioned as money should. Perhaps it was sufficient that the government bestow "legal tender" status for a medium to be money. These questions also raised the issue of how to repay the greatly enlarged national debt, and whether to repay the bonds issued during the war with paper money, specie, or paper money backed by specie.

As money became more and more controversial, two basic positions emerged: greenback and bullionist. Greenbackers took a "soft money" position, advocating inflation, retention of the greenbacks, nonconvertibility of bank notes into specie, rejection of the gold standard, and repayment of the national debt with paper currency. On the other side, bullionists drew on the monetary orthodoxy of English economists and embraced the traditional gold standard, sought convertible bank notes, insisted that the national debt be repaid with gold-backed currency, and supported deflationary policies. Roughly speaking, Republicans tended to take the hard money position while Democrats were divided on the issue but more likely to embrace soft money policies (Ritter 1997: 34–6, 41–2).

While the controversy entailed sharp disagreements over public policy, it also raised philosophical questions about the nature of value and the basis for money that would have been familiar to Aristotle. The bullionists insisted that money had to possess intrinsic worth if it were to function as such. One powerful analogy they relied upon was that a measure had to possess the same quality as that which it measured: to measure length, a ruler had to possess length; to measure volume, a vessel had to possess volume, and so on (Carruthers and Babb 1996: 1566–7). Similarly, a measure of value could not work unless it possessed value. Gold and silver had real value, and so did all coins made of precious metal. That value did not depend on the government, and so granting legal tender status (so-called "fiat money") in the absence of "true" or "underlying value" was a strategy doomed to failure. In fact, the falling gold price for greenbacks was taken as proof by bullionists that government couldn't create or bestow value where it did not already exist. Paper money, in bullionist eyes, didn't have true value, no matter what the government said. And when paper money was convertible into gold, on demand, then at least it *represented* true value. Convertibility allowed paper money to enjoy the true value of gold.

Greenbackers took strong issue with such arguments. Materials and objects, including gold, possessed value only because society conferred value upon them. In modern societies, this meant that money was a creature of law. Indeed, greenbackers claimed that if gold itself were demonetarized and only used for jewelry and tooth repair, it would lose much of its value, too. Their arguments about paper money were correspondingly different: what determined the value of paper money was not its convertibility into gold (or silver) but whether it could be exchanged for goods and services (Carruthers and Babb 1996: 1571). If people treated paper money as if it were money, it would indeed function as money. The declining gold price for greenbacks reflected not the inherent weakness of fiat money but rather the fact that, when issued, the greenbacks had been granted only limited legal tender status (e.g., they couldn't be used to pay import duties). Hobbled by law, they possessed less value than they could have.

Greenbackers opposed a return to the gold standard. Not only was such a return based on a false premise (i.e., that gold possessed "intrinsic worth"), but it required deflationary policies that were hurtful to debtor interests, especially workers and farmers, and that benefited creditors, banks, and financiers. Since agrarian groups were concentrated in the Southern and Western regions of the country, and since financial institutions were most numerous in the Northeast, this conflict exacerbated domestic sectional differences. In addition, the gold standard would keep the U.S., as a whole, economically dependent in relation to Great Britain. Bullionists, by contrast, viewed continued reliance on fiat money as dangerously inflationary, and made reference to the near-valueless paper money of the Revolutionary Era. They believed that the return to gold convertibility would also return the U.S. to the ranks of civilized, rich countries. They also denied that the gold standard had the kind of sharp distributional consequences that greenbackers perceived, and felt that a sound monetary system was good for all citizens.

Politically, the greenbackers lost out and so the U.S. returned to the gold standard. However, money stayed on the political agenda during the 1880s and 1890s, when populist groups pressed for the monetarization of silver. Embracing a bimetallic standard by adding silver to gold as backing for U.S. currency was an inflationary move, but it was not as extreme as pure fiat money. The "free silver" movement came to a head in the 1896 election when William Jennings Bryan, the Democratic nominee, made his famous "Cross of Gold" speech against the gold standard. However, despite the political controversy surrounding money, the U.S. returned to the gold standard and stayed on it. The Gold Standard Act of 1900 put an end to bimetallism or silver standard alternatives (Myers 1970: 221).

In joining the international gold standard, supporters believed the U.S. would have a monetary system that would automatically adjust to international trade imbalances, without political interference. A country running a trade deficit (more imports than exports) would have to make up the difference by exporting gold to pay for the excess imports, and the subsequent contraction of the money supply would automatically lower domestic prices, raise interest rates, and make domestically produced goods more competitive. This would eventually lead to higher exports, the trade deficit would disappear, and money would flow back into the country. Countries with trade surpluses would experience the opposite effect: gold inflows would raise prices, make exports less competitive, and their surpluses would automatically disappear. In addition, since national currencies were tied to gold, exchange rates would be stable (which encouraged foreign trade). Finally, since the money supply was tied to the underlying amount of gold, politically driven inflation would become a thing of the past. To its supporters, the gold standard seemed like an automatic, self-equilibrating system that resisted political interference. In actual fact, the operation of the gold standard conferred more discretion on monetary authorities than they cared to admit (Eichengreen 1996: 32), but at least in theory it tied the hands of government. Further, the central bankers who organized and ran the gold standard system in the nineteenth century really had no sense that they were responsible for national macroeconomic goals like stability or growth (Bloomfield 1959: 24). They focused on much more narrow goals like maintaining convertibility.

While controversy raged over money in the latter nineteenth century, a more gradual change occurred to the U.S. banking system. State-chartered banks had effectively been put out of business by the National Banking Act's provision to tax the bank notes they issued. But these banks made a comeback in the decades that followed, chiefly because they came to depend less on note-issue as a profitable activity, and more on taking deposits and making loans (see figure 2.1). The composition of the U.S. money supply shifted away from currency and towards demand deposits (i.e., checking accounts), and once again it became profitable to charter a state bank. Furthermore, to encourage the formation of new banks in areas that lacked them, some states put in place relatively weak capital standards and reserve requirements (Friedman and Schwartz 1963: 19). By the end of the century, the U.S. financial system was populated by a varied collection of banks. Those in the West and South were more likely to have a state charter and were generally weaker (smaller and more poorly capitalized). Furthermore, many states prohibited branch banking, and so banks could only take deposits and make loans at one specific geographical location. During a financial crisis or credit crunch, this made state-chartered banks particularly vulnerable to bank runs.[4]

Although financial panics were not uncommon, the panic of 1907, marked by the failure of New York's Knickerbocker Trust Company, proved to be particularly consequential. This panic prompted a series of Congressional investigations and deliberations that culminated in the National Monetary Commission. The Commission's 1910 report offered a diagnosis of the shortcomings of the U.S. financial system, and criticized it for having an "inelastic currency" that could not easily accommodate periodic "waves" in business activity and demand for credit (Myers 1970: 247–8). Furthermore, there was no central agency to coordinate rescue efforts during the financial crises that threatened illiquid but solvent institutions. The Commission's findings led to the establishment of the Federal Reserve System in 1913, and gave the U.S. its first functioning central bank (Friedman and Schwartz 1963: 171). Although it wasn't until after World War I that the Fed was truly up and running, it was designed to fulfill one of the chief functions of a central bank during a financial crisis: to act as a lender-of-last-resort by lending freely but at high rates. Thus, the Fed offered its "discount window" to its members, which allowed them to bring some of their commercial paper (so-called "real bills") to the Fed for re-discounting. By privileging real bills, the bank was following standard banking practice of the time (Bodenhorn 2000: 91). In effect, the Federal Reserve would lend to its member banks on the strength of their holdings of commercial paper ("real bills"), and give them the kind of liquidity they sought during a financial panic. Vigorous re-discounting would add "elasticity" to the money supply and allow the financial system to survive whatever panics and crises occurred (Mints 1945: 223, 233).

The post-war financial situation was very different from that envisioned by the architects of the Federal Reserve System (Friedman and Schwartz 1963: 189, 192). For one thing, world conflict had disrupted operation of the international monetary system (see Obstfeld and Taylor 2004: 27). The Governor of the Bank of England and the head of the Federal Reserve Bank of New York worked together to restore the gold standard, but wartime financial dislocations made this a very difficult thing to accomplish (Moggridge 1969). Their hope was that a reconstructed gold standard would bring back some of the positive aspects of the pre-war international economy, in particular free flows of goods, capital, and labor (James 2001: 34). Several countries suffered through hyperinflation during the early 1920s, and the obvious vulnerability of flexible exchange rates to financial speculation increased their resolve to return to gold (Eichengreen 1996: 51, 57). Thanks to their efforts, the number of countries on the gold standard increased from only a handful in 1921 to over forty by 1928. But once achieved, the restoration of the gold standard proved fleeting as the onset of the Great Depression soon pushed the international financial system back into disarray. From a highpoint in 1931, many countries followed Britain's decision to suspend convertibility and left the gold standard *en masse*, so that by 1937 there were no adherents (Eichengreen 1996: 48). Freed from its constraints, countries were better able to pursue independent economic policies aimed at recovery from the Depression. Many of them embraced protectionist policies that raised barriers to international trade, and the world retreated from a free trade regime.

Another major change following World War I was that the U.S. itself went from being a debtor to a creditor country. To pay for their military expenses, many European countries liquidated their foreign assets and eventually had to borrow money to fund their imports from the U.S. In relatively short order, the U.S. went from being a capital importer to a capital exporter. Finally, despite higher wartime taxes, the U.S. government had to borrow to pay for its own military expenses, and so the volume of Treasury securities in private hands grew very substantially with the expansion of the national debt. These laid the basis for what eventually became a new mode of policy intervention by the Federal Reserve: open market operations (Friedman and Schwartz 1963: 251; Mints 1945: 265). The money supply could be affected by buying or selling government securities, as well as by shifting interest rates charged at the Federal Reserve's discount window.

The Great Depression and After

The Depression revealed in stark relief some of the shortcomings of the U.S. banking system. In particular, fears of insolvency set off bank runs that led to the closure of many small weak banks, an instance of self-fulfilling prophecies of the worst kind. President Roosevelt had to declare a bank holiday shortly after his inauguration in order to stop the panic and enable solvent but illiquid banks to survive. But despite various measures many banks failed, and so the number of banks declined dramatically. For example, the number of state banks in the U.S. decreased from 18,113 in 1928 to 9,310 in 1933, and their assets similarly declined from $33,298,000,000 to $19,698,000,000 (Historical Statistics of the U.S.: table Cj158–68). Similarly, the number of national banks dropped from 7,685 in 1928 to 4,897 in 1933. To protect their own liquidity, banks shifted their portfolios towards the safest investments and heavily restricted credit (Chandler 1971: 95). Such widespread tightening of credit made it hard for the U.S. economy to recover.

Widespread bank failures were one reason for the establishment in 1933 of the Federal Depository Insurance Corporation (FDIC), which offered insurance to bank depositors. Some deposit insurance schemes had been tried before at the state level, but it became clear that only a national program would be robust enough to fulfill its purpose. A year later, a similar scheme (FSLIC) was established to protect depositors at Savings and Loans Associations. Together, these public insurance arrangements helped to make bank runs a rarity, and enhanced the stability of the banking system. Another important measure was the Glass–Steagall Act of 1933, which separated investment from commercial banks, in an attempt to dampen the speculative excesses that had helped to drive up the stock market during the 1920s.

The Great Depression produced a flurry of federal policy innovation, and increased regulatory oversight over banks and financial markets. In addition to FDIC, FSLIC, and the separation of investment from commercial banking, Regulation Q (which set interest rate ceilings on checking and savings deposits) was put into place in 1933. Further, the Securities and Exchange Commission (SEC) was established in the following year to enforce securities laws and oversee stock markets. Many parts of this regulatory apparatus continue to function today. For instance, bank runs by depositors at U.S. commercial banks are still rare because of the confidence instilled by FDIC, and the SEC continues to regulate publicly traded securities. However, financial innovation has gone hand-in-hand with financial deregulation, and significant parts of the New Deal era regulatory apparatus have been taken down. Regulation Q was repealed in 1980, and so interest rates for savings accounts were allowed to float. The separation of commercial from investment banking was repealed in 1999.

Some deregulatory results have been disastrous. During the 1980s, the U.S. savings-and-loan industry was quickly deregulated and before too long speculators were using savings-and-loans associations like piggy banks to fund their own risky or even fraudulent real estate undertakings. Many individual institutions failed and the entire industry had to be bailed out by the U.S. government in 1989 at a cost of at least $160 billion (Calavita, Tillman and Pontell 1997; Glasberg and Skidmore 1997). More recently, the subprime loan crisis occurred in part because of the development of exotic new financial instruments that challenged the ability of rating agencies to assess accurately the true risks of default, coupled with the unwillingness or inability of regulatory agencies to provide rigorous oversight.

Laws prohibiting branch banking have been repealed, and so the commercial banking industry has consolidated nationally. Furthermore, the strict separation of commercial from investment banking was also repealed, and the largest U.S. financial institutions have become conglomerates that can offer a wide variety of services. JPMorgan Chase, for example, resulted from the merger in 2000 between J.P. Morgan & Co., a well-known investment bank, and Chase Manhattan Corp., a large commercial bank. In general, there were many bank mergers during the 1980s and 1990s, and so the overall number of banks in the U.S. declined. The abolition of legal barriers allows financial institutions to offer a full range of financial services to individuals and has helped to spark a great deal of financial innovation over the last two decades. But as the current crisis shows, regulators were not able to keep pace or curtail overly risky behavior.

International Developments

Towards the end of World War II, when it was becoming clear that the Allies would defeat Germany and Japan, Britain and the U.S. began to consider the post-war international financial system. The famous negotiations led by John Maynard Keynes, representing Great Britain, and Harry Dexter White, from the U.S. Treasury Department, occurred in Bretton Woods, New Hampshire, in 1944. The resulting arrangements came to be known simply as the "Bretton Woods System." The discussions were shaped by fears that the post-war economy would relapse into a depression, by memories of the failure to rejuvenate the gold standard during the interwar period, as well as by the plain fact that the world's economic center of gravity had shifted to the U.S.

The agreements created a set of institutions that are still with us today, including the International Monetary Fund (IMF) and the World Bank. Rather than try to reimpose fixed exchange rates, as occurred under the gold standard, the Bretton Woods arrangement allowed for rates to be flexible under certain conditions. Furthermore, temporary balance of payments problems were no longer simply left to the market for resolution. The first priority of the IMF was to make short-term loans to countries to help them solve such problems (Eichengreen 1996: 93), and international capital flows were restricted in many countries. By contrast, the purpose of the World Bank (then called the International Bank for Reconstruction and Development) was to make long-term loans to assist with national economic development. Initially, World Bank development loans went to advanced countries for post-war reconstruction (e.g., France), but later its lending activity targeted the poorer countries of the third world (e.g., Sub-Saharan Africa). Today, World Bank lending goes to developing economies exclusively.

The post-war international monetary system largely succeeded in helping war-damaged economies to recover, and in combination with arrangements like the General Agreement on Tariffs and Trade (GATT, and its successor, the World Trade Organization, or WTO) eventually led to a system of freer international trade. But it offered nothing like the gold standard, in which gold flows and interest rates would automatically counteract trade imbalances or government deficits, and in which exchange rates were fixed. The world's monetary system no longer depended on gold, or any other precious metal. Furthermore, after the war, countries enjoyed greater ability to manage their economies as they saw fit, in keeping with domestic political realities and the dominance of Keynesian economic doctrine. Recessions were no longer regarded as painful but necessary economic medicine to correct speculative excesses, or even as bad spells that simply had to be endured. Instead, domestic monetary and fiscal policies were aimed at minimizing the impact of economic downturns and speeding up the recovery. In particular, deficit spending became a tool with which to manage the economy.

As European colonial empires were dismantled during the 1940s and 1950s, a large number of new countries gained their independence, particularly in Africa and Asia. As a token of their nationhood, and following European countries, almost all of them set up their own territorial currencies (Helleiner 2003: 186). They also established their own central banks. Despite much optimism at the moment of independence, only a few of the poorer countries enjoyed long-term economic growth. In the late 1950s, Ghana and South Korea were equally impoverished, with roughly the same per capita GDP (gross domestic product). Forty years later, South Korea had outstripped Ghana and became a much wealthier country. Unfortunately, most developing economies were like Ghana, and South Korea had few peers. As poor countries stayed poor, they also remained vulnerable to the evolving strictures and ministrations of the IMF and World Bank. Particularly when poor countries suffered balance-of-payments problems or faced a financial crisis, they often had to look to the IMF for financial assistance. Such assistance was usually forthcoming in the form of a large short-term loan, but the money had strings attached ("conditionalities"). These stipulated a variety of policy reforms that the recipient country promised to undertake as a condition for receiving the loan, and often-times they were quite onerous (Babb and Carruthers 2008).

The Bretton Woods system survived until 1973, when President Nixon favored domestic political considerations over international finance and made his famous decision to suspend gold convertibility of the U.S. dollar at $35 per ounce (Gowa 1983). Nevertheless some key Bretton Woods institutions (e.g., the IMF and World Bank) continue operating to this day, although their credibility has waxed and waned. Capital controls were loosened over many decades so that now investment capital flows around the globe, largely (although not entirely) unrestricted. Much foreign direct investment circulates among developed countries (e.g., Europeans investing in the U.S., Japanese investing in Europe), but some of it goes to a few favored developing countries, in particular to China (Gilpin 2000: 24, 169).

Today, countries are no longer constrained by the gold standard, but they do not have the freedom to pursue whatever economic policies they wish. In particular, they operate under a policy "trilemma" which means that only two of three macroeconomic policy goals can be met at the same time. Countries can have either capital mobility across national boundaries, or fixed exchange rates, or an independent monetary policy. They can even have two of these, but not three (Gilpin 2000: 122; Obstfeld and Taylor 2004: 30). Since all three policy goals are desirable, the key question has always been which one to forgo. An orthodox gold standard, for example, meant capital mobility and fixed exchange rates, but not independent monetary policy. After World War II, domestic political forces in many countries made it more important to pursue counter-cyclical fiscal and monetary policy and to ensure smooth economic growth, so countries shifted from fixed to floating exchange rates (Obstfeld and Taylor 2004: 39). But floating exchange rates add uncertainty to international trade, and threaten competitive devaluations as countries try to boost exports by cheapening the value of their currency.

The world economy in the early twenty-first century is a global economy, with a high degree of interdependence. What happens in one country can affect many others, whether they like it or not. A good example concerns how recent problems in the U.S. subprime mortgage market have hurt credit markets and financial institutions all over the world – even famously conservative Swiss banks have been hurt by these problems. In an interdependent world, troubles have a way of spreading far and wide. Despite these interconnections, the effects of globalization have been quite uneven. More so than in the pre-World War I period of global integration, today's international monetary system functions so that international capital flows occur more among rich countries than from rich to poor (Obstfeld and Taylor 2004: 241–3). British investors, for example, are more likely to put their money into the U.S., Canada, or Australia than into sub-Saharan Africa. Similarly, U.S. investors are more likely to invest in Western Europe or Japan than in Ghana, Madagascar, or Sri Lanka. In effect, foreign investment pursues diversification (among rich countries) more than economic development, although there are exceptions (like China).

On this score, figure 2.2 provides some revealing information. It shows how much foreign direct investment (FDI) expanded between 1970 and 2007, but also that most FDI is flowing into developed economies. The percentage of total FDI allocated to

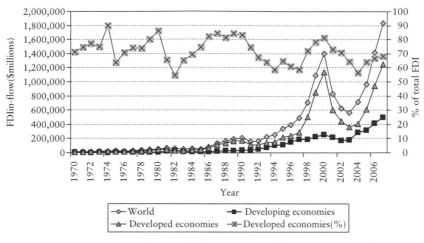

Data source: UNCTAD FDI, table 1970 to 2007

Figure 2.2 In-flow of world foreign direct investment, 1970–2007

developed economies varies over time, but it generally stays around 70%. FDI generally does not go from capital-rich to capital-poor countries, but rather it flows among the capital-rich countries.

On the monetary front, sovereign countries still issue their own territorial currency. However, there have been some notable instances where countries have adopted someone else's currency (what happens is that a small nation like Ecuador or El Salvador uses the U.S. dollar, or pegs the value of its domestic currency to the U.S. dollar). In addition, most members of the European Union (EU) have entered a monetary union that replaced French francs, Italian lira, German marks, Spanish pesetas, and Irish pounds with a single regional currency, the euro. The effect of monetary unification has been to further integrate the economies of EU members, to support commerce within the EU by reducing foreign exchange risks for international trade among members, and to curtail members' ability to pursue independent monetary policy. Along with the euro came a new institution, the European Central Bank, responsible for the monetary policy of member countries. At the same time as member countries gained the advantages of closer economic integration, they lost their ability to set their own monetary policy. No longer could France adopt an expansionary policy while Germany tightened credit.

Informal Monies

While formal monies have a long and storied history, informal money waxes and wanes in importance. The money that we are all familiar with today is, as noted above, what Eric Helleiner (2003) calls "territorial currency." It is issued by sovereign governments (or groups of governments), adheres to well-known iconographic conventions (so that most money "looks" the same), and functions as legal tender within a bounded geographical region. Legal tender status means that money can be used legally to satisfy all debts, public and private. Sometimes, however, informal monies emerge. These are unofficial and are not issued by national governments, they circulate locally, and they are not legal tender. But for certain purposes and within particular communities, they can function like money.

Informal monies emerge for a variety of reasons: scarcity of official money, breakdown of central government authority, competing monetary standards, tax evasion, or community solidarity. Each can motivate people to create something like money. A couple of examples help to illustrate how these reasons operate. Today in Ithaca, New York, the home of Cornell University, one can find a peculiar kind of local currency, denominated in terms of time (Good 1998). First developed in 1991 by a community activist and called "Ithaca Hours," these printed notes function like a special currency, and they are intended to help develop the local economy (*New York Times*, May 31, 1993, p. 28; Jan. 21, 1996, p. 21). Local businesses and individuals voluntarily agree to join the "system" and so accept and issue special notes denominated in hours (one hour = $10). Since only locals participate in the system, Ithaca Hours notes can only be spent locally, which (according to the proponents) helps to ensure that spending power stays inside the community. Some other small American towns have followed Ithaca's example and developed their own time-based local currency (*New York Times*,

May 28, 1998, p. B1). There too the goal has been to boost the local economy (Crowther et al. 2002; Witt and Lindstrom 2004).

Although contemporary examples of local and alternative currencies are easier to document, there is also evidence of informal money in the past. Often, people created their own money because of severe shortages of official legal tender. Such problems arose in both national and colonial situations. During the nineteenth century, as we have seen, regional differences in the number of banks meant that some parts of the U.S. (e.g., the Northeast) had much greater access to currency than did others (e.g., the West). Where currency was scarce, promissory notes issued by well-known local merchants sometimes circulated in the community and functioned like money (see Guyer 2004; Hoagland 2002). Inadequately served by the formal monetary system, people created local money to support local market activity.

People also seek out alternative monies during episodes of hyperinflation or economic crisis, when the value of their nation's official money is unstable. For example, in Bulgaria in the late 1990s people shifted from market exchange to an extensive barter system in which potatoes featured as a kind of informal monetary equivalent since they could be exchanged for almost everything else (Cellarius 2000). Economic transactions in Israel during the early 1980s often involved a variety of currencies in addition to official Israeli money, as people operated in a situation of monetary disunification (Dominguez 1990). In transition-era Russia during the 1990s, the central government tried but largely failed to impose a single monetary standard on the entire country (Johnson 2000: 226; Woodruff 1999: 53, 68, 95). As a consequence, many firms resorted to complex barter arrangements and had to rely on alternative commodity monies or IOUs as a way to conduct their transactions and survive the economic downturn (Johnson 2000: 97, 107, 163). The failure of official money prompted one local government to try to pay its public school teachers' salaries using sausages and other food items it received in lieu of tax revenues (Woodruff 1999: 138).

An informal system for international money transfers became extremely topical after the September 11, 2001 attacks on the World Trade Center and the Pentagon. In determining how the airplane hijackers managed to fund their operation, U.S. authorities became aware of an international system for money transfers, the *hawala* system. This network operated especially in the Middle East and South Asia (India and Pakistan), and has developed in areas where the formal banking system is weak (El Qorchi et al. 2003: 6). It has mostly been used by migrant workers who go abroad in search of higher wages (e.g., Filipinos and Mexicans moving to the U.S.), and who then wish to send money back to their families in their country of origin. They cannot mail cash, and do not have access to checking accounts or other bank services. Instead, an expatriate worker in country X who wants to send a sum back home to country Y can pay the money to a *hawaladar* (member of the *hawala* network) in country X. The *hawaladar* then communicates with another member of the network in country Y who makes the sum (minus a fee) available to the worker's family in that country (El Qorchi et al. 2003: 12–14). At some point, the two network members have to settle up between themselves, but there are a variety of ways to do this. Using such a system, remittances can be transferred over long distances quickly, informally, and with (almost) no paperwork. Most such remittances are done with the best intentions, but the system can also be used for illegitimate purposes, such as to launder money, avoid taxes, or fund terrorist activities.

Territorial currency has almost never entirely monopolized exchange within national territories. Informal monies have persisted alongside formal territorial money, never quite disappearing but always operating on the fringes of the economy. Informal monies can function quite effectively within particular geographical regions or social communities, and there are a number of reasons why their use might prove advantageous to someone. Nevertheless, in the modern world political sovereignty normally encompasses the right to create money and set the medium of exchange. While there have been some important instances where countries have given up that right (the European Union is the most obvious), most countries have retained it and will tolerate rival monies only in special circumstances.

Conclusion

Today no-one in the U.S. worries much if the cash in their purse or wallet is any good. Those familiar pieces of paper, issued by the Federal Reserve System, can reliably be exchanged for whatever good or service we wish to purchase. We can take money for granted because, in our experience, it does what we want it to do. This brief overview of the history of money shows, however, that our current and enviable situation is an unusual accomplishment. Money has often been problematic, not simply because people want more of it, but because money itself doesn't always work. People have used a variety of methods to construct effective money, coining precious metals or issuing paper based on such metals, but the solutions have never been perfect. People have had to accommodate exchange through a variety of means in addition to money: barter, credit, and informal monies. The creation of money has often been the special project of sovereign governments, and so money as an institution has been closely linked to political power. That linkage has remained despite dramatic changes in the nature of government (from kings and emperors to democratically elected prime ministers and presidents), the locus of governance (from city-states to nation-states, and now to groups of countries), and in money itself (from gold to paper to virtual money). So whether money works well or not, it always has a political dimension.

Discussion Questions

1 Imagine you had to survive for one week on the basis of barter alone. Instead of using cash, checks or a payment card to acquire the goods and services you normally use, you had to rely on barter. What would you barter with? Could you survive? What would happen to the economy if everyone had to barter?

2 Look at some paper currency (dollars, euros, yen, pesos, or whatever) and regard it as a piece of public art. What messages do the pictures, symbols, and images convey? Across different currencies, are there common patterns of symbolism? Why would political authorities wish to signal these particular messages?

3 Suppose you went to Ithaca, New York, and were impressed by the local currency, Ithaca Hours. In fact, you were so impressed that you decided to launch your own local currency, modeled after what you saw. How would you organize your local community to support your new money? How could you give it credibility, trustworthiness, and value?

3

The Social Meaning of Money

Schindler: For each thousand you invest, I will pay you with. . .
Stern [Schindler's right hand]: Two hundred.
Schindler: Two hundred kilos of enamelware a month to begin in
    July and to continue for one year. After which we're even.
    That's it. It's very simple.
Old man: Not good enough.
Stern [surprised]: It's not good enough?
Schindler [raising his voice]: Not good enough? Look where you're
    living. Look where you're being put. Not good enough. . . .
    A couple of months ago, you'd be right, not anymore.
Old man [stressing each word]: Money is still money.
Schindler: Not, it is not. That's why we're here [bargaining in a
    car]. Trade goods. That's the only currency that will be
    worth anything in the ghetto. Things have changed, my
    friend.[1]

This scene from Steven Spielberg's movie *Schindler's List* illustrates a set of ideas we will discuss at length in this chapter. In
contrast to economists' depiction of money as a fungible and universal medium of exchange, we will analyze the institutional limits
to money's circulation and liquidity. We will refer to changes
across cultures and over time in what money can and cannot buy.
And we will trace culturally embedded distinctions between different currencies and among "special monies" (Zelizer 1989, 1994)
fashioned out of uniform legal tender. Additionally, we will show
how both in the contemporary West and in other cultural settings,

money's meaning can change according to its sources, its users, and its uses (Belk and Wallendorf 1990; Carruthers and Espeland 1998).

This chapter discusses money as a vehicle for conveying meaning. We are concerned not just with the capacity of money to express quantitative value, but more broadly with the symbolic power of money as a marker of status, power, and social values (Carruthers 2005). Drawing on the work of anthropologists, social psychologists, and sociologists, we examine different ways in which social relations and culture shape and transform money (Bloch and Parry 1989). But we also reflect on the consequences of monetarization and the cultural and social struggles around it, as money extends to new social spheres and practices. When doing this, we pay attention to how contemporary scholars position themselves – or can be situated – *vis-à-vis* Marx and Simmel's critique of modern capitalism.

General-Purpose Money, Special-Purpose Money, and "Special Monies"

Much of the recent sociological research on the meaning of money criticizes the standard definition of money as an object that fulfills four basic functions: it is a universal medium of exchange, a standard of value or unit of account, a means to store wealth, and a standard of deferred payment (Furnham and Lewis 1986). This view portrays money as an entity "devoid of meaning" beyond its capacity to represent value in quantitative terms (Belk and Wallendorf 1990: 35). Furthermore, it highlights money's uniform appearance, its divisibility, and its exchangeability, all qualities that sum up money's superior ability to facilitate exchange, measure value, and store wealth (Lea et al. 1987: 319–20).

A first critique to this general view of money came from historical and ethnological research on exchange and other economic activities. Polanyi (1957a, 1968) and his followers proposed a broad classification of money into "general-purpose" money used in the modern West, and "special-purpose" money found both in the ancient world and in contemporary, non-Western societies. Money circulating in modern, Western economies was "general-purpose" money, in the sense that it fulfilled all four functions listed by economists. However, in historical and in contemporary non-Western settings, the uses conventionally associated with money were distributed among multiple objects. "Primitive" money was generally "special-purpose" money, in the sense that one class of objects might circulate as a medium of exchange, another category might function as a means to measure value and to store wealth, and yet another type of object might serve as a means of payment in political or ceremonial transactions.[2] Polanyi (1968: 189–90) illustrated this conceptual framework with an example from the eighteenth-century African kingdom of Dahomey. In Dahomey, there were different types of money, including cowries, gold dust, and slaves. While cowries did serve all four purposes – a medium of exchange, a unit of account, a store of value, and a means of payment – gold dust complemented cowries as a means of exchange, and slaves were used to measure value, to store wealth, and to pay tribute to foreign kings, but not as a medium of exchange.

Polanyi and his school added a second meaning to the concept of "special-purpose" money, beyond the idea that different categories of objects might perform separate monetary functions. Some studies within this school linked the circulation of different currencies to the existence of separate exchange spheres or circuits (Einzig 1966; Polanyi 1957a). Bohannan (1955, 1959, for example, used this frame to analyze exchange among the Tiv, a society of subsistence farmers in Kenya, prior to their colonization by the British. Bohannan (1959: 492) characterized the Tiv as having a "multi-centric" economy, "an economy in which a society's exchangeable goods fall into two or more mutually exclusive spheres, each marked by different institutionalization and different moral values." The Tiv's economy was comprised of a sphere associated with subsistence, a sphere connected with prestige, and another related to marriage. Within the subsistence sphere – including foodstuffs, household utensils, tools, and raw materials – people exchanged goods through barter. Within the prestige sphere, whose exchangeable goods included slaves, cattle, medicines, and magic, among others, brass rods served as "general-purpose" money. Finally, within the marriage sphere, brass rods could function as a means of payment, but only for "second-best" marriages, conferring rights over women but not over their descendants. Furthermore, the Tiv did not see the brass rods used in these transactions as a standard of value for assessing the women exchanged.

Without contesting the validity of their historical and ethnographic studies, Melitz (1970) questions the Polanyists' clear-cut opposition between modern, "general-purpose" money and primitive, "special-purpose" money. Modern money may also be considered "special-purpose." First, money in our society takes different forms, such as coins, paper currency, money orders, savings accounts, and personal checks, to name only a few. None of these different forms is equally suitable for all four monetary functions. Thus, for example, coins and paper currency are best used as means of exchange, but are less adequate as a store of wealth. By contrast, savings accounts function well to store wealth, but they do not serve as a medium of exchange. Second, modern Western economies also consist of distinct exchange spheres, associated with restrictions on the circulation of different money forms. It is easy to see how, in our society, the use of certain money forms is acceptable in some types of exchange, but inadequate in others. For instance, we use coins only in small transactions, while leaving personal checks for relatively larger payments. Moreover, as we will discuss in detail below, both our legal and moral codes forbid the use of money in exchange for certain goods, such as political offices, professorial chairs, or children.

Melitz's critique notwithstanding, the Polanyists' attention to the existence of different currencies associated with distinct exchange circuits continues to be fruitful in contemporary anthropological studies. A case in point is Rogers' study of differential liquidity and social stratification in post-socialist Russia. Rogers (2005) examined the interaction among rubles, moonshine (homebrewed liquor), and labor, and showed how the different degrees of liquidity of each currency resulted in new lines of social stratification, both within the household and among households.

Rogers' starting point was the explosive growth of subsistence agriculture in the post-socialist period. As he pointed out, in the rural town of Sepych in the 1990s, "only a handful of townspeople could rely on enough salary income to go without raising some combination of pigs, cattle, and fowl, and growing potatoes in multiple scattered plots" (Rogers 2005: 66). To meet the growing labor needs arising from subsistence agriculture, households in Sepych would rely, depending on their resources, on mutual aid arrangements, hired labor, or some combination of the two. In all these cases, homemade moonshine played a key role in economic exchange. People would use moonshine as part of the commensality surrounding mutual aid arrangements, but also as direct payment for hired labor, given the ubiquitous cash shortages of the post-socialist period.

Rogers showed how money and moonshine were gendered media of exchange, used in different spheres, and endowed with differential degrees of liquidity. Women were more likely to be employed in cash-paying jobs, as nurses, teachers, or workers in the culture department. As the main cash-earners, women were responsible for expenditures requiring rubles, including consumer durables, store-bought food, bills, and taxes. Men, in contrast, were more likely to work for the privatized collective farm, which often paid workers in kind, for example construction materials, agricultural products, or farm services. However, men secured other essential goods for the household, most importantly, labor help for domestic agriculture, through mutual-aid arrangements involving moonshine. As Rogers (2005: 68) explained, both within the household and among households, the "settings could slip back and forth between moonshine as contributing to commensality and moonshine as currency object exchanged for labor."

However, the coexistence between different currencies with differential degrees of liquidity was loaded with tension. The fault lines between rubles and moonshine produced fissures within marriages themselves. Women welcomed male sociability and drinking, as long as it was the counterpart of their husbands' securing labor for the household's agricultural chores. However, women resented men who drank only recreationally with friends, that is, when drinking did not lead the men to call on their friends for assistance with agricultural work. Men, in turn, resented women's greater purchasing power, arising from money's greater degree of liquidity as compared to moonshine. Although vulnerable to inflation, money was an acceptable medium of exchange in a "much wider array of exchanges," including exchanges beyond the town's borders. In Rogers' words, "many marriages struggled to find a balance point between women's money and men's moonshine, struggles that were not aided by the unpredictable shifting levels of liquidity and exchange rates in the economy, reflected in late salaries, in-kind payments, and inflation" (Rogers 2005: 68).

Psychological Studies on the Meaning of Money

Like anthropologists, psychologists have also paid attention to the limited exchangeability of money. Money, they have shown, is not a generalized medium of exchange, but has limited purposes, as it is excluded from some transactions and even made non-fungible in certain contexts (Belk and Wallendorf 1990; Lea et al. 1987). Furthermore, cognitive and social psychologists have examined the multiple meanings of money, beyond its economic functions. In contrast to anthropologists, though, psychologists have focused on contemporary Western money and based their discussions not on historical or ethnographic accounts but on behavioral experiments and survey studies.

Webley and Lea (1993) illustrate the cultural limits on the exchangeability of modern Western money in a survey study of neighborly help conducted in Britain. The authors find that people may offer money to their neighbors in return for consumable items such as oil or sugar, but they do so only as a formality, expecting from the outset a negative reply. However, if a neighbor helps somebody out with yard work or another form of practical help, even mentioning money as a form of repayment will seem offensive. It is not that the recipient of help will not feel indebted. However, according to British social norms, reciprocation should take place later, preferably with a favor of the same kind.

Another example of limits to the use of money in contemporary Western society comes from experiments involving money as a "reinforcer" (Lea et al. 1987). Can money buy greater effort, better performance, or greater satisfaction with the job done? Is money always the best incentive? Psychologists have shown that, in certain contexts, the use of money may reduce rather than enhance intrinsic motivation. Calder and Staw (1975), for example, conducted an experiment involving students solving jigsaw puzzles. The results showed that students who were paid found the task *less satisfying* than those who did not get any money. Discussing Calder and Staw's example, Lea et al. (1987: 331–2) conclude that, in this case, money did not work as an incentive to strengthen intrinsic motivation.

In addition to illustrating limits to the use of money, studies in cognitive psychology and behavioral theory show how people make qualitative distinctions within formally homogeneous money. Heath and Soll (1996), for example, study how consumers manage the household's monetary resources with the aid of "mental budgets," which assign labels to money allocated to different categories of expenditures. People keep track of their expenditures and adjust their spending decisions to their mental budgets. This budgeting process takes into account the sources of money (Thaler 1999: 193). People classify income derived from different sources into different mental accounts, and then tie money from these accounts to different spending items. For example, a couple may spend $225 on a restaurant dinner only if they can draw on what they label a "windfall gain" account (Thaler 1985: 199–200). But they wouldn't spend as much if they had to use money coming from their "regular income" account. People resort to "mental accounting" as a way of "making rational trade-offs between competing uses for funds" (Thaler 1999: 193). Besides, mental accounting can serve as a mechanism of "self-control"; classifying money into different accounts makes it easier to keep spending in check (Thaler 1999: 193; see also Thaler and Shefrin 1981).

Psychological studies generally point to the insufficiency of economists' conventional definition of money as an account of how people view and use money in the real world. However, it is hard to come up with a better definition of modern money that covers its different uses, accounts for its multiple meanings, and remains applicable to different "species" of money. But, if money is so difficult to define, how do people manage to identify money items and to use them successfully in everyday life? Snelders et al. (1992: 71) propose to characterize money as a "polymorphous" concept, "a concept whose definition and boundaries cannot be specified precisely, but which nonetheless can be used consistently and efficiently." From this point of view, no definition may settle on what objects are included or left out of the category "money." Instead, different instances of money, such as coins, cash, credit cards, bonds, gold, and other value objects, share among themselves a "family resemblance" (Wittgenstein 1958).

Like other polymorphous concepts, money possesses some interesting psychological properties. People are able to rate different objects as more or less typical instances of money. Thus, for example, people may judge coins as more typical money items than bonds. In addition, people are capable of comparing different money items and judging how similar or different they are. Thus, people may decide that checks and debit cards are similar to each other – based on their connection with banking – but not similar to postal stamps. Moreover, we can find significant "inter-subjective" agreement about this type of judgment. People's judgments on the typicality and similarity of money items are not merely a matter of personal opinion, but reflect monetary practices in the real world.

Snelders et al. (1992) tested these ideas in an experimental study on the meanings of money in Britain and the Netherlands. In both countries, participants would judge cash items as the most typical instances of money, followed by foreign currencies, and bank accounts and other items associated with banking. At the other end, in contrast, were investment goods and "near-money" items such as shares and diamonds. There were, however, some differences between the British and the Dutch samples, when people compared money items based on their value. For example, British participants attributed lower value to the credit card than Dutch participants did. This had to do with differences in money habits between the two countries: in the Netherlands, people used credit cards for expensive purchases, whereas in Britain the credit card was more widely used.

Zelizer's Model of "Special Monies"

The anthropological tradition on "special-purpose" money and social psychology's findings on the symbolic meanings of money served as building blocks for Viviana Zelizer's influential analysis of "special monies."[3] Zelizer (1989: 343) developed her conceptual frame in opposition to what she called the "dominant utilitarian understanding of money, which sees it as exempt from extraeconomic influences." Zelizer (1989, 1994) set her model apart from the conventional view of money through five basic propositions. First, cultural and social structures profoundly influence money, which circulates not only in the modern economic market, but also in other social spheres such as the family, caring relations, gift giving, and charity. Second, instead of economists' idealized "single, uniform, generalized money," what we find in the modern world are "special monies," for example multiple currencies with special rules of allocation, differentiated uses, and different users. Third, social relations and culture may transform externally homogeneous money into separate, heterogeneous, and non-exchangeable currencies. Fourth, there is no radical opposition between unique, personal, subjective, indivisible non-monetary objects and fungible, impersonal, objective, divisible money. In certain conditions, "money may be as singular and unexchangeable as the most personal or unique object" (Zelizer 1994: 19). And fifth, cultural codes and social relations limit the monetarization of certain spheres and practices and create restrictions on money's uses, liquidity, and circulation.

One case Zelizer analyzes concerns the transformation in the meanings, uses, and allocation rules of married women's money from the 1870s to the 1930s. The turn of the century coincided with an important growth in real incomes, which accompanied the expansion of the consumer economy and culture. As the economic environment changed, families found it necessary to reevaluate their financial practices and spending habits. However, changes in household budgeting and spending were not a mechanical response to economic transformations, but were shaped by cultural definitions of the family, gender divisions, and age roles. In the author's words, "regardless of its sources, once money had entered the household, its allocation, calculation and uses were subject to a set of domestic rules distinct from the rules of the market" (Zelizer 1989: 368).

Zelizer showed how, within the domestic sphere, money became divided into qualitatively different currencies, with different methods of allocation and uses, according to gender and age. In upper- and middle-class households, men gave a discretionary portion of what they earned to their wives, first in the form of irregular "doles" and later on in the form of regularly disbursed "allowances." Zelizer (1989: 356–7) relates how women dependent on the dole found themselves in a situation of "relative poverty," as they confronted the challenge of managing housekeeping expenditures without a regular cash supply. To secure additional cash, wives "were limited to a variety of persuasion techniques: asking, cajoling, downright begging, or even practicing sexual blackmail." Although first welcomed as an improvement, the regular "allowance" maintained men's financial control and supervision.

In working-class households, in turn, men were the ones who received "allowances," after turning their pay over to their wives. However, men still kept control of the household income, because "the husband's envelope was not necessarily intact on arrival" (Zelizer 1989: 364). Like men, working children also got "allowances" after giving away their pay to their mothers, and they, too, "withheld or manipulated their earnings." As Zelizer notes, there was a crucial difference between the allowances received by working-class men and children and the allowances granted to upper- or middle-class women. Working-class men and children would spend their allowances on personal expenses, while upper- and middle-class women would devote theirs to household needs. As Zelizer (1989: 365) points out, "women's money retained a collective identity, while men's and children's money was differentiated and individualized."

When women earned money outside of the household, their money became "pin money," and was "trivialized" and treated differently than men's income. Regardless of the amount, women's money was seen as less important than men's money, and was either added to the housekeeping fund, without differentiation, or used for discretionary expenses such as buying clothes or paying for recreation.

Studies of other cultural settings provide additional evidence on the collective use of wives' money and the trivialization of women's income. In a study of Mexico City, Benería and Roldán (1992) tell how women would approve of their husbands keeping some money for their personal use – even if they questioned the amount withheld by their spouses. In contrast to their husbands, though, women would devote all of their earnings to the common household fund, without keeping anything for their own personal expenses. Whenever they would spend any money on themselves, women would feel guilty and find themselves at fault "for depriving their children." Furthermore, the women studied were dismissive towards the money they earned.

Like households, organizations also classify money into separate categories, treating some funds as more fungible then others (Carruthers and Stinchcombe 2001). The budget is a way of regulating liquidity within the organization; it makes certain funds liquid at the department or project level, thus making those funds unavailable at higher levels. Conversely, the budget preserves other funds as liquid for the executive levels as "strategic reserves," which prevents the circulation of such funds to particular departments or projects. Thus, "flexibility below is created by rigidity above, and vice versa" (Carruthers and Stinchcombe 2001: 128).

Through earmarking in this way, organizations can solve the cognitive problem of calculating a complex "vector of risks." For organizational actors, it is hard to manage the vector of risks faced by the whole organization. Organizational actors, however, are used to assessing the risks related to the particular departments or projects where they work. By segmenting resources and income streams, the budget helps to segregate risks among hierarchical levels, departments, and divisions. In this way, each section of the organization gets to manage the type of risks it routinely calculates. This is much simpler and more feasible than calculating the vector of risks pertaining to the organization as a whole (see also Stinchcombe 1990).

Money and Its Sources

Money's meaning depends not only on how it is allocated but also on its proximate sources (how money was acquired) and its "ultimate" sources (who issued that money) (Carruthers and Espeland 1998). In the West as well as in non-Western societies, money's sources affect its meaning and condition its use. Money obtained through morally objectionable activities, such as bribes, illicit trade, theft, or prostitution, becomes "dirty" money. Similarly, as Belk and Wallendorf (1990: 53) point out, in a culture that honors hard work, people may regard money acquired without labor as "evil." As an example, they refer to the comments of an informant who worked as a tour guide in a big mansion. The guide – who presumably did not consider the mansion a product of hard work – warned a tourist that such wealth had been "deadly" for the men who had acquired it.

Furthermore, the categorization of money as "dirty" or "evil" limits its use. Its holders may try to keep that money separate and avoid using it for long-term life goals, since they may fear that impure money may contaminate the goods or activities on which it is spent. Research on Oslo prostitutes (Hoigard and Finstad 1992) – an example also discussed by Zelizer (1994: 3) – shows how sex workers would keep separate their prostitution revenues from their legal income. While they would quickly expend prostitution money on recreation, addictions, and clothing, they would carefully put aside their welfare income to cover housing and bills. Individuals, corporations, and governments, however, may be able to "launder" dirty money by devoting it to socially respected uses, such as building an art collection or donating it to charity.

They may also, in some cultural contexts, attempt to "purify" evil money through special rituals, devised to cleanse not only the money but also its holders, so that they can regain their status as full members of the community (Shipton 1989).

Dangerous Money, Blood Money, and New Money

In an ethnographic study of Benares, a city in northern India, Parry (1989) studies the moral classification of money. Benares attracts hundreds of thousands of pilgrims each year, many of whom perform part of the rites owed to the dead. A large class of priests (including ritual technicians, pilgrimage priests, and funeral priests, among others) assist them in this enterprise, while acting as immediate recipients of the pilgrims' donations. Such gifts, called *dana*, consist usually of cash payments and are intended to reach a god, a ghost, or an ancestor, without any expectation of return, either in this world or in another. Although the priests are supposed to stand as mere intermediaries for the donations' ultimate recipients, in practice the *dana* contribute substantially to the daily livelihood of the priestly class.

The *dana* are thought to contain the donors' sins, and it is up to the priests to "digest" and "evacuate" those sins by elaborate rituals and by giving away more than they receive. In reality, however, the priests have neither the capacity to conduct those rituals nor the resources to disburse in excess of what they receive. As a result, not only do they amass unearned, unreciprocated gifts, but they also become a sort of "pit" of accumulated sin, with disastrous consequences for themselves and their progeny. The donations collected by the priests become a source of misery, illness, and death for their recipients and their families, so much so that, whenever opportunities arise, the priests opt out of their hereditary job. As Parry (1989: 71) stresses: "It is not money or the material world that they claim to renounce – few become ascetics. It is the proceeds of *dana*."

Parry contrasts the "moral peril" engulfing Benares' priests to the moral neutrality shielding its merchants. Despite their "eagle-eye for quick profits and their dubious commercial practices," the city's merchants are not usually the target of moral indignation (Parry 1989: 77). Nor is the money they earn from trade considered tainted or perilous. As long as they give away some of this money, merchants can safely conduct their trade and even engage in morally questionable transactions, without fear of consequences for either themselves or their families.

Moral codes imposing distinctions onto seemingly homogeneous money are common not only in the religious or "traditional" realm but also in "modern," professional practice. For example, Baker (2001) studies how the sources of money affect tort litigation in U.S. personal injury cases. Plaintiffs, defendants, and their lawyers orient their behavior by two "mutually reinforcing norms," the "blood money" norm and the "new money" norm. The first norm dictates that, except in the case of institutional defendants or an "outrageous wrong," the compensation money awarded to plaintiffs should not be defendants' own money, also called "blood money." The second norm states that part of the defendant's insurance money should be used to directly compensate the victims, instead of being entirely devoted to reimburse institutional players, such as the worker's compensation carrier. This portion used to compensate victims – who, in general, by the time of litigation, have already received some compensation benefits – is termed "new money." As Baker (2001: 314) points out, "although very little blood money is paid, this does not mean that blood money is unimportant to personal injury litigation. A credible claim that a trial could result in a legal obligation to pay blood money provides a significant inducement to settle."

The "Purification" of Money

Individuals as well as governments often face the challenge of how to rub off the stigma adhering to money obtained through morally condemned activities. State governments that depend on legalized gambling, for instance, may try to "launder" the revenues derived from gambling by allocating them to "higher" purposes such as public education (Carruthers and Espeland 1998: 4). Individuals, too, may try to "purify" dirty money by devoting it to "sacred" uses (Belk and Wallendorf 1990), from helping the poor and supporting the arts to protecting the environment.

In some societies, the purification of money requires carefully performed rituals, in order to placate the spirits offended by the transgression of social norms. For the Kenyan Luo, for example, the money derived from the sale of certain goods, including lineage land, tobacco, gold, or a homestead rooster, is "bitter money," which cannot be used for any transaction involving the preservation of the family and the continuation of patrilineal lineage (Shipton 1989). When used to buy livestock – the Luo believe – the animals will perish, and so will the bride if those animals are used in bridewealth payments. The owner of bitter money can convert it into "good" money, though, through a purification ceremony aimed to thank the spirits for providing it. As Shipton explains, such ceremony amounts to a "rite of passage" which rehabilitates the money's holder as a member of society.

Sometimes, rituals are also necessary when money crosses the boundaries between different institutional spheres or "transactional orders" (Bloch and Parry 1989). Carsten (1989), for example, studies the opposition between the fishing trade and the domestic world in a Malay fishing community. The fishing trade, the main source of cash for the families in the study, is a male-dominated world, founded on "temporary, commercial, and hierarchically-based" relations (Carsten 1989: 134). By contrast, in the household, which includes more than one family, consanguineally related women perform communal tasks embedded in egalitarian, enduring relations. These two opposed worlds, however, become connected when men hand over cash to women for household daily needs. As it enters the household, money becomes socialized and is spent on domestic consumption, including collective meals cooked and eaten in the unified household kitchen, called *dapur*. As the author explains: "Women, then, purify or socialize money, endowing it with the values of kinship morality, by cooking it in the *dapur*. By so doing they transform the one kind of community, based on differentiation, exchange, and alliance, and primarily male, into the other, based on the notion of a collection of similar female-dominated houses" (Carsten 1989: 138).

Cultural Barriers and Social Struggles against Monetarization

In addition to creating distinct moral categories out of uniform money, social relations and culture generate barriers against the monetarization of certain spheres and practices. As social psychologists have shown, even in a cultural setting as deeply individualistic and capitalist-oriented as the modern West, social norms constrain the use of money in certain exchanges and limit the application of market-pricing rules. Thus, as we mentioned earlier, money cannot be openly exchanged for political office, professorial chairs, or children. Neither is it accepted in exchange for things that circulate in a reciprocity system, such as car pools or neighborly help (Belk and Wallendorf 1990; Webley and Lea 1993). This, however, is a moving frontier, the object of compromises and struggles that keep redrawing it over time.

To think about cultural struggles over the extension of monetarization, it can be useful to draw on McGraw and Tetlock's (2005) discussion of morally acceptable exchanges. Analyzing decision-making in various contexts, the authors find a clear contrast between what they call "routine trade-offs" and what they identify as "taboo trade-offs." In a routine trade-off, people compare values that can be treated as fungible under our social norms and values. To use the authors' example, think of routine comparisons we make when grocery shopping, as we ponder sacrificing higher quality for lower price, or vice versa. By contrast, a "taboo trade-off" would entail putting secular values such as affordability, time, and convenience side by side against "sacred values that are supposed to be infinitely significant" (McGraw and Tetlock 2005: 4). Within our culture, for example, people would consider it normal and acceptable to wait another year to buy a better computer, hoping that prices would decline. But how would we judge a parent who could easily afford to give the tetanus vaccine to his or her child, but decided to put it off until vaccine prices dropped? Protecting a child's health, a sacred value within our culture, is not something we would normally trade off for a foreseeable price discount.

In fact, many of the current debates over the extension of monetarization to new spheres concern the moral consequences of accepting the generalization of taboo trade-offs. Thus far, social norms in the West exclude the pricing of mothering and children (Cohen 1987; Firth 1967). Nevertheless, some commentators fear that new developments in reproductive technologies and practices are visibly lowering the bar on what we consider marketable goods, tolerable comparisons, and acceptable exchanges. Thus, Shanley (2002: 272), for example, questions the sale of human eggs and sperm in an open market – currently a legal practice in the U.S. – because, among other things, it opens the door to "differential pricing of gametes" depending on the donor's skin color, height, athletic or musical skills.[4] Knowledge of differential pricing of genetic material, in the author's words, "may undermine the proposition that all persons are of equal dignity" (Shanley 2002: 272). Furthermore, Shanley criticizes the notion that people's relationship to their genetic material corresponds to that of saleable property. Instead, following Dickenson (1997), the author claims that we are not owners but "stewards" of our genetic material, which forms an enduring bridge across generations (Shanley 2002: 272–3).

Anderson (1993) strongly censors contract pregnancy on similar grounds. In contract pregnancy, the future father hires a broker, who finds a suitable surrogate mother, arranges for her medical care during the pregnancy, and handles the eventual relinquishment of the child. In Anderson's view, this practice transforms parental rights over children from a relationship of stewardship into transferable property rights. Anderson argues that this commodification of parental rights clearly weakens the norms of parental love. In fact, part of the job of the broker, who represents the interests of the intended parents, is to undermine any parental love that the gestational mother may develop towards her child. To accomplish this, the broker may resort to a combination of legal threats, persuasion, and financial incentives.

Moral norms regarding what can be priced and exchanged for money vary over time and from one culture to another (Bloch and Parry 1989). As discussed by Bloch (1989), in Western societies money is morally charged and the introduction of monetary exchange may color the meaning of social relations. Thus, for example, a direct cash exchange in the context of sexual relations makes such relations immoral and turns them into prostitution. By contrast, in societies where markets are not as extensive, money can have a more neutral meaning. This is the case of the Merina people of Magadascar. As reported by Bloch (1989: 166), in this society, "the right thing for a man to do is to give his lover a present of money or goods after sexual intercourse." What's more, this occurs not only within pre-marital or extra-marital relations but also within the context of marriage. This does not mean – the author stresses – that there are no distinctions between such relations and prostitution, which "is defined by the casualness of the relationship rather than by the kind of objects exchanged" (Bloch 1989: 166).

A similar contrast can be found in the sphere of gift giving. The Merina people do not find it odd to give money as a present, whereas in Western societies social norms strongly restrict giving money as a gift. Money fails to communicate what ought to be the defining traits of a present in our culture, namely, the effort and thought put into selecting it and the surprise felt in receiving it (Webley et al. 1983). If Western people do use money as a present, though, they put special care into "personalizing" the money, and even changing its physical appearance, by fitting money into special cards, using brand-new bills, selecting symbolically meaningful amounts, and imposing specific uses, thereby distinguishing money-as-a-present from otherwise homogeneous, impersonal money (Zelizer 1994: 105–18).

Social norms restricting the use of money change not only across cultures but also over time, within the same society. As it occurred historically with the introduction of wage labor, the extension of the monetarized economy to new spheres often became an extremely contested issue. Analyzing changes in the French textile industry in the eighteenth and nineteenth centuries, Reddy (1984) explains how, at the beginning of this period, the industry players were unsure about how to handle labor as a commodity. What was the entrepreneur buying? How could labor be measured, commensurated, or appraised? Mill owners and laborers solved these issues through conflict.

One of the changes most resisted by laborers was a transformation in compensation, from pay for the product of labor, the yarn, to variable paying rates according to the laborer's effort. Mill owners introduced this change to make new power-assisted mules cost-effective, under hardened competition in product markets. As Reddy (1984: 137) points out, laborers rebelled against "the need to finely calculate the value in monetary terms of every move of the finger, every break for a little drink and talk, every decision to take an extra moment fixing up a piece of work to look the way it ought to." On this point, as he contends, even laborers' own political supporters misunderstood them, narrowing laborers' grievances to shorter hours and higher pay. Instead, the main grievances behind laborers' struggles had to do with their loss of independence. What was at stake for laborers, and what they found themselves at pains to defend in an effective language, was a conception of work that resisted quantification in favor of continuing control over their bodies, routines, and methods of work.

Money and the "Corruption" of Social Life

But what is the impact of money on our relations to things and to other people? Does the introduction of money in new social spheres affect social relations? Classical social theorists took up this question as part of their more general analysis of capitalism and modernization. For Marx and Simmel – among others – money "revolutionized" people's relation to their work, to objects, and to other people. However, recent developments in economic anthropology and economic sociology have challenged some of the premises of the classics' work and helped to assemble a growing body of work on the reciprocal interaction among money, social relations, and culture. At the same time, certain themes from the classics' intellectual legacy continue to reemerge in new sociological analyses of monetarization. In the rest of the chapter, we briefly review Marx's discussion of commodity fetishism and Simmel's analysis of money. Then, we introduce recent theoretical and empirical contributions that either dispute or come to terms with the classics' critique of modern capitalism.

In his critique of classical political economy, Marx (1978: 207) brings into relief the social character of production: "In production, men not only act on nature but also on one another. . . .They enter into definite connections and relations with one another and only within these social connections and relations does their action on nature, does production, take place." Relations of production are historical, and change over time. In a capitalist society, relations of production involve capital and labor. Capital requires labor to realize itself. Unless exchanged for "direct, living labor," capital has no capacity to create new value (Marx 1978: 209). Labor, in turn, perishes if capital does not buy it; wage workers, who only have their own labor power to sell, are completely dependent on capital for securing their means of subsistence.

While labor and capital presuppose each other, they have conflicting interests. The exchange between the two amounts to an exploitative transaction. When selling his labor power, the worker gets in return a monetary wage to cover his means of subsistence. What the capitalist obtains, in exchange, is the worker's labor power, which creates new value for the capitalist, in excess of what is necessary for the worker's sustenance. The capitalist, in other words, "appropriates" the surplus value produced by the worker. Furthermore, the exploitation of workers worsens over time, as a result of competition among capitalists. In Marx's words: *The more productive capital grows, the more the division of labor and the application of machinery expands. The more the division of labor and the application of machinery expands, the more competition among the workers expands and the more their wages contract"* (Marx 1978: 216, the author's emphasis).

Marx's critique of capitalism blends with a general critique of commodification. Marx (1978: 322) characterizes commodities as "social hieroglyphics." In exchanging commodities, we equate the products of our labor as values. Each commodity appears in our eyes as possessing inherent, objective value, which can be measured against all other commodities. However, as objects of value, commodities are nothing but the "material receptacles of homogeneous human labor" (Marx 1978: 322). When equating commodities, "we also equate, as human labor, the different kinds of labor expended upon them" (Marx 1978: 322). Yet, producers see commodity exchange as "a relation between things," and not as what it is, a relation connecting producers among themselves and to the aggregate of their own labor (Marx 1978: 321). The deceptive character of commodities is more difficult to expose when production for exchange becomes the "predominating and characteristic manner" of production, as in modern capitalist society (Marx 1978: 328).

Like Marx, Simmel (1978) is interested in scrutinizing commodity exchange in a modern capitalist economy. However, Simmel's analysis is concerned not with the concealment of social labor but with money's unique power to make things and people commensurate. Simmel (1978: 128) highlights money's abstract, divisible, and convertible character, in essence, those qualities that turn money into a "common denominator of value." For Simmel (1978: 124), money is nothing but "the distilled exchangeability of objects"; money represents in abstract form "that element or function of things," that aspect of objects, that makes them exchangeable (Simmel 1978: 130). Simmel (1978: 126) points out that only in "a fully developed monetary economy" does money acquire its "distinctive significance," as the embodiment of the exchangeability of things.

Through its power to make any object commensurate – thus solving the problem posed by barter – money casts a mantle of relativity on the material and social world (Simmel 1978: 128). Money makes each individual object more replaceable and, at the same time, less meaningful. Similarly, money allows us to expand and diversify our relations to other people, and, at the same time, to reduce the depth of those relations. Even if we grow dependent on a large number of people for satisfying our daily needs, we focus only on the functional aspect of those relations, while each particular person becomes less significant to us. Thus, in Simmel's (1978) view, both the material and the social world become increasingly impersonal and superficial with the creation of a fully monetarized economy.

Yet, as we saw, contemporary economic sociologists have challenged the conception of money as inevitably uniform, multipurpose, and fungible (Zelizer 1989, 1994). Instead, Zelizer and others have shown the power of social relations and culture to imprint meaning on money, carve up multiple distinctions on it, and impose restrictions on its use, divisibility, and circulation. Furthermore, economic sociologists have rejected the notion that the extension of monetarization inexorably unravels and corrupts family, friendship, and community relations, or eradicates the meaning of our material and social world. What emerges instead is a more complex view on how individuals, families, and organizations act on the monetarization of new spheres by selecting different forms of compensation, monetary and non-monetary, to signal the quality of social relations and to distinguish among them (Zelizer 1996).

In *The Purchase of Intimacy* (2005), Zelizer explores in depth the relationship between intimate relations and economic transactions. Her starting point is the empirical evidence that people routinely mix economic transactions, including transfers of money, with intimate relations, and that economic transactions actually "sustain," rather than destroy, the world of personal, caring, and trust-based relations. Take the example – she suggests – of immigrants' remittances to their relatives in their home countries. These transfers, as Zelizer (2005: 27) points out, "have large macroeconomic consequences, for example, in generating large flows of cash from rich countries to poor countries and in transmitting wealth from one generation to the next." But these transfers have also deep personal consequences, as they help to nurture not only materially but also emotionally strong family and ethnic ties across national boundaries.

But why is it – Zelizer asks – that jurists, moralists, observers, and people in general worry so much about the interplay of economic interactions and intimacy? And why is there so much controversy about the extension of monetarization to new spheres, be it childcare, human reproduction, or organ transfers? Zelizer (2005: 37) does not dismiss such worries as groundless or irrational, but takes them instead as a sign of our preoccupation with "creating viable matches" when connecting social relationships, economic transactions, and forms of compensation. People work hard to distinguish among different types of social ties, with concomitant sets of rights and obligations, and to select appropriate kinds of transactions and forms of compensation. Thus, as Zelizer notes in the case of caring services, people make sure to distinguish among care provided by nurses, spouses, or live-in-servants. For each of these relationships, they draw boundaries between "permissible" and "forbidden" forms of care, and between proper and improper forms of compensating the provider. Bitter conflicts can erupt when one or both parties involved, or even third parties, judge existing arrangements a "wrong mix" of relationship, transactions, and forms of repayment.

A clear example brought up by Zelizer (2005) is the legal dispute involving a professional couple and Gabina Lopez, a Bolivian-born immigrant nanny, who worked for three years in their household in the Washington D.C. area (*Lopez* v. *Rodriguez;* 500 F. Supp. 79 (D.D.C. 1980)). Gabina had met her employers in her native Bolivia and accepted their offer to travel to the U.S. to do housework and look after their three children. In the U.S., Gabina labored non-stop, with no breaks and no vacations, getting as compensation room and board, paid medical expenses, and pocket money, together with the promise of wages to be deposited in a bank account. When her employers refused to hand over that money to her, she sued. Her employers argued that their relation to Gabina was not an employment relationship, but a family-like bond, in which case Gabina was not entitled to monetary wages. Gabina's lawyers disputed such a claim and the court ruled in favor of the former nanny, awarding her back wages plus damages and court costs, minus the amount spent by her employers on room and board. For the court, Gabina fit the profile of an employee and thus deserved wages as compensation.

Healy (2006) draws on Zelizer's ideas to conduct a comparative analysis of blood and organ donation. As his study shows, organizations that procure and distribute what he calls "human goods" have been successful at promoting donation by embedding it on the template of the "gift exchange." Participants understand the transfer of blood and organs as a gift, without expecting material compensation in return. This is the case even when the exchange does not occur within the context of face-to-face relations and when the donor and the recipient have not met each other.

However, the increasing gap between organ demand and supply has led procuring organizations to review their practices. They are currently evaluating and testing new programs that use money as an incentive to increase organ donation. Not surprisingly, these new programs have triggered a new round of debates about the role of money in social relations and the inevitable "debasement" of social life. Healy acknowledges that, despite opposition, money is likely to play a role in organ donation. Yet, he denies the claims that the introduction of money incentives is tantamount to the complete commodification of organ exchange and the dissolution of the "gift" framework. Instead, Healy forecasts an *expressive role* for money, where money will act as an implicit incentive but not as overt compensation for organ donation. Even when mediated by money, organ donation will continue to be understood as solidarity-driven.

Monetary Exchange, Commodification, and Exploitation

While Healy (2006) focuses on the legal, regulated, and organizationally driven market for human goods, other researchers have peered into a darker side of the organ trade. Scheper-Hughes (2002a, 2004), for instance, has looked at illegal organ sales, which connect wealthy buyers from both developed and developing countries with poor, vulnerable sellers in the latter. The analysis of the logistics of this trade, the ideological categories used to justify it, and the underlying inequality in wealth, living conditions, and symbolic power share key common themes with the Marxian critique of capitalist society. Critics of the organ trade like Scheper-Hughes do not merely talk about a "corruption" of social relations or a "depletion" of meaning and solidarity, but center instead on the exploitation of destitute populations by over-privileged groups and the concealment of exploitative relations of production behind the façade of "voluntary exchange."

Scheper-Hughes (2002a: 32) studies the illegal organ traffic in what she defines as "a hybrid of experimental, multi-sited, ethno-graphic research" and "medical human rights documentation and surveillance." Her goal is to throw light onto the normally hidden practices of procurement and sale of human tissues and organs. As she points out, such practices remain in the dark thanks, in part, to "the invisibility and social exclusion of the population of organ suppliers" and to the seldom-challenged authority and legitimacy of transplant medicine (Scheper-Hughes 2002a: 34). The motto guiding the project's data collection is to "follow the bodies," an enterprise which leads researchers to travel back and forth from elite medical centers to inner cities and shantytowns. Researchers start that itinerary by asking "whose needs" are favored and whose "sacrifices" are dismissed in the ideology of transplant medicine (Scheper-Hughes 2004: 35).

The picture emerging from the research is that of a clear "divi-sion of society into two populations, one socially and medically included and the other excluded, one with and one utterly lacking the ability to draw on the beauty, strength, reproductive, sexual, or anatomical power of the other" (Scheper-Hughes 2002b: 4). The organ traffic is built upon a deep gulf between poor, disen-franchised organ givers and wealthy, socially privileged organ receivers. Beyond the abysmal differences in material conditions, these two populations are also separated by their differential position in the world of medical attention and medical discourse. While transplant physicians treat organ receivers as deserving individual patients, with known names, biographies, and medical histories, organ suppliers tend to become an unknown zero in the transplant equation, who count only as bodies whose biological properties "match" the donor's needs.

Going beyond the simplified image of a "voluntary exchange"

of money for organs, Scheper-Hughes (2002a) seeks to uncover the social conditions that allow for paid organ transfers from unrelated living donors, from the social deprivation sustaining the supply side to the multifaceted ideological mantle that nurtures the growing demand. Thus, to the idea of a "scarcity of organs," the author counters the notion of an artificially created demand, fostered by technological developments and medical decisions resulting in the continuous expansion of the pool of transplant candidates. Furthermore, to the image of the "gift of life" from organ givers to recipients, Scheper-Hughes opposes the picture of a "bodily sacrifice" by members of a subordinated population on behalf of more powerful, richer individuals. Finally, against the poorly tested assumption of a "risk-free" kidney removal, the anthropologist brings up detailed, abundant evidence of real physical and psychological costs for organ givers, who "face extraordinary threats to their health and personal security through violence, injury, accidents, and infectious disease" (Scheper-Hughes 2002a: 56).

Cost–Benefit Analysis and the Commensuration of Incommensurables

Another line of criticism that overlaps with classical analyses of monetarization deals with the notion of commensuration. As we have seen, Simmel's (1978) analysis of monetarization centers on the power of money to make things and people commensurate and interchangeable, and thus render human relations to the material and the social world purely functional and superficial. Simmel's preoccupation with the cognitive and social consequences of unlimited exchangeability has reemerged in contemporary critiques of cost–benefit analysis and related models of decision-making. Contemporary critics highlight the threats to people's culture and identity which underlie attempts to transform incommensurable values into monetary estimates and stress the power inequalities disguised in the use of cost–benefit analysis as a basis for policymaking. Besides, empirical studies have underscored cost–benefit analysis's limitations in assessing hard-to-quantify aspects of objects and situations, even within the sphere of capitalist production for a competitive market.

Espeland (1998), for example, challenges the assumptions behind rational choice decision-making as a tool for evaluating policy outcomes. She builds her argument on her experience with the decision-making process involving the construction of a dam to improve Arizona's water supply. Orme Dam – which was finally called off – would have flooded the lands of the Yavapai tribal community and threatened their identity as a people. Espeland's analysis revolves around the Central Arizona Water Control Study, a research project on the social and environmental impacts of suitable alternatives to Orme Dam. Even though the ancestral lands of the Yavapai were saved from inundation, Espeland remains skeptical of rational choice methods for assessing and comparing the costs and virtues of contrasting policy alternatives.

Espeland's skepticism focuses on the notion of commensuration, a technique at the core of rational choice decision-making models. The author defines commensuration as a process "concerned with measuring different properties normally represented by different units with a single, common standard or unit" (Espeland 1998: 24). As she explains, commensuration in the policy evaluation of Orme Dam entailed predicting "the impacts of various alternatives" and expressing the "values or preferences about these projected impacts" by using a "common scale" (Espeland 1998: 25). Espeland acknowledges that commensuration is a powerful tool, as it allows decision-makers to integrate and compare radically "disparate" forms of information. For the scientists and technicians in charge of the Central Arizona Water Control Study, commensuration appeared as the solution to the dilemma on how to reconcile such disparate values as farmers' improved water supply, increased land values, and the potential losses for the Yavapai community.

Espeland, however, finds fundamental flaws with commensuration techniques used in cost–benefit analysis. The technical complexity of these models does not guarantee their neutrality when assessing disparate values: "But just as commensuration can create new relationships among disparate things, it can also undermine other relationships" by violating culturally and socially relevant "boundaries" (Espeland 1998: 28). Commensuration techniques inevitably misrepresent and distort what we conceive of as "incommensurable" values, values which we explicitly situate outside of the sphere of choice. For the Yavapai community, land was one of those values; land was an inseparable dimension of their identity as a distinct people, and could not be made commensurable with other values without deeply altering its meaning and "what it means to be Yavapai" (Espeland 1998: 205).

Like Espeland, Anderson (1993) opposes the use of cost–benefit analysis as a technique for assessing public policies. One problem with this form of analysis is that it adopts an extremely narrow vision of how people value and appreciate public goods. In the case of environmental policies, cost–benefit analysis only contemplates the value of nature and the environment as "amenities," consumed as "privately appropriated, exclusively enjoyed goods" (Anderson 1993: 193). This view fails to take into account any intrinsic value that people may attach to the environment as a shared good or as a part of a nation's collective heritage, which is worth preserving independently of any personal enjoyment or direct welfare that particular individuals may derive from it. As Anderson (1993: 205–6) points out: "Many people dedicate themselves to preserving and protecting these goods for their own sakes, even at significant cost to their own welfare. And they care about preserving the pristine character of parts of the biosphere, such as the Antarctic, which few people will visit or use."

Furthermore, Anderson (1993) objects to the political implications of accepting "market-willingness-to-pay" as a measure to value alternative policy outcomes. By treating citizens as consumers and measuring their political choices by the money they are ready to spend, cost–benefit analysis endorses a very restrictive definition of citizenship and democracy. Anderson (1993: 194) argues against adopting public policies on the basis of how much people are willing to pay, instead of taking into account how competing ideas fare "in public debate." Moreover, there is only a short step from privileging consumers' willingness-to-pay as a guide for policymaking to upholding their actual *capacity* to pay. As Anderson (1993: 194) puts it, cost–benefit analysis implicitly "weighs the preferences of those with larger incomes more heavily than the preferences of those with smaller incomes."

But are the problems with cost–benefit analysis and commensuration limited to what we hold as emotionally dear, culturally sacred, or constitutive of our identity? Baldwin and Clark (1994) present evidence on how, even within modern capitalist firms, monetarization can limit people's capacity to perceive and fully take advantage of hard-to-quantify qualities. The authors seek to explain the decline of American corporations' competitiveness after World War II. Dismissing the explanations centered on the high cost of capital or short-term horizons, they offer evidence of sustained corporate investment throughout the 1970s and the 1980s. What was missing – the authors stress – was investment in hard-to-measure "organizational capabilities." One of these capabilities, for example, was external integration, which the authors define as "the ability to link knowledge of customers with the details of engineering design in creating and improving products" (Baldwin and Clark 1994: 89–90). The problem for corporations was that this and other organizational capabilities – usually entangled with day-to-day operations – were not captured "within the 'cash inflow–cash outflow' framework of the existing financial systems" (Baldwin and Clark 1994: 79).

Conclusions

We started the chapter by revisiting economists' conventional definition of money and its purposes, and then introduced three streams of literature that brought up different kinds of evidence to challenge this definition as an account of money's changing meanings in the social world. Ethnographic and historical studies showed the coexistence of multiple objects serving different monetary functions and the presence of separate exchange circuits associated with different currencies. Psychological surveys and experimental studies confirmed restrictions to the use of money in the contemporary West and characterized money as a "poly-morphus concept," whose meaning reveals itself in judgments on the "typicality" and similarity of different money items. Finally, following Zelizer's lead, sociological studies showed how social relations and culture transform externally homogeneous legal tender into "special monies," endowed with different meanings and earmarked for different purposes.

We would like to end the chapter with a brief comment on another discussion that crosses the three streams of literature pre-sented here, but especially the anthropological and sociological traditions. Contemporary anthropologists and sociologists con-tinue to disagree over the classics' critique of modern capitalist economy and its fruitfulness for thinking about the inclusion of new spheres and practices in the money economy. While some prefer to put aside the classics' ideas, because of their assumptions about a quasi-linear historical development, others continue to either explicitly borrow from or implicitly share themes with the classics' preoccupation with money's "disruptive" effects on social relations.

As Zelizer (1989) and Bloch and Parry (1989) have pointed out, Marx and Simmel's critiques of modern capitalism overstated money's power to erode social ties, introduce a wedge between people and the products of their labor, and erase qualitative dif-ferences under a quantitative mantle. Blending the classics' bias with the Polanyists' narrative of a "great transformation," numer-ous studies of monetarization have also overstated the division between "traditional," pre-capitalist and "modern," capitalist societies. This magnification of contrasts has often come with a longing for a "lost world" of authentic economic transactions that were grounded on – rather than disembodied from – cultural norms and social relations (Maurer 2006).

Many of the examples reviewed in this chapter have served to counter the notion of a radical opposition between "traditional" and "modern" societies, and to reaffirm the idea of monetary practices' embeddedness in social structures and culture in con-temporary capitalist economies. However, it is not necessary to endorse the "great transformation" narrative to acknowledge the continuing relevance of the classical critique of modern capitalism. As we have seen, the idea of commensuration continues to illuminate the problems with decision-making methods widely used in the contemporary world. Similarly, the notions of concealment and social exploitation are still useful to question the ideological image of "voluntary exchange" when portraying unregulated monetarized transactions between over-privileged and dispossessed groups.

With the "great transformation" narrative abandoned, more research is necessary beyond the recognition of the social embeddedness of monetary practices. What regularities and differences exist across societies in monetary habits and the meaning of money? Parry (1989) gives us some hints. In all societies, there are certain goods beyond exchange, certain values that belong to the sphere of reciprocity, and certain rules that classify exchanges as "fair" or "unfair." Furthermore, Bloch and Parry (1989) offer the idea of opposed, but interconnected, transactional orders, an order of short-term, individually oriented transactions and an order of long-term, transcendental exchanges. Money changes its sign, from morally neutral to positive, as it passes from the short-term to the long-term order, and can become morally perilous when sacrificing long-term, transcendental needs on behalf of short-term wants. However, having focused their inquiry on non-Western societies, Bloch and Parry have less to say about regularities and variations in the meaning of money across contemporary, Western societies, a topic which deserves greater attention in future sociological studies.

Discussion Questions

1 Think of a precious family heirloom. Would you or your family ever sell it? Could you ever replace it? Why is it so valuable? Can this value be accurately expressed in monetary terms? What do heirlooms and similar objects reveal about the limits of money?

2 Think about the ways in which you manage your personal income and carry out your spending decisions. How do you decide how much money to spend on housing, food, books, and entertainment? Are you committed to not exceeding a certain figure when buying non-essential items such as new clothes or movie tickets? What do you do whenever you get an extra, unexpected income flow? Could you spell out your personal budgeting rules? Have you adjusted them as you have grown older or whenever your financial situation has changed? How?

3 Suppose that you live in an economically depressed community near a pristine mountain range and a multinational company initiates negotiations with local authorities to start a large-scale mining project. The project would bring much-needed jobs and economic development, but it might also pose environmental risks and visually deteriorate the landscape. How should your community respond to this project? How should citizens assess and weigh its potential costs and benefits? By which methods should authorities reach a decision?

4

Credit and the Modern Consumer Society

In chapter 3, we argued that the connection between money and market exchange is complicated by the fact that money has meaning. In this chapter, we consider another complication: market exchange without money. Individuals, households, and families in the U.S. have always made ample use of credit in addition to money. Long before the invention of credit cards, people had to borrow money, or purchase on credit, in order to obtain the necessities of life (and the luxuries) for themselves and their families. If all market transactions were for cash only, many people would have suffered for their inability to obtain money.

Cash was always scarce in early America. Borrowing allowed people to bridge the gap between their variable and sometimes intermittent cash income, on the one hand, and their household expenditures, on the other. Money didn't always come into the family just before it had to be paid out again, and people used credit to bridge the difference. A family farm, for example, was beholden to the crop cycle, as we noted in chapter 2. Farmers had to make major investments in seed and equipment in the spring, during the planting season, but they would not generate significant cash income from their crops until the harvest. They couldn't pay for their supplies in cash, so they typically bought from their supplier on credit. And, of course, farm families had to be fed and clothed year round. So, typically, farm families would borrow for most of the year, and settle their accounts annually, after the fall harvest put money in their pockets. Wage earners faced similar problems when using their uneven income streams to satisfy more continuous expenditures: many household necessities had to be bought on credit. Matters could get worse for this economic balancing act if the family breadwinner lost his or her job, or if someone got hurt or became ill. In an era without unemployment or health insurance, families were particularly vulnerable to unexpected expenses or loss of income.

With foresight, one solution to the income/expenditure mismatch problem was to accumulate a financial nest-egg – to save by spending less than one's income. Savings would then be available to deal with financial shocks or interruptions to income. But in fact many lower- and middle-income consumers could not save and so had no choice but to depend on credit to get by. In addition, some goods were so expensive relative to average income that financing was almost always required for someone to be able to make a purchase. Furthermore, even substantial personal savings could be wiped out during a period of extended unemployment or a serious medical emergency. Overall, savings weren't always a very practical way to deal with mismatches between family income and expenditures.

Despite this perpetual need for credit, in the past ordinary people could not turn to banks in order to borrow. Commercial banks simply didn't make personal loans like they do today, and their lending patterns were quite unlike those of contemporary banks. Banks generally made only short-term business loans, and individuals had to borrow elsewhere. Instead, individuals obtained credit from their suppliers, merchants, country stores, department stores, and friends and family. For particular purchases, they could secure particular types of credit: a mortgage to purchase land or a home, or an installment loan to acquire a durable good like a piano, sewing machine, or piece of furniture. Indeed, sellers realized that they could sell more goods if they also offered credit to their customers. If a person already owned a valuable object (like a watch or piece of jewelry), they could visit a pawnshop and use it to secure a short-term loan. And if none of these kinds of loan were available, people who were desperate could always turn to a philanthropic lender (like New York City's Provident Loan

Society), commercial small loan lenders (like Household Finance), or, more likely, to a loan shark. Only in the mid-1920s did commercial banks begin to make personal loans directly to individuals, and at first only wealthier customers were eligible.

In general, credit seldom flowed to consumers in a single, even stream. Rather, it came in dribs and drabs, tied to particular purchases or coming from specific sources for specific purposes. The overall growth in credit for individuals has occurred in part because methods developed to support the extension of credit for one kind of purchase have spread to other kinds of purchases. More credit has allowed individuals to consume more (by anticipating future income), and it has allowed suppliers to sell more. Credit has also grown as a direct result of government policy, particularly in the case of home mortgages. Overall, the number of sources and the total volume of credit have increased substantially, and so now ordinary American families carry a large debt burden. As we are discovering in the current economic crisis, that debt burden may have become too large.

Although many groups benefited from the long-term growth of credit, credit has always presented serious problems on both sides of a loan transaction. Not only is it sometimes hard for the people who need credit to get it, but those who extend credit don't always get repaid. Lenders want to distinguish between individuals who are creditworthy and those who are not. They are happy to lend to the first group, but not the second. And those who need credit the most are often among the least creditworthy of would-be borrowers. It is an old irony that lenders are happiest lending to those who need the money least, but in fact it is sometimes very hard for lenders to tell who is truly creditworthy.

Compared to lenders, borrowers are quite knowledgeable about their own willingness and ability to repay a loan: they know their own financial situation best, and know their "true" commitment to meeting their own obligations. Lenders do not possess such "inside information" about borrowers' hearts, minds, and wallets. This disparity in knowledge is referred to in economics as an "information asymmetry" (Stiglitz 2000). Such asymmetries affect many different kinds of markets, but are especially important in credit markets. In general, borrowers know much more about the likelihood that they will repay a loan than do lenders, and it is not easy for them to convey their knowledge to lenders in a credible manner. For example, few bankers would take a borrower at her literal word if she simply asserted that she would repay her loan. Anyone seeking a loan, whether creditworthy or not, is going to assure the lender of their best intentions, and so lenders quite reasonably discount such claims. However, lenders remain very interested in being able to tell the difference between who is, and who is not, creditworthy. Thus, they turn to other sources of information, besides what the borrower says. And they have also developed new ways to manage their vulnerability to debtor default.

Although credit in some form has always been a part of the American economy, its overall volume, shape, sources, and purposes have evolved considerably. In this chapter we will discuss these changes, and examine how they have figured in the larger process of economic change. The invention and spread of new forms of credit have been vital in shaping the modern social landscape (e.g., post-World War II suburbanization would have been impossible without government programs to promote mortgage lending) and in laying the economic foundation for the modern consumer economy. And the sources of credit have been both public and private. Today's economy relies very heavily on credit extended to the individual consumer, who can easily buy a house or car on credit, and can use a wallet or purse full of credit cards to cover virtually all other expenses. Credit has been the handmaiden of modern consumer demand.

Individual Credit in Early America

Exchange relations in early America were substantially affected by the absence of cash. The traditional media of exchange, coins made out of precious metals like gold and silver, were perpetually in scarce supply (Bailyn 1955: 100; Clark 1990: 166; Sellers 1991: 13). In response, people adapted both individually and collectively. Individually, people performed in-kind or barter exchanges with their neighbors and so avoided the need for money (Billings and Blee 2000: 83). Of course, barter wasn't always possible since it required a "double coincidence of wants" between the two parties. But when the circumstances were right, people could exchange without money. If one person really needed something, they could always offer their own labor power in return (e.g., paying someone by working for them). At the individual level, people also used credit. This meant that people could acquire goods and then wait until later to pay for them. Indeed, if two parties frequently traded among themselves, then reliance on credit allowed them to offset each other's accounts and settle only the net balance in cash. Very often "book credit" accounts got settled annually, and so there was need for cash only once a year. A family might "run a tab" at the local country store, and pay up intermittently as cash became available. Even urban wage earners during the nineteenth century were paid only every three or six months, and so depended on store credit (Gelpi and Julien-Labruyère 2000: 98). Lastly, people could and did forgo exchange, and simply relied on themselves or their families to provide what they needed. To a much greater extent than today, early American families were self-subsistent.

Collectively, people responded to the shortage of money through democratic politics, and pressed for monetary reforms that would increase the supply of money. For instance, a number of colonial governments tried to satisfy popular demand for money by issuing paper money (Shammas 1982: 81). Paper money did not have the legitimacy or value of specie, but under the circumstances people regarded it as better than nothing. The demand for money also influenced the politics of banking regulations. Where money was scarce, state governments were more likely to make it easier to establish a state bank (through, for example, lower capital requirements) since banks issued paper money and so increased the local money supply (Bodenhorn 2003: 95). Chartering a bank was one way to reduce the scarcity of money, and passage of "free banking laws" provided a considerable boost to the founding of new banks. New York state passed such a law in 1838, and many other states followed suit (Bodenhorn 2000: 39; 2003: 5). Unfortunately, banks chartered under weak regulations were more likely to fail during a financial crisis, and so the value of paper currency could be quite unstable depending on the solvency of the banking system. States worked hard to craft regulatory laws that would ensure bank-supplied currency that was both stable in value and plentiful, but this was hard to achieve (see Moss and Brennan 2001 on New York state).

Before the establishment of railroads and other forms of long-distance transportation, most people traded locally. The rules of local exchange were quite distinctive. According to Clark (1990) and Bruegel (2002), people living in late eighteenth- and early nineteenth-century rural New England were involved in two quite different kinds of trade: local and long distance. Local exchange embedded people in their own personal social networks, and entailed obligations of neighborliness and civility (Mann 2002: 33). Good neighbors showed forbearance when dealing with an unpaid debt, and did not press their claims unilaterally or inflexibly (Clark 1990: 123; Mann 2002: 12, 17). As compared to the written financial instruments that became common later, book credit was more informal, flexible, and could serve social functions (Mann 1987: 23, 26). Similarly, in rural antebellum Kentucky and colonial Massachusetts, good neighbors didn't insist on strict legal rectitude (Billings and Blee 2000: 89; Konig 1979: 85, 88). Breen (1985) found that credit relations among Virginia tobacco growers were also governed by a kind of social etiquette. Generally speaking, economic choices were heavily shaped by social imperatives, and debtors and creditors were linked together in webs of long-term mutual dependence (Bruegel 2002: 42–3). As in early modern England (Muldrew 1998), many early American credit relations followed a social logic that makes modern definitions of "debt" somewhat anachronistic (Kulikoff 1993: 350).

Long-distance trade, in contrast, was conducted more in accordance with a strict market logic: social considerations were weaker, the degree of formality was higher, and deals were deals. Furthermore, long-distance trade was more likely to involve cash rather than in-kind or labor exchanges (cash connoted greater anonymity and social distance, see Clark 1990: 33). Long-distance trade was simpler in the sense that trade relations were less likely to be encumbered by other social ties (i.e., trading partners weren't also friends, neighbors, kin, etc.). But such trade was more complicated in that it exposed people to distant economic forces beyond their influence or ken. Frequently, it was merchants who operated at the interface between local and long-distance exchange. A local merchant would buy and sell with his neighbors, but he might also act as intermediary between the local community and more distant towns and cities (Jones 1936: 134). Local merchants often acquired locally produced goods (e.g., agricultural produce) and then shipped these to cities, for example New York. And they frequently imported commodities (e.g., dry goods) from distant sources and sold them to local customers. Merchants operating general stores in the upper Hudson River Valley typically imported goods from New York City suppliers on sixty- or ninety-day credit (Bruegel 2002: 163). In antebellum Clay County Kentucky, it was salt production that linked the local economy with national trading networks (Billings and Blee 2000: 46, 61). Thus, local and long-distance trade may have had a distinct ethos, but they were also intertwined.

Over time, the balance between local and long-distance exchange shifted strongly in the direction of the latter. Increasingly, farmers, merchants, and ordinary people became entangled in trade networks that reached outside of their local communities, and so the relative volume of exchanges influenced by the ethos of neighborliness and informality shrank. Over the nineteenth century, developments in transportation (e.g., canals, railroads) and communications (e.g., the telegraph) encouraged the development of trade on a regional and eventually national basis. Thanks to cheaper and faster transportation, Midwestern farmers could provide agricultural products to consumers on the East Coast. Textiles manufactured in New England were shipped nationally. Through expanding trade and credit relations, people became exposed to external economic forces that were beyond their ability to control or even to anticipate. The network of credit ties could quickly transmit a credit crunch outward from New York City and cause distress in the rest of the country. The development of long-distance trade and credit brought new uncertainties into people's lives.

Mortgages in Early America

One particularly important type of credit was the mortgage. This was an ancient form of secured lending, going back in the English Common Law tradition to the early Middle Ages (Simpson 1986: 141), and it involved loans secured by real estate. In the U.S., such real estate typically consisted of land, a house, or a farm (or some combination). Collateral distinguishes secured from unsecured lending. A secured loan means that the lender has the legal right to seize an asset (the collateral) owned by the borrower if the borrower defaults on the loan. That asset is specified in the loan contract. Unsecured loans, by contrast, do not involve collateral. Today, borrowers can mortgage intangible property like their patents, accounts payable, or other future revenue streams, but land served as the earliest mortgage collateral, for two reasons: centuries ago, land was the predominant form of wealth, and it was a permanent and difficult-to-conceal asset that could be seized by a creditor.[1] Mortgages started with land but later on other types of property became mortgageable (e.g., crops or other chattels).

The use of collateral encouraged lending because it reduced the financial vulnerability of potential lenders: if the debtor couldn't repay the loan, the lender seized the collateral to offset the loss. Mortgages were also advantageous for borrowers since they maintained possession (and hence use) of the collateral while they repaid the loan. The success of mortgage lending thus depended on the stable value of the collateral (so that in the event of default it could be used to repay the loan), and on the unambiguous private property rights of the borrower (so that the collateral could indeed be seized by the lender). But even if the lender possessed a clear right to enforce a mortgage, much depended on the exact details

90

of the enforcement procedure (Riesenfeld 1973). A very slow or cumbersome foreclosure process could make it difficult for lenders to enforce their legal rights. In addition, the value of some assets was easier to calculate than others, and, as we will see below, the widespread success of home mortgage lending depended very much on the emergence during the 1920s and 1930s of consensus methods for appraisal of home values.

In the past, people sought mortgages for a variety of reasons. One important motive would be very familiar to us today: to finance the purchase of a home, farm, or piece of land. A buyer who lacked the cash to cover the entire purchase price would try to finance the balance with a loan from the seller, secured by the property being purchased. Owners also used mortgages to pay for improvements to the farm or house, or to generate cash to "buy out" co-heirs (Clark 1990: 91). Indeed, land was a notoriously illiquid asset that, thanks to a mortgage loan, could be turned into cash.

Today's home mortgage loans come in an almost bewildering variety: fixed vs. floating, fifteen-year vs. thirty-year, junior vs. senior, balloon mortgages, negative amortization mortgages, and so on. Furthermore, borrowers can obtain a home mortgage with very little money of their own, sometimes less than 5% of the total cost of the home. Today, government-sponsored entities play a very big role in the mortgage market (e.g., "Fannie Mae," the Federal National Mortgage Association, and "Freddie Mac," the Federal Home Loan Mortgage Corporation). In the past, however, mortgages looked very different: they were considerably simpler, and did not involve third-party entities. Instead, mortgages were typically for much shorter periods of time (nothing like thirty years), they involved much bigger down-payments, and they were not self-amortizing.[2]

There is not much systematic evidence on the details of early mortgages, but Frederiksen's study from the late nineteenth century offers some useful information. Based on data gathered by the U.S. Census, Frederiksen (1894: 205) found that the average length of a mortgage varied from state to state, but that it was far below the fifteen- or thirty-year period that is usual for contemporary mortgages. In Massachusetts, for example, the average length of a mortgage was 6.24 years; in California it was 2.95 years, and in New Mexico it was only 1.47 years. Farm mortgages had a typical maturity of five years (Eichengreen 1984: 998). Clearly, lenders were generally unwilling to lend money for as long as they are now, and there were significant differences depending on where the borrower lived. Consistent with later work on interregional differences in interest rates (Eichengreen 1984: 996; James 1978; Snowden 1988: 278), Frederiksen (1894: 206) noted that mortgage interest rates tended to be lower in the Northeastern U.S. than in the West and South.

Severson et al. (1966: 154) examined mortgages in one Illinois county during much of the nineteenth century and found that over time the average length of a mortgage loan increased: rural loans went from about twenty months in length to sixty months (five years) by the 1890s. Furthermore, as time passed, more and more funds came from out-of-state lenders. These lenders tended to make larger loans for longer periods of time (Severson et al. 1966: 159). Thus, Midwestern mortgages became more like those characteristic of the Northeastern states.

Frederiksen also examined who was lending to borrowers. A substantial amount came from various kinds of financial institutions, including insurance companies, mortgage loan companies, savings banks, and building and loan associations. The latter started out as cooperative financial institutions with a mission to bring moral uplift and social stability to the working class through savings and homeownership (Mason 2004: 12–15). Some institutions, like national banks, were restricted by law from direct mortgage lending activities (although there were ways to circumvent these prohibitions, see Keehn and Smiley 1977). But a great proportion of the investment in mortgages still came from individuals, who loaned money so that someone else could buy their property (Frederiksen 1894: 208–9; see also Rozman 1927: 374).

Almost regardless of who made mortgage loans, lenders tended to hold the mortgage in their own portfolio. That is, if a homeowner took out a five-year mortgage from a savings bank, then for five years that bank would receive payments from the borrower. Selling a loan to a third party (such as happens with modern-day securitization) was relatively rare in the early nineteenth century, although it became more common towards the end of the century as Western mortgage companies steered Eastern and overseas investment capital into farm mortgages in states like Nebraska, Texas, and Kansas (Brewer 1976; Eichengreen 1984: 997; Kerr 1963; McFarlane 1983).

In the nineteenth century, states passed laws to restrict or encourage investment in mortgages, and they adjusted those restrictions over time. For example, after the 1830s, New York City mutual savings banks were allowed to invest in mortgages (Olmstead 1976: 91), and in many states insurance companies were induced to invest in farm mortgages in the home state (Keller 1963: 127). During severe economic downturns, state legislatures were often tempted to pass laws making it hard for mortgage lenders to foreclose on insolvent debtors, especially if it meant protecting local debtors from out-of-state lenders (Bogue 1955: 187; Sellers 1991: 163–4). Some states simply prohibited land ownership by foreigners, which meant that foreign lenders could never seize the land used to collateralize a loan (Davis and Cull 1994: 51–2). States also passed homestead exemption laws, which protected debtors' homes from seizure by creditors, even when the debtor had defaulted on a loan (Goodman 1993). In the early twentieth century, a few states followed the lead of South Dakota, which in 1917 set up a program to provide mortgages to farms (Moore 1949: 169). But to support mortgage lending directly, there was nothing like the elaborate institutional machinery put in place at the national level during the New Deal.

Mortgages started with land, but lenders eventually found other forms of collateral to secure their loans. In the antebellum South, for example, slave-owners could use their slaves as collateral for loans. After the Civil War and the abolition of slavery, however, Southerners had to find some other way to secure their loans and so many Southern states passed crop lien laws (Woodman 1995: 4–7). Farmers could borrow on the security of their crops, and landlords could obtain liens on the crops grown by their tenants (Woodman 1995: 39).

Consumer Credit

Mortgages were commonly, although not exclusively, used to support the purchase of real estate. This connection between credit and sales became both deeper and wider as new forms of credit were used to encourage the sale of consumer goods. One important development occurred with the rise of installment lending in the middle of the nineteenth century (Lynn 1957). This form of credit was closely associated with the sale of relatively expensive durable goods like sewing machines, reapers, furniture, tractors, pianos, encyclopedia sets, and, later on, automobiles (Calder 1999: 161–2; Clark 1930: 19). Such commodities were relatively costly, and it was hard for consumers to save up enough money to purchase them with cash. Sellers realized that they could boost sales by, in effect, lending buyers the money needed to make the purchase. In an installment arrangement, the buyer would make an initial down-payment, take possession of the good, and then make a series of cash payments (often monthly) so as to cover the full price. In the meanwhile, the buyer would be able to use and enjoy their purchase. If the buyer failed to make a payment, the seller would then have the right to repossess the good. Installment lenders typically used chattel mortgages or conditional sales contracts to enforce the right of repossession (Lynn 1957: 414), and the installment price was higher than the cash price because it factored in interest. Installment loans transformed the meaning of "affordability" by turning the hefty purchase price, which could seem quite daunting to a buyer, into a sequence of much smaller payments. Instead of having to come up with $300 cash for a piano, for example, a family simply had to be able to afford a monthly payment of $10. Installment loans also had the advantage (to the seller) of evading usury laws since, legally speaking, the installment contract was a hire-purchase arrangement, not a loan (Gelpi and Julien-Labruyère 2000: 103). This method was so successful that by 1930, more than 80% of furniture and about 75% of washing machines were sold using installment credit arrangements (Calder 1999: 201).

The biggest effects of installment lending were felt in the automobile industry. At the start, cars were expensive durable goods for the wealthy, and most Americans simply couldn't afford to buy them. However, with the right kind of financing, ordinary Americans could afford low monthly payments and purchase a cheaper, mass-produced car (Grimes 1926). Furthermore, it was expensive for automobile dealers to maintain large inventories of cars on their lots. Following the lead of other durable goods manufacturers, automobile companies realized that one effective way to increase sales was to help with credit, and so General Motors established GMAC (General Motors Acceptance Corporation) in 1919 to provide financing to both dealers and customers. Henry Ford was initially opposed to installment lending and so Ford Motor Company didn't follow suit until later, but other manufacturers did (Clark 1930: 25; Clarke 2007: 109, 117). Besides boosting sales, these new kinds of financing allowed manufacturers to maintain smooth and steady production on the automobile assembly line (Olney 1989).

With this systematic extension of credit, automobile ownership multiplied throughout the country, starting with high-income families and then spreading down to middle- and lower-income families. For instance, out of consumer spending on durable goods, the percentage spent on automobiles went from a paltry 1% in 1900, when the car was a pure luxury item, to 10.6% in 1910 and then to 31.4% in 1925, when it became a mass commodity (*Historical Statistics of the United States*, table Cd411-423). Figure 4.1 shows the dramatic rise in the consumption of cars. Starting at the end of the nineteenth century, spending on cars went from 0% and climbed through the 1900s and 1910s until it reached a stable level of between 30% and 40% of total consumption of durable goods. There was a big dip during World War II, when the U.S. produced tanks instead of cars, but things quickly resumed after the war.

Throughout the 1920s and 1930s, most new cars were purchased

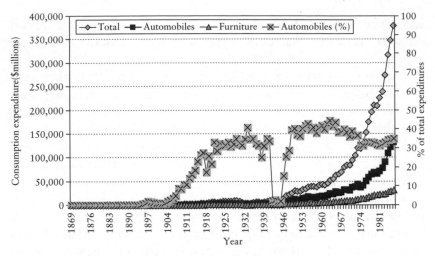

Data source: *Historical Statistics of the United States*, table Col411-423

Figure 4.1 U.S. consumption expenditures, 1869–1986

on some kind of installment plan (Olney 1999: 324), and automobile companies systematically eased the terms of auto loans, further stretching out payment schedules and reducing the size of the initial down-payment (Clarke 2007: 234, 255). Americans fell in love with cars they could afford, and so by 1950 the typical urban American family devoted about 12% of their total annual spending to their cars (*Historical Statistics of the United States*, table Cd558-577). Cars became even more important within family budgets as cities and suburbs were rebuilt around automobile transportation: by 1972–3, more than 18% of total family spending was on cars (*Historical Statistics of the United States*, table Cd597-616). This system of credit greatly expanded the market for cars and ownership spread from well-to-do Americans into the middle class and deeply into the working class. The percentage of families owning cars rose from about 1% in 1910 to 60% in 1930, and then to 82% in 1970 (Clarke 2007: 239).

Producers and retailers appreciated that they could boost their sales by extending credit that was earmarked for the purchase of their goods by their customers. Thus, installment lending and other forms of store credit became a central part of sales and marketing, although this development did not exactly turn producers and retailers into banks. Retailers, including the dry goods stores that preceded the modern department store, helped to cover the cost of credit by charging a credit price for goods that was higher than the cash price. And some stores sold a great deal on credit: in Montana in 1899 and 1900, for example, credit sales for the T.C. Power & Bro. department store were about 78% of total sales (Klassen 1992: 709). Successful management of store credit was one of the keys to success: insisting on timely collections, pursuing delinquent accounts, and avoiding bad risks before they were able to borrow. Credit could be used to lure customers into buying, but excessive or indiscriminate extension of credit would soon get a store into serious difficulty. Credit became widespread enough that some of the new department store chains (e.g., Macy's, Sears and Roebuck) distinguished themselves from the competition in the late nineteenth century by selling for cash only, at substantially lower prices (Calder 1999: 71). However, they all eventually relented and gave credit to their customers. Credit was simply too effective as a tool for selling to consumers (see, e.g., *New York Times*, September 20, 1914, p. 10).

As more people shifted away from self-sufficiency and participated as consumers in the cash economy, and as retailers grew in size and dealt with larger numbers of customers, the old reputation-based methods for assessing creditworthiness lost their value. Mass retailers could not know their customers as the owner of a small New England town store knew his. There were too many dealings with too many anonymous people for a seller to know much about the trustworthiness of customers who wanted to buy on credit. So merchants came to rely on credit bureaus (Hunt 2005: 10). These were cooperative organizations formed by local business communities to keep track of individual credit records: which customers paid their bills on time, who was heavily in debt, who was occasionally late in payments, and who had ever gone bankrupt. The rise of consumer credit bureaus mirrored prior developments in business credit, as starting in the middle of the nineteenth century mercantile agencies provided credit ratings for small businesses. Consumer credit bureaus arose in the late nineteenth century and remained largely local institutions. By one report (*New York Times*, December 25, 1921, p. 32), the main credit bureau operating in New York City kept track of over 75,000 individuals. The information gathered by bureaus helped to define what "creditworthy" meant in the eyes of retailers. According to Hert (1938: 117), department stores and clothing stores were especially reliant on credit reports generated by credit bureaus.

Pawnshops offered another way for people to use their tangible assets to obtain general credit (Woloson 2007). Functioning somewhat like a mortgage, pawning a valuable object encouraged lending by giving the lender extra protection in the event of default. The borrower would give something valuable to the lender (the pawnshop owner) to hold until the loan was repaid. If the loan wasn't repaid, the lender kept the object and usually sold it. Unlike with a mortgage, however, the borrower did not retain possession of the collateral. And unlike store credit, pawnshop loans weren't earmarked for the purchase of a specific good and so could be used for any purpose. Thus they offered flexibility to borrowers. Pawnshops have been particularly important in meeting the credit needs of the poorer segments of the U.S. population usually overlooked by other financial institutions (Calder 1999: 43; Caskey 1991: 87).

As the U.S. economy industrialized, the proportion of the population living on farms shrank, while the proportion supported by wage earners grew. Urban workers could not borrow like farmers on the security of their farmland. At the end of the nineteenth century, and into the early twentieth, policymakers grew concerned that workers did not have sufficient access to credit: banks did not do personal lending; mortgages were generally inappropriate; pawnshops couldn't meet workers' needs; and workers needed access to credit that wasn't always directly tied to the purchase of particular goods. Workers needed to be able to borrow when dealing with unanticipated expenses (often for medical care) or lost income (due to unemployment). So, lacking better alternatives they turned to informal credit institutions, including loan sharks (Haller and Alviti 1977). Indeed, at the turn of the century, loan sharks were regarded as a serious social evil, and philanthropic organizations like the New York City-based Russell Sage Foundation mobilized public opinion against them (Anderson 2008; Ham 1912; Hodson 1919). Loan sharks charged exorbitant interest rates and threatened violence as a way to ensure repayment. They operated informally, but possessed none of the "neighborly ethos" that characterized informal credit relations in earlier times. Although most states had usury laws on the books, which capped interest rates, these were largely ineffectual and did little to stop predatory lending.

In response to loan sharking, the Russell Sage Foundation pursued several policy options before firmly backing one in particular. Initially, the Foundation's personnel supported remedial loan societies, which offered below-market-rate small loans to poor borrowers. The best known of these non-profit organizations was the Provident Loan Society of New York City but nationally there were simply not enough remedial loan societies to really challenge the loan sharks. The Foundation also supported the formation of credit unions, but before long it settled on a Uniform Small Loan Law as the solution. Such a law, intended to be passed in all the states, would regulate small loan lending (loans worth $300 or less), ensure a measure of transparency for borrowers, and permit a high enough interest rate (3.5% per month) to encourage legitimate lenders to enter the market and so drive out the loan sharks. The Russell Sage Foundation played a key role both in determining the specific content of the Uniform Small Loan Law, and in lobbying state legislatures to pass it (Calder 1999: 134). By the early 1940s, some version of this law was in place in 34 states, and a number of small-loan lenders and personal finance companies (e.g., Household Finance, Beneficial Industrial Loan Group) operated under its auspices.

Although they were not actively supported by the Russell Sage Foundation, credit unions were another financial institution that developed to provide credit to poor and working people. Credit unions were an idea imported from abroad (from Germany, via Canada) and brought together people employed by the same workplace so that they could, in effect, lend and borrow from each other. Credit unions could also be organized around common membership in a parish, fraternal lodge, or labor union. The idea was that members of the same group knew a lot about each other, and possessed some measure of social solidarity, so that information asymmetries were less of a problem and borrowers would feel a social (as well as a legal) obligation to repay their loans. Credit unions typically made small uncollateralized loans to their members, in the $50–$150 range, and could do so at lower interest rates than many other lenders (Froman 1935: 291, 295; Ham and Robinson 1923).

The Russell Sage Foundation was initially in favor of credit unions, but decided to concentrate its efforts on passage of the Uniform Small Loan Law. Instead, a different philanthropic foundation founded by a different philanthropist, Edward Filene's Twentieth Century Fund, became the chief proponent of credit unions, and helped to establish the Credit Union Extension Bureau (CUNEB) in 1921 (Clark 1930: 83, 87; Froman 1935). CUNEB became a vigorous promoter of state laws for credit unions (Bergengren 1937: 146). Legislation enabling credit unions was first passed in Massachusetts in 1909, followed by New York and Texas in 1913, Rhode Island in 1914, and then many other states. By 1915, sixty-four credit unions had been established. In 1925, there were 284 credit unions in the U.S., and by 1929 their numbers had grown to 974 (Neifeld 1931: 321). Credit unions continued to spread even during the Great Depression, so that by 1939 there were over 7,000 of them (*Historical Statistics of the United States*, table Cj437-447). Despite this success, the proportion of credit accounted for by credit unions remained fairly small (e.g., credit union assets totaled only $146 million in 1939), and so credit unions remained less important as a source of consumer credit than, for example, personal finance companies (Foster 1941: 155; Ryan 1930: 404).

Commercial banks did not make loans to individuals until the 1920s. Previously, they had loaned to businesses, preferring to support business activity or investment rather than individual consumption. But matters changed after the National City Bank of New York opened a personal loan department in 1928 (Clark 1930: 75; Paddi 1938). A number of other prominent banks quickly followed. Although at first banks concentrated their lending activity on higher-income individuals (Foster 1941: 170), gradually they shifted into middle- and lower-income families and provided another source of credit.

In combination, the different ways that consumers could borrow, and the sources of credit, grew substantially between 1900 and 1930. Credit unions, small loan lenders, commercial banks, store credit, installment loans, and so on, supported a higher debt burden on American households. Olney (1999: 321) shows that non-mortgage consumer debt, as a proportion of household income, rose from 4.6% in 1919 to 11.4% in 1939, more than doubling in relative size. With higher indebtedness, individuals could boost their consumption even if their incomes were interrupted. And, some argue, Americans underwent a kind of cultural transformation by changing their attitudes towards borrowing (Calder 1999). Early on, thrift was celebrated and debt was something to be ashamed of. But taboos against debt diminished as more and more families willingly assumed an ever-growing debt burden to support their consumption. The downside of greater indebtedness was more individual bank-ruptcy. Indeed, wage-earner bankruptcy filings grew almost continuously from about 1921 until 1938 (Hansen and Hansen 2005).

In their famous community study of Muncie, Indiana, the Lynds noted that: "Today Middletown lives by a credit economy that is available in some form to nearly every family in the com-munity" (Lynd and Lynd 1929: 46). In Middletown, installment loans were available to purchase durable goods, there was credit to buy new cars, and local building and loan associations allowed young wage earners to afford homes (Lynd and Lynd 1929: 82, 104, 255). Credit clearly added vitality to the local economy and supported a higher level of consumption, but there was an inter-esting downside. Muncie's adult inhabitants were caught in a never-ending search for credit, and to obtain it, they had always to seem creditworthy in the eyes of their fellow small-town citizens. This induced widespread conformist social pressure as everyone sought to "fit in" with everyone else (Lynd and Lynd 1929: 278). Too much of an idiosyncratic personality would make someone seem a little untrustworthy and perhaps not the best sort of person to lend to. Credit and conformity seemed to go hand in hand.

Mortgages after the New Deal

The Great Depression was a huge shock to the U.S. economy, and the system of domestic finance and credit that entwined firms, banks, and families simply froze up. Many firms and individuals were unable to pay their debts, and so waves of insolvency and foreclosure swept the country. In attempting to reverse course, first the Hoover Administration and then especially the Roosevelt Administration created a new set of institutions to encourage credit flows and protect the banking system. Some, like the Federal Deposit Insurance Corporation (FDIC), were designed to restore confidence in banks. But others were explicitly intended to encourage mortgage lending, to support home ownership and benefit the construction industry, and to support farmers.

In 1933, President Roosevelt set up the Home Owners' Loan Corporation (HOLC), intending to provide quick relief to distressed homeowners. Many families had fallen behind on their mortgage payments, and either faced foreclosure, or were actually in foreclosure, as lenders moved to seize the collateral for their loans (Jackson 1985: 196). HOLC extended new mortgage loans to homeowners, with longer maturities, full amortization, and lower monthly payments. Someone struggling to pay a ten-year mortgage would find it easier to service a new twenty-five-year mortgage. Although the loan terms were different, these new mortgages were like the old ones in that the total amount of the loan depended on the market value of the home (i.e., there were maximum loan-to-value limits). Since home prices had dropped so much, HOLC was creative in measuring value, and applied an "intrinsic worth" formula that put home value about 25% above current market price (Stuart 2003: 46). By injecting about 3 billion dollars into a million home mortgages, HOLC gave short-term support to housing markets (French 1941: 54), but its long-term consequences were even more significant. HOLC helped to shift home mortgage lending conventions so that the new "standard" mortgage was longer-term, self-amortizing, and with a higher loan-to-value ratio (which meant that new buyers could purchase homes with smaller down-payments). HOLC also helped to standardize appraisal procedures, although this had some detrimental effects.[3]

HOLC was a temporary measure, but the Federal Housing Administration (FHA), established in 1934, was not. Together with the Veterans' Administration (VA), the FHA insured long-term self-amortizing high loan-to-value mortgages that conformed to their standards (for appraisal, underwriting, and documentation). By providing mortgage insurance, the FHA encouraged mortgage lending. In 1935, its first full year of operation, the FHA insured over 23,000 loans worth almost $94 million. After the recession of 1937, the FHA made its terms even more generous and began to insure mortgages with up to twenty-five-year maturity, and with a loan-to-value ratio of 90% (French 1941: 63). In 1940, the FHA insured 177,000 mortgages worth $762 million (*Historical Statistics of the United States*, table Dc1105-1121). Publicly provided mortgage insurance was a huge boost to U.S. housing markets, particularly in the new suburbs, and stimulated their growth starting in the 1930s and continuing into the post-war period. After the war, the VA also guaranteed mortgage loans to support homeownership by veterans, and added a further long-term push to the housing sector (Cohen 2002: 141). In 1946, for example, the VA guaranteed over 400,000 mortgages worth over $2.3 billion.

The Federal Savings and Loan Insurance Corporation (FSLIC) was founded in 1934, and did for savings-and-loans what FDIC did for banks: it insured their deposits. However, because savings-and-loan associations did almost nothing but take in deposits and make mortgage loans, bolstering them through deposit insurance directly supported mortgage lending (Mason 2004: 93–4). The kinds of home mortgages loaned by savings-and-loans were also affected by HOLC and the FHA.

Another New Deal institution was the Federal National Mortgage Association (aka "Fannie Mae"). Founded by the FHA in 1938, Fannie Mae supported mortgage lending by helping to create a secondary market in FHA mortgages (Green and Wachter 2005). The primary mortgage market consists of the borrower and the (initial) lender: the lender provides cash to the borrower, and in return is promised a payment stream extending over the term of the loan. The lender doesn't get all its money back until the loan is fully repaid (say, twenty years later). So mortgage lenders who hold on to their loans have to be patient and take a long-term perspective on their investments. In the secondary market, the borrower's promises are traded. So if the initial lender wants to recover its capital sooner than the final payment, it can sell the debtor's promissory note to someone else. An active secondary market boosts the primary market by enabling primary lenders to regain their capital and lend again. Thus, mortgage lenders could make a loan to a homeowner, sell the loan to an investor, and then make another loan. By purchasing, holding, and selling FHA-insured mortgages and in effect creating a secondary mortgage market, Fannie Mae supported the primary mortgage market. Later on, Ginnie Mae (the Government National Mortgage Association) and Freddie Mac (the Federal Home Loan Mortgage Corporation) were established in 1968 and 1970, respectively, to provide similar support for secondary markets in mortgages made by savings-and-loan institutions.

Direct government intervention largely succeeded in increasing homeownership in the U.S. by steering more credit into the housing market. Mortgages were supported by a new set of institutions, and in addition homeowners were given tax incentives to purchase homes: mortgage interest payments were deductible from federal income taxes (Howard 1997: 96), and as the income tax became a mass tax during World War II, the incentive became widely felt. Homeownership rates increased from 43.6% in 1940 to 66.2% in 1997 (*Historical Statistics of the United States*, table Dc653-669). Figure 4.2 shows the long-term trend for homeownership, and it

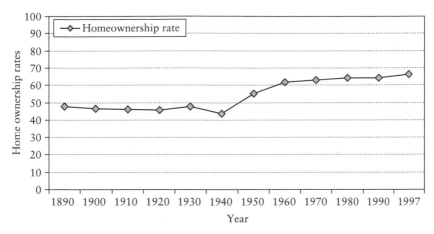

Data source: *Historical Statistics of the United States,* table Dc653 669

Figure 4.2 U.S. homeownership rates, 1890–1997

shows a relatively stable level through the first part of the twentieth century. Homeownership declined between 1930 and 1940 because of the Depression, but it climbed quickly in the 1940s and 1950s, and then rose at a slower rate in the succeeding decades. The encouragement of "subprime" mortgage lending during the administration of George W. Bush represented an attempt to increase homeownership still further.

Unfortunately, the growing benefits of homeownership went hand in hand with enduring racial inequality. Mortgages funded suburban growth, but neglected the older inner cities, and many mortgage lenders were strongly opposed to public housing (Mason 2004: 153). Consequently, white neighborhoods did much better than minority neighborhoods, and racial disparities in homeownership remained dramatic. In 1900, the homeownership rate of white households was 62.3%, as compared to only 30.6% for black households. Ninety years later, white homeownership had increased to 81.7% while for black households it was 58.2% (*Historical Statistics of the United States,* table Ad740-743). Discrimination in mortgage lending also remains a problem (Cohen 2002: 171; Munnell et al. 1996; Yinger 1995). Figure 4.3

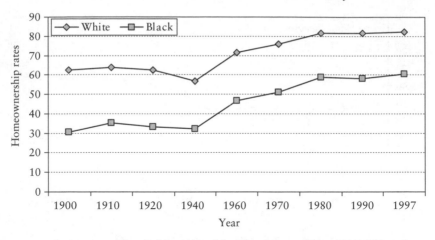

Data source: *Historical Statistics of the United States*, table Ao1740-743

Figure 4.3 U.S. homeownership rates by race, 1900–1997

reveals that the racial disparity in homeownership has persisted for many decades and shows no sign of disappearing any time soon.

The government also intervened in farm mortgages, setting up a variety of programs and institutions to support the flow of credit into rural America. Since family farms were stressed even before the Great Depression, these interventions preceded the New Deal. Before World War I, the primary sources for farm mortgages were individuals, insurance companies, and commercial banks (Clarke 1994: 74). In 1916, Congress created a national system of land banks to make mortgage loans to farms, and these Federal Land Banks soon began to lend. In the early Depression, as farm foreclosures climbed, the land banks were held back by rules that restricted loans to a maximum value set by the market price of the farm: since the value of farms had dropped so much, the maximum possible loans shrank accordingly. However, like HOLC, the land banks became creative in valuation, and set their loans to the "normal" value of a farm, not its current market value. The former was invariably higher than the latter, and so land banks were able to make bigger loans and provide more aid (Clarke 1994: 141). By 1936, the land banks had become the single biggest source of farm mortgages, willing to lend even when others would not. To offer additional assistance to farms, Roosevelt added a number of other institutions in 1933: the Federal Credit Administration, the Agricultural Adjustment Administration, and the Commodity Credit Corporation. The FCA and CCC provided more credit while the AAA attempted to raise prices for agricultural commodities so that farmers' incomes would increase enough for them to be able to service their newly renegotiated loans.

The recovery and expansion of mortgage lending was not something that happened just because of market forces. Rather, the federal government intervened quite deliberately and dramatically in credit markets, favoring some sectors (suburban single-family dwellings, farms) over others (urban multi-family dwellings). Although today mortgage lending is in crisis, and some institutions have become infamous (e.g., Fannie Mae), over the long run these interventions were successful in helping families to borrow and in raising homeownership. However, those benefits were not evenly distributed.

Consumer Credit after World War II

With the economy recovering from the Depression, and with wartime interruptions over, developments in individual credit came to full fruition in the post-war era. The depth and duration of the Great Depression made many people doubt the long-term viability of capitalism, but fears that military victory over the Axis powers would be followed by a return to economic depression proved groundless. Through a variety of means, American citizens were able to go deeper into debt than ever before, buying houses, automobiles, durable goods, and other commodities at an increasing rate. After World War II, America became a mass consumer society. A "consumer republic," as Cohen (2002) terms it, recognized consumers as the primary engine for economic growth, and used consumer well-being as a way to bolster America's capitalist democracy without having to turn to a planned economy or a redistributional welfare state (Cohen 2002: 116, 127). Consumers became a priority for politicians and policymakers, and this focus derived from some of the underconsumptionist diagnoses of the interwar period and Great Depression (Cross 1993: 38). These pre-Keynesian analyses stipulated that the main economic problem was insufficient demand leading to underconsumption, low prices, low investment, and slow growth. One of their recommended solutions was to make credit more readily available (Jacobs 2005: 83–6). But such worries seemed to disappear in the post-war economic boom.

Consumer credit took a big step forward with the invention and spread of payment cards. First the credit card, and then the debit card, allowed people to substitute plastic money for cash, and to obtain a new source of credit, known as "revolving credit." Unlike store credit or installment loans, payment cards offered credit that wasn't tied to the purchase of a particular good, or to a purchase from a particular retailer. Credit cards offered a welcome degree of flexibility and convenience. From the standpoint of the card issuer, so long as the cardholder stayed under their credit limit, they could use it to make whatever purchases they wished. Indeed, since cardholders who do not pay off their balances every month are more profitable, card-issuers welcomed borrowers who carried a balance.

Credit cards originated in the early 1950s, as a convenient way for well-to-do restaurant customers in New York City to pay their bills. Instead of paying cash for each meal, they could use their Diners Club card at a number of restaurants (only fourteen at first), and then simply pay a single monthly bill that combined all their charges. In effect, this arrangement gave card holders credit until the end of the month (or next payment cycle). Diners Club earned money by charging card holders an annual fee and by charging participating restaurants a percentage of the amount billed for each transaction (7%). The arrangement was profitable and soon many other restaurants and cardholders joined up (Evans and Schmalensee 2005: 53–5). Diners Club was able to solve a key problem faced by all new credit card companies: merchants will only accept the card if they think that large numbers of consumers carry the card, and consumers will carry the card only if they think large numbers of merchants will accept it. Both sides must be satisfied for the card to succeed, and since initially there are neither cardholders nor participating merchants, the hurdle is non-trivial to surmount.

In 1958, competition began to catch up with Diners Club: in California the Bank of America issued its own credit card, Hilton Hotels started up Carte Blanche, and American Express launched a national card. Before long, Mastercard and Visa were also established (in 1966 and 1970, respectively) by networks of banks, and credit cards could be used to pay for all kinds of purchases. Card issuers started at the upper end of the income distribution, giving credit cards to individuals whose high incomes made them a good credit risk. In 1970, only 9.2% of households had one of the so-called "travel-and-entertainment" cards (Evans and Schmalensee 2005: 61). But with growing competition, and the desire to increase market share, card issuers began to move down the income distribution.[4] The number of card holders grew, and so by 1983, 37% of American families had a credit card (Federal Reserve Board 1992: 12) while by 1992, 62% of U.S. households had at least one card (Evans and Schmalensee 2005: 76). In 2004, over 72% of households had a credit card (*Statistical Abstracts* 2008, table 1158). Use of credit cards became increasingly common, and now they are even used by college students to pay for small purchases like Starbucks coffee.

More significantly, however, even low-income Americans have increased access to credit cards, despite their greater vulnerability. Bird et al. (1999) find that the proportion of poor households (defined as those with incomes below the poverty line) holding a credit card increased from 17.0% in 1983 to 36.2% in 1995, and over the same period, the magnitude of credit card debts (as a proportion of all non-mortgage debt) of poor households increased from 18.0% in 1983 to 39.1% in 1995. More recently, over the period from 1989 to 2001, the proportion of U.S. households in the bottom income quintile (the poorest 20% of the population) with credit cards increased from 29.3% to 42.9% (Federal Reserve Board 2005: 475).

Once card issuers were able to circumvent state-level usury laws (thanks to the Supreme Court's 1978 decision *Marquette National Bank* v. *First of Omaha Service Corp*), they could charge higher interest rates to riskier borrowers (and impose various other fees), but the fact remained that providing credit to less creditworthy individuals was a tricky proposition. To help sort through individuals and determine who should, and who should not, receive a card, credit card companies have increasingly relied on credit scores issued by companies like Fair Isaac (Evans and Schmalensee 2005: 106; Lewis 1994). Such numerical scores (e.g., a FICO score) are based on credit reports compiled about individuals and are determined by their payment history, prior defaults, income, employment history, assets, indebtedness, and so on. Since calculation of a credit score is a proprietary process, it is hard to know exactly what information gets used and how. One such consumer credit reporting company, Experian, maintains detailed files on over 200 million Americans. But access to credit cards was sometimes influenced by gender bias rather than just economic rationality. Cohen (2002: 147, 282) points out that for decades credit card issuers discriminated against women applicants on the basis of their marital status, withholding credit from married women.

Credit scoring emerged from credit rating, which started in the early 1840s as the firm that eventually became Dun and Bradstreet sold information relevant to the trade credit extended by New York City wholesalers and suppliers. The buyers of this information were often asked to supply goods to firms they had never heard of before, and who were at a considerable distance. Normally, trade credit was unsecured and short term (for thirty or sixty days), and suppliers shipped the goods to their buyers and simply awaited payment. For those thirty or sixty days, the supplier was creditor to the buyer, and suppliers wanted to know if the buyer was likely to pay. Rating agencies aimed to provide this information, on a national basis. The credit information business was a quick success and soon there were many rating agencies (Sandage 2005: 121). Furthermore, buyers of credit information emerged nationwide because, as trade expanded over the latter nineteenth century, virtually every firm became embedded in complex webs of debt and credit. Most firms were simultaneously debtors and creditors.

Using a national network of informants and other sources, after the 1850s firms like R.G. Dun (or the Mercantile Agency) published reference books listing thousands of small firms and giving them a specific credit rating. These books were organized by location (so there was, for example, one for Chicago, and another for Boston, etc.) and were made available to the rating agency's paying subscribers. The entry for a firm described its line of business, named the proprietor, and then gave a summary measure of creditworthiness (in either one or two dimensions, depending on the decade). Instead of trying to determine a customer's general reputation or using social networks to learn about the company's creditworthiness, a subscriber could simply look up the firm and receive a simple and summary piece of information (Olegario 2003: 120–3).

The provision of credit ratings as a way to summarize the creditworthiness of a debtor proved very successful, and spread into other kinds of credit, both upwards to the largest firms and downwards to individual consumers. By 1900, R.G. Dun reference books contained entries on over 1.2 million firms (Olegario 2003: 123). When bond rating agencies started to analyze railway and then corporate bonds at the beginning of the twentieth century, they adopted a similar format for their ratings. Today, Moody's and Standard & Poor's place high ratings (AAA) on the safest bonds and give the riskiest ones "junk bond" status. These summary measures affect the cost of a bond issue, and indeed whether a debtor can borrow at all. Credit scoring emerged as a way to summarize the creditworthiness of individual consumers, and so today most adult Americans have a FICO score that determines, among other things, what kind of a credit card or mortgage deal they can obtain (Miller 2003: 2), and more recently how much they will pay for insurance. Credit card companies know almost nothing about the personal character or individual trustworthiness of their card holders, but they do know FICO scores and credit histories.

Card companies were also able to get growing numbers of

merchants to accept credit cards for payment, despite the transaction fees. Starting with restaurants, card issuers managed to enroll department stores and other retailers, gas stations, car rental agencies, airlines, fast food chains, and hotels and motels. In 2001, 66.9% of department store sales were paid for using credit cards, and 89.6% of car rentals (Evans and Schmalensee 2005: 118). Use of credit cards has become almost essential for retail e-commerce since purchases on the internet are so hard to consummate using cash or checks. Thus, credit cards have become increasingly useful as a medium of payment, and for many kinds of transactions have displaced cash. Credit cards have also been used by small businesses as a substitute for bank loans: it is much easier for a proprietor to run up his or her credit card balances than to take out a formal loan (Evans and Schmalensee 2005: 107–8).

The U.S. economy is uniquely dependent on credit card debt, and in this respect the rest of the world isn't necessarily converging with America. In other parts of the world, people rely on different arrangements to make non-cash payments. In Europe, for example, debit cards are much more common than credit cards, although both are a type of payment card (and to the untrained eye, they both look like "plastic money"). Cash remains important in developing economies (outside of tourist enclaves), while in the transition economies of Eastern and Central Europe, the shift from command to market economies has posed unique challenges. Not only have countries like Hungary, the Czech Republic, and Russia had to privatize state-owned assets, liberalize markets, and develop legal systems suitable for capitalist economies, but they have also had to transform their monetary and financial systems. Guseva (2008) has analyzed in detail the difficulties faced by Russian banks as they tried to develop their own payment card and credit card systems. The fundamental problem was a familiar one: how can lenders figure out which borrowers are trustworthy? At first, they issued cards only to prominent individuals or people who were somehow connected to the bank, but this was too slow. Then they started recruiting organizations (firms, collectives), issuing cards to everyone who worked for the organization (Guseva 2008: chapters 4 and 5). Eventually, the overall number of card holders grew, but it was only because of very deliberate efforts by banks that took the Western credit card model and adapted it to Russian circumstances (Guseva 2008: 101, 147). An American tourist may be able to use his or her Visa card (almost) anywhere, but that doesn't mean that the rest of the world has emulated America's dependence on the credit card.

Informal Credit

Just as credit pervades the formal economy, it also operates in the informal economy. Informal markets (also called "black markets") involve transactions that occur beneath or outside the formal legal framework offered by governments. Thus, informal transactions aren't taxed or even measured by government statistical agencies. They may involve illegal commodities (like drugs or pirated software) or illegal services (prostitution, loan sharking, smuggling, etc.). Informal transactions aren't always criminal, however, because they may involve something as simple as employing someone "off the books" and paying them in cash (e.g., a nanny or housekeeper). And they usually do not involve formal contracts. Informal economies vary in size from one country to the next, and in some places (e.g., Nigeria, Moldova) they rival the formal economy in size.

There are a number of informal financial institutions that make credit available to ordinary people. One of the best-known is the "rotating credit association" (Biggart 2001; Light and Bonacich 1988), found in many countries around the world and within certain immigrant communities in the U.S. This is a private, informal arrangement among a group of people that allows them to save money and borrow from each other. Typically, a group of individuals will agree to make weekly (or monthly) monetary contributions to a "pot." And every week (or month) that pot is given to one of the participants. These periodic contributions continue until everyone has had a turn receiving the pot. Thus, if twelve people form an association and agree to contribute $100 per month, then after a year everyone would have received a single lump sum of $1,200 at some point. No formal contract binds the group together, but social and reputational bonds do. The "numbers racket," an institutionalized form of illegal gambling, also functioned like a financial institution within inner city communities, mobilizing and reallocating savings (Light 1977).

For those who wish to make long-distance monetary transfers, instead of using banks or Western Union, they can rely on the *hawala* system (El Qorchi et al. 2003). This, as we saw in chapter 2, is an informal global network that can allow, for example, migrant workers to repatriate their earnings and support their families at home. For example, there are many individuals from India and Pakistan currently working in the Gulf States (Saudi Arabia, Bahrain, Qatar, Abu Dhabi) and they use the *hawala* system to send their wages back to South Asia. Using the informal network of *hawala* brokers means that the wage earner can pay a cash sum to a broker where he works, and that same cash amount, minus a fee, will be paid out to the wage earner's family by a broker who lives near the family back in South Asia. No formal organizational apparatus or binding legal contract links the broker network together: they are bound by informal social and reputational ties. Remarkably large sums have been transferred by this method. The IMF estimates that between 1981 and 2000, a total of about $75 billion was remitted to Pakistan this way (El Qorchi et al. 2003: 52).

Bankruptcy

When the system of credit works, lenders make loans to borrowers who need them, and then borrowers dutifully repay their loans. But sometimes borrowers are unable to meet their commitments and repay loans as they promised. If the financially troubled debtor is lucky, he or she may be able to renegotiate the terms of the loan so that repayment again becomes affordable. If the debtor is not so lucky and stops paying, the lender can take legal action: enforce payment, garnish wages, seize collateral, and so on, depending on the nature of the debt contract. A debtor who has trouble meeting one debt obligation, but can take care of the rest, may try to muddle through. But a debtor who is overwhelmed by multiple debts, and whose liabilities are greater than their assets, still has one other option: to file for personal bankruptcy. This legal process accomplishes two basic things for insolvent individuals: it takes their assets, liquidates the assets, and turns the proceeds over to creditors to help satisfy the debtor's obligations; and it discharges the debtor from any remaining obligations. Creditors get the debtor's assets (which because the debtor is insolvent do not entirely satisfy their claims), and the debtor gets a fresh start. Bankruptcy law offers an encompassing framework to deal with all the obligations of a troubled debtor.

A number of complications have been added to this basic process. For example, current U.S. law stipulates that some debts are non-dischargeable. That is, obligations like payment of child support or certain taxes cannot legally be extinguished by going through bankruptcy. This may reflect the belief that some financial obligations have a special moral status – parents really must support their children. Furthermore, certain kinds of property are exempt from the liquidation process, and so insolvent debtors are allowed to keep some of what they own (including the proverbial clothes on their back). Bankruptcy law can be modified to favor debtors, or creditors, by adjusting the procedures that filers must go through, by making certain kinds of debt harder to discharge, or by changing the property exemptions. The most recent changes to U.S. bankruptcy law (2005) made it harder for individuals to discharge their credit card debts.

Bankruptcy law is provided for in the U.S. Constitution, but there were long periods of time during the nineteenth century when there was no federal bankruptcy law. For instance, the first law was passed in 1800 and repealed in 1803. Another law got passed in 1841 and then repealed in 1842 (Balleisen 2004; Mann 2002: 248, 255). This pattern of intermittent passage and repeal occurred several times until 1898, when Congress passed the first bankruptcy law that was not subsequently repealed (although it has been substantially modified several times). When there was no federal law, state insolvency laws helped to fill the gap (Skeel

2001: 23). The nineteenth-century pattern typically went as follows: an economic crisis would lead to widespread insolvency, and numerous debtors would apply political pressure for relief from their debts. Congress would pass a new bankruptcy law, and debtors would discharge their debts, *en masse*. Then there would be a political backlash from creditors arguing that debtors were abusing the law and unfairly escaping from their obligations, and so the law would be repealed, until the next economic crisis.

Bankruptcy is driven by the availability of credit. That is, if individuals could not borrow money and accumulate debts, they could not be overwhelmed by their debts. Were people forced to control their expenditures so that spending was always equal to or less than income, then they could never accumulate debts. But credit allows people to spend beyond their means, and so the greater the amount of credit, the greater the danger of bankruptcy. A recent study of personal bankruptcy examines in detail the precipitating conditions and events that drive people to take this extreme measure. In general, people who file for personal bankruptcy are burdened by debts that are substantially greater than their annual income (Sullivan et al. 2000: 70), so bankruptcy truly is a measure of economic desperation. Several kinds of events can so worsen people's economic circumstances that they file, and these affect either incomes, expenditures, or both. Job loss, a demotion, or a job downgrade (e.g., from full-time to part-time work) often precipitates bankruptcy, as do unexpected medical expenses and divorce (Sullivan et al. 2000: 75, 105, 142, 173). But Sullivan et al. (2000) also point to some underlying factors as helping to set the stage for increasing rates of personal bankruptcy, in particular the new ways developed to give more credit to more people (more credit cards, greater use of home equity loans, etc.). In effect, the system for personal bankruptcy functions like a social safety net – it offers a (painful) way for people experiencing serious economic problems to escape from those problems. To be sure, insolvent debtors will lose all their non-exempt property to the creditors, but they will also get a discharge from their debts and thus have a fresh start (Skeel 2001: 242). Depending on how deep of a hole they were in, the magnitude of economic relief can be very substantial. Unlike the social safety net provided by the welfare state, however, the costs of the bankruptcy safety net are born by creditors.

Conclusion

The long-term trend in the U.S. has been for greater amounts of credit to be offered to larger numbers of people. According to a recent Survey of Consumer Finances done by the Federal Reserve, in 2004 47.9% of American families had some kind of debt secured by residential property (either a mortgage or home equity loan), 46% of families had some kind of installment debt (e.g., a car loan), and 46.2% of families had credit card debts (Federal Reserve Board 2006: 28). In 2004, over 76% of American families were indebted to someone in some fashion. This extraordinary expansion of credit has fueled the post-war consumer economy. But the growth of credit occurred unevenly, with wealthier and high-income individuals being the first to receive it, and only with the passage of time did the more numerous lower-income households join the trend. The spread of credit cards exemplifies this process. Inevitably, lenders began to offer credit to people who were less creditworthy, and the question is, why? It seems irrational for them to have done so because people who are poor credit risks are less likely to repay their loans. However, as they loaned to people with worse and worse credit records, lenders have realized that such borrowers can be enormously profitable. Higher risk borrowers pay higher interest rates. A card holder who occasionally misses a payment can be charged enormous fees, in addition to seeing the debt balance grow. Overall, marginal borrowers can make a lot of money for lenders.

The development of consumer credit has depended on a number of underlying institutions. Some were publicly initiated (like those organizations established to support home mortgages) and others were privately established (credit rating agencies). The growth of credit has not been a purely private matter, or something driven solely by invisible market forces. Over time, credit has largely (although not entirely) escaped the local ethos that encapsulated it during the colonial era. Credit used to be extended through personal networks and on the basis of dense, local social ties. Lenders knew borrowers: they were friends, neighbors, kin, or members of the same church or fraternal organization. Informal connections helped to provide the information that creditors sought about debtors. Today, credit is extended much more anonymously, and it flows between people who do not otherwise know each other. No personal social tie joins Visa to millions of Visa card holders. Instead, Visa and the other card issuers and creditors rely on the standardized, quantitative information that is collected and sold by credit raters and scorers. Credit ratings now provide some of the key information about both individuals and businesses that creditors seek, and the development of credit rating represents a big change in how credit operates in America.

Today, credit for individuals involves the same basic trust problems that pertained two centuries ago: creditors are vulnerable to their debtors, and creditors don't know for sure if their debtors will repay. If there is too much vulnerability, or too little information, then creditors will be reluctant to lend. But because the extent of credit has grown so much over those two hundred years, the problems are more daunting than ever. To help manage vulnerability, lenders have greatly expanded the use of collateral and can now use almost any tangible or intangible asset possessed by a borrower to secure a loan. Lenders have also developed secondary markets for individual debt (via securitization), so that lenders can recapture their capital even before the debt is fully repaid. To help reduce uncertainty, lenders now make use of great volumes of information about borrowers (their payment histories, earnings, concurrent debts, spending habits, etc.), frequently summarized in a single number, a credit score. Credit is now much more open-ended and flexible than in the past, and can be used for (almost) whatever purpose the borrower intends.

As Adam Smith would have predicted, this massive extension of credit has mostly not occurred for altruistic reasons.[5] Rather, lenders are selfishly seeking profits, either through the interest (or fees) they charge on a loan, or through the goods they sell on credit. Indeed, the overall well-being of the U.S. economy depends very much on whether consumers are buying goods, homes, or new cars with sufficient vigor. Today, American consumers are feeling pessimistic and are scaling back their purchases. Credit is tight and the economy is slowing down. But as has often been the case in the past, the U.S. government is not just letting this situation unfold. Rather, it is intervening in financial markets to get the credit flowing again, bailing out banks and providing fresh injections of capital. The goal is to get the banks lending again so that economic activity will pick up. Consumer credit is recognized by government as one of the linchpins of the modern capitalist economy, and government will prop it up if necessary. But intervention isn't just crisis-driven, for governments have supported credit markets both in good times and in bad.

The hand of government brings with it politics. And political clout is certainly evident in the heavy support for farm credit, or in the way that the home mortgage system benefits the middle class, sustains the construction industry, and favors suburban growth over urban renewal. Political influence is even apparent when credit fails and insolvent debtors file for bankruptcy. Credit card companies lobbied for years to revise the rules that governed personal bankruptcy, and in 2005 these were changed to favor credit card companies. Perhaps this wasn't a coincidence. Political influence is also obvious when an economic crisis undermines the credit system, in part or as a whole. In the 1980s, for example, the savings-and-loan industry was quickly deregulated and, absent any prudential oversight, large numbers of savings-and-loans soon got into trouble by making too many risky or imprudent loans (Mason 2004: 213–29). The costs of savings-and-loans failures were first borne by FSLIC, which insured their deposits. But these costs grew so high that FSLIC was itself overwhelmed and became insolvent in 1987. Congress had to intervene directly with a massive bailout that ultimately cost taxpayers more than $150 billion.[6] Clearly, housing markets were still of great concern to politicians and they would spend a lot of money to maintain stability. And if the events of the savings-and-loans crisis bear an unfortunate resemblance to what is going on today, they also underscore that governments recognize the importance of credit markets and will in a crisis make vigorous and expensive interventions. *Laissez-faire* ideology does not last long under such circumstances.

Discussion Questions

1 Someone once said that if a woman owes her bank $100,000 and can't pay, then she has a problem. But if she owes her bank $100 billion and can't pay, then her bank has a problem. What does this suggest about the balance of power between debtors and creditors? Can you think of some real-world examples?

2 Consider that today many people have too much debt, and face the prospect of personal bankruptcy or spending years repaying all the money that they owe. Since debt only occurs when someone wants to borrow and someone else is willing to lend, who is to blame for this situation? What distinguishes an "irresponsible" from a "responsible" borrower? What differentiates between "responsible" and "irresponsible" lenders? Does it make sense to pass laws that protect "responsible" lenders and borrowers, or to penalize "irresponsible" lenders and borrowers?

3 An individual who is overwhelmed by their debts can file for bankruptcy. Typically, such a person has more liabilities than assets. Bankruptcy is a legal process that seizes the debtor's assets and uses them to repay creditors. It also discharges the balance, and gives the debtor a "fresh start." However, some debts are "non-dischargeable" in that the debtor is still obliged to repay even after going through the bankruptcy process (e.g., income taxes, child support payments). As well, some personal assets are exempt from bankruptcy in that the debtor is allowed to keep them (e.g., clothing and personal effects). Do you agree that some debts should still encumber the post-bankruptcy debtor? What kinds of debts should be non-dischargeable? And what kinds of exemptions are appropriate? Is there property that bankrupt debtors should be allowed to keep?

4 Over many decades, a variety of federal policies have tried to boost homeownership among American families. What is so special about owning a home? Why does ownership of this particular commodity deserve political support, as opposed to, for example, ownership of cars, telephones, computers, or toasters? What are the arguments in favor of owning a home? Are the benefits worth the cost of the federal programs?

5 What role does credit play in your life? What sources of formal and informal credit do you rely on to finance your regular and unexpected expenditures? What expenditures would you have to forgo if you couldn't resort to these sources of credit?

5

Credit and the Modern Corporate Economy

With the spread of markets, the disappearance of socialist command economies, and the neoliberal shift in economic policy in many capitalist nations, the for-profit firms and corporations that populate markets have become increasingly important as basic units of the modern economy. Unlike the consumers and individual borrowers who were our focus in chapter 4, modern corporations are "fictive individuals." They aren't real persons, but under the law they have some of the same economic rights and privileges as living individuals: they can own property, sign contracts, sue in a court of law (and be sued). They can also borrow and lend. But even though they are legal "fictions," corporations command a substantial proportion of our society's economic resources.

Like the people we discussed in the previous chapter, firms are also embedded in credit networks. Large corporations raise long-term funds through retained earnings, equity (issuing corporate shares), and debt (borrowing from banks, or issuing bonds), and in the short term they obtain trade credit from suppliers or issue commercial paper.[1] Small businesses usually raise money through other means. Generally, they do not issue publicly traded securities (like stock and bonds), but rely on bank loans, family funds, and may even use an owner's credit cards as a way to finance operations. Like large firms, however, they depend on their suppliers for trade credit.

In this chapter, we focus on credit in the modern corporate

economy. We begin our discussion with a review of microsociological studies of capital markets. Studies in this area return to the classics' ideas on economic action – in particular, the characterization of economic action as "social" and "embedded" in culture, institutions, and social structure, and tackle problems traditionally seen as the exclusive purview of economics, such as trading volumes, price formation, and price volatility. After looking at capital markets, we turn to broader institutional arrangements that structure credit flows in modern capitalist economies. First, we explore cross-national variations in credit institutions within the capitalist world, including contemporary China's mixed economy, and then we examine in greater depth the role of the state and financial institutions in the United States.

Following our discussion of institutions, we address some of the problems which threaten credit for large, publicly traded corporations and for small businesses. Our analysis of credit for large corporations – largely centered on the U.S. – pays attention to what is known as corporate governance, for example the relationships among investors, boards of directors, and managers, and the rules that structure these relationships (Roe 2004b: 1). We look at issues which have frequently made the headlines, such as "excessive" executive compensation and corporate fraud, and situate them within their historical and institutional context. When addressing small business finance, we emphasize issues of trust between borrowers and lenders, and how they are managed by "embedding" commercial transactions in social ties (Uzzi 1999).

In the last part of the chapter, we adopt again an international perspective and review existing discussions regarding the effects of the internationalization of capital flows. We examine the literature on governments' power to control or reverse this trend and assess arguments about the fragility of the welfare state in the era of international financial integration. We conclude the chapter by revisiting three themes that underlie the previous sections: the embeddedness of economic action, the problem of trust, and the diversity of institutional arrangements.

Economic Action and Social Structures in Capital Markets

We will first look at economic behavior in capital markets. These markets form the core of modern capitalism, and are where large organizations, both public and private, raise money and manage risk. If the state of Illinois wishes to borrow, it will go to U.S. capital markets and issue bonds. When Google needed to raise equity in order to finance its continued growth, it went to Wall Street, hired an investment bank, and made an initial public offering (IPO) of Google stock. A multinational firm worried about foreign exchange rates can hedge its risks by purchasing currency options or futures contracts. And as we have recently come to appreciate, capital markets don't just affect big firms and governments, but influence the ability of ordinary individuals to borrow money to buy a car, to use their credit cards, or to obtain a home mortgage. Given their importance, it is critical to understand how these markets operate.

Studies of this topic build upon two core premises of Weber, Marx, Durkheim, and Polanyi (Swedberg and Granovetter 1992). First, economic action is "social action." In contrast to mainstream economics' treatment of economic action as "maximizing, rational behavior," uncomplicated by non-economic motives, sociologists consider non-economic motives in the study of economic behavior. In Swedberg and Granovetter's words: "It is clear that economic action cannot, in principle, be separated from the quest of approval, status, sociability, and power" (Swedberg and Granovetter 1992: 6–7). Second, economic sociologists challenge the mainstream depiction of economic action as a series of discrete and atomistic encounters. Instead, sociologists examine economic action as anchored in the institutional arrangements and social relationships connecting economic actors, be they individuals, groups, or organizations (Smelser and Swedberg 1994). Based on these two premises, economic sociologists have sought to explain buying, selling, and pricing practices in capital markets, while questioning the ideal-typical images of actors and markets derived from mainstream economics.

It is not uncommon for sociological studies of capital markets to use fieldwork research in order to better understand how economic actors behave in the real world (see Keister 2002: 48). Baker (1984), for example, combined ethnographic fieldwork with a network approach to study a national stock options market which traded through open outcry (i.e., traders gathered face-to-face). Baker focused on two particular "crowds," for example two groups of buyers and sellers – a smaller one and a larger one – who gathered on the exchange floor to trade different types of stock options.[2] In each crowd, Baker examined the networks of social relationships connecting buyers and sellers. Furthermore, he looked at how different networks affected stock options' price volatility. Baker found, first, that the two crowds differed significantly in the kind of networks linking traders. The larger crowd was more differentiated, for example segmented into smaller groups of traders, when compared to the small crowd. Drawing on organizational theory – supported by his qualitative interview data – Baker attributed the larger crowd's stronger segmentation to traders' limited communication abilities. Unable to communicate smoothly in a large, noisy crowd, buyers and sellers restricted trade to those in their vicinity. Second, Baker found that differences in networks were associated with differences in price volatility, which he measured as the variance of prices. While the larger crowd's greater segmentation tended to increase price dispersion, the smaller crowd's more unified character had the opposite effect. Baker's findings illustrate the importance of understanding economic behavior as "embedded" in networks of social relationships (Granovetter 1992).

The traders studied by Baker interacted face-to-face, which rendered all the more plausible the argument for economic action's "embeddedness" in social relationships. But what happens with electronic trading? What if traders conduct their business on a global scale, so that their "partners" are located thousands of miles away? Is it still reasonable to search for "social structure" in this global context? Knorr Cetina and Bruegger (2002) offer an answer to these questions with their study of global microstructures in international currency markets. As the authors explain, "the foreign exchange market is not organized mainly in centralized exchanges but derives predominantly from inter-dealer transactions in a global banking network of institutions" (Knorr Cetina and Bruegger 2002: 906). Although physically based at investment banks, participants in this market trade with each other through technological means and turn to a computer screen, rather than to another person, as their central focus of attention. The authors conducted field research at the trading floors of three "globally operating investment banks" based in Zurich. Like Baker, they discovered an underlying social struc-ture that contradicted the traditional view of the market as "anonymous, discrete exchanges ruled by supply-and-demand adjustments rather than intersubjectivity" (Knorr Cetina and Bruegger 2002: 920).

In fact, Knorr Cetina and Bruegger found that despite their pre-dominantly virtual, disembodied character, international currency markets possess some of the traits of local, face-to-face interaction. These markets could be best characterized as "communities of time," where intersubjectivity is born out of time coordination rather than a shared local setting. Time coordination is evident, for example, in calendars and schedules which organize traders' time around the delivery of important economic news and indica-tors. As the authors point out: "Synchronized collective emotional arousal around weekly, monthly, and quarterly calendar events can plausibly be assumed to further enhance the integration of dispersed global groups" (Knorr Cetina and Bruegger 2002: 930). Moreover, like other communities, the international currency markets depend on their participants' shared expectations and social governance mechanisms. Observation shows that traders orient their behavior by rules of conduct which seek to avoid unlimited profit-seeking, maintain traders' commitment to their stated prices, and preclude price negotiations within the trading interaction. Furthermore, "these institutionalized expectations are extended by an informal code of honor, by which traders are informally assessed and by which trading behavior is constrained" (Knorr Cetina and Bruegger 2002: 936–7). Time coordination, shared expectations, and social governance reveal the presence of "global microstructures" in these de-territorialized, virtual markets.

In contrast to most economic sociologists – preoccupied with "enriching" the models of actors and markets advanced by mainstream economics – some, like Michel Callon (1998), have taken another path. Rather than argue that real-world economic actors are not rational, calculative, maximizing agents, Callon claimed that *homo economicus*, as depicted by economic theory, is not a mere fiction. In fact, market participants who behave like the theoretical model can be found, not as a "natural occurrence," but as a product of economic theory (MacKenzie and Millo 2003). Perhaps, the very success and acceptance of economic theory *in the real world* has resulted in market participants' adjustment to the theoretical model. Thus, economic sociology's main task is to explain the social process by which real people have gotten to think and act like *homo economicus*.

MacKenzie and Millo (2003) set out to test Callon's ideas in the Chicago Board Options Exchange. In their view, this was an ideal setting to explore the notion of "performativity," for example the argument that economic theory helped to create the very things it sought to explain. This was because the area of economic theory which dealt with the pricing of options, option theory, achieved considerable success in explaining economic outcomes: there was a close (but not perfect) fit between the theoretical model and empirical patterns. MacKenzie and Millo decided to take a closer look at option theory's success. One possibility was that option theory succeeded in a purely scientific way, that is, it helped to explain "preexisting price regularities." Another possibility – following Callon – was that option pricing theory helped to forge the reality it described, as market participants learned the theoretical model and began to use it to price options. To solve this puzzle, MacKenzie and Millo undertook a historical sociology of the options exchange and interviewed some of the people who had participated in the market since its creation.

MacKenzie and Millo's findings, although generally fitting into Callon's framework, reveal a more nuanced story. On the one hand, the authors find evidence of the "performative power" of option pricing theory. Thus, for a time following the establishment of the options exchange, options theory fit poorly with empirical data; only later did pricing patterns conform to theoretical predictions. This temporal evolution is not consistent with the notion that options theory merely described a preexisting economic reality; instead, it seems that market actors eventually learned to act in ways prescribed by the theory. On the other hand – the authors argue – Callon's framework alone is not enough to explain the creation of the Chicago Board Options Exchange. In particular, Callon's framework overlooks the central role of "collective mobilization" by a group of active members of the Chicago Board of Trade. These people committed their own time, money, and social ties to establish the Chicago Board Options Exchange and keep it going; and they did so not in pursuit of their own profit but guided by what they believed was the "public interest." MacKenzie and Millo conclude that the idea of economic theory's "performative power," though insightful in some contexts, should be combined with economic sociology's traditional interest in broader cultural frameworks, institutional arrangements, and interpersonal networks of social relationships.

Market-Based and Credit-Based Financial Systems

While the work reviewed in the previous section is focused on the microdynamics of capital markets, other research centers on macro-level institutional arrangements, both as outcomes to be explained and as historical forces shaping economic and political outcomes. Within this body of research, researchers have studied how credit varies depending on the structure of the financial system (Carruthers 2005). Different institutional arrangements, born out of particular historical circumstances, condition available options for business agents and policymakers, and shape relations among government, banks, and non-financial corporations. How do non-financial corporations raise funds? What sources of credit are available to them? How much influence do banks have on the non-financial corporations they lend to? And how much does government affect the allocation of funds among different sectors, industries, and firms? The answers to these questions vary from country to country and depend on the structure of the financial system.

Based on Zysman's (1983) typology, a broad distinction can be made between *market-based* and *credit-based* financial systems (see also Allen and Gale 2000; Davis 2009: 35). The defining trait of a market-based financial system is the existence of an active and developed capital market, where investors can buy and sell corporate stocks and bonds, government securities, and other financial instruments. A well-developed capital market allows investors to acquire corporate stocks or bonds, under the assumption that they can sell them later with relative ease. When these conditions are met, access to capital markets makes non-financial corporations less dependent on commercial banks for long-term investment, although they still depend on the services of investment banks (Morrison and Wilhelm 2007: 3–5). Occasionally a bank may interfere with the affairs of a financially troubled firm, but generally direct bank control is not routine in market-based financial systems (Mintz and Schwartz 1985).

The United States and Great Britain stand as the clearest examples of countries with market-based financial systems (Allen and Gale 2000: 4). In these countries, capital markets supplied credit to industry. In contrast, in "late-developers" such as Germany and Japan, banks, rather than capital markets, became the main external sources of corporate finance. As Zysman (1983: 61) points out: "where capital markets were neither adequate nor reliable sources of development funds, banks or specialized institutions filled the gap with loans." Banks' pivotal role in financing industrial growth usually developed under the state's sponsorship; to ensure the availability of credit, governments assumed part of the risk involved in transforming short-term savings into long-term lending (Zysman 1983: 62–3).

A financial system where bank loans take precedence over funding from capital markets is a credit-based financial system. France and South Korea are examples of countries with this kind of financial structure. In credit-based systems, non-financial firms tend to be highly indebted (or "leveraged"), and their dependence on bank credit increases bank influence on corporate affairs. As they have a big stake in non-financial firms' survival, banks are more likely to closely monitor firms' performance and to intervene in managerial policies and decisions. Moreover, credit-based financial systems grant policymakers greater room to influence the sectoral allocation of credit flows: government officials can pressure the banks, who then steer credit accordingly. This contrasts with the state's role in market-based financial systems, where the government focuses on preserving competition and controlling a few key macroeconomic variables, such as interest rates, but generally avoids direct resource allocation (Zysman 1983: 69).[3]

In France, as well as in South Korea, the state relied on the credit-based financial structure to spur industrial development. Both countries benefited from the U.S.'s steady support, a financial largesse founded in part in America's geopolitical interests during the post-war era. In the 1950s and 1960s, the French state took advantage of a benign international environment to promote the modernization of the country's industrial base (Loriaux 1991). For its part, the South Korean state – a privileged target of bilateral aid and multilateral lending – used external funding in the 1950s "to build a social basis of support for a strong state"; after that, it devoted foreign lending to fund heavy industrialization (Woo 1991: 8). In the two countries, the credit-based financial structure allowed the state to give businesses access to cheap credit and regulate the sectoral allocation of resources.

These two countries' financial structure entailed a high level of interdependence among businesses, the banking system, and the state. Loriaux (1991: 66) characterized the French economy in the mid-1970s as a "pyramid of credit extending from the Banque de France to the individual firm." Woo stressed how the South Korean state's control of the banking system, combined with firms' high level of indebtedness to banks, resulted in strong business compliance with state policies. Although instrumental in encouraging industrial development, allocation of finance by the state had both strengths and weaknesses. As Loriaux (1991: 13) pointed out, abundance of finance at negative interest rates in real terms "caused the French economy to become one of the more inflationary economies of the developed world." As for South Korea, Woo (1991: 13) argued that the system itself "promoted bankruptcy" because strongly subsidized credit gave firms little incentive to become financially sound. Moreover, when large, highly leveraged firms became unable to meet their financial obligations, the state could not afford to let them go bankrupt and was often forced to come to their rescue (they had become "too big to fail").

Policymakers can use the banking system not only to promote economic development, as in the cases of France and South Korea, but also to enhance their own political fortunes, as in the case of recent financial centralization in China. According to Shih (2004), Chinese policymakers chose to consolidate financial power at the central level instead of adopting a more market-oriented approach. He seeks to explain why market liberalization stalled in the area of bank finance, even when it occurred at a fast pace in other areas. His answer points to "power politics," in particular to top bureaucrats' interest in securing their political standing and avoiding any reforms that could lead to short-term instability.

The "power politics" framework helps to explain Premier Zhu's measures towards the country's accumulated US$400 billion in non-performing loans. This issue jumped to the top of policymakers' agenda when they faced the Asian financial crisis in the late 1990s. However, rather than taking steps to change the structure of incentives, so that banks could enjoy greater autonomy and make "lending more market-oriented," the Zhu Administration focused on accumulating financial power by centralizing control of the banking sector (Shih 2004: 934). Shifting financial power from state authorities to the central government did not address the root causes of non-performing loans. What it did accomplish, instead, was a "simplification" of bureaucratic control of resource allocation, thereby enhancing central leaders' capacity to advance their own political interests. As Shih (2004: 929) explains, with the centralization of finance, the Premier was able "to use the distribution of financial resources as a political bargaining chip at the Politburo level, building a support coalition through disbursing funds to the pet projects of other leaders."

The Role of the State and Financial Institutions in the U.S. Context

In contrast to what happened in France or South Korea, the American state has largely shied away from an active role in the allocation of finance. However, this does not mean that the American state has remained passive in the construction of the financial system. On the contrary, government action and politics have shaped the organization of financial markets and constrained the participation of banks in corporate finance. Historically, two sets of regulations have strongly narrowed banks' role in the American financial system: rules limiting bank consolidation and branching, and rules restraining banks' ability to own corporate equity, in particular controlling portions of company stock. These mutually reinforcing regulations have weakened banks' involvement in corporate finance and curtailed banks' chances of becoming active players in corporate governance (Roe 1994: 21–2).

As Calomiris (2000: 43–4) recounts in his history of banking regulation, citizens in early America were not permitted to freely establish banking corporations; instead bank charters were "seen as a privilege and as a tool of the state (and, possibly, federal) governments to be used to achieve specific, appropriate objectives." In 1781, the Confederacy issued a bank charter establishing the first commercial bank in the United States, the Bank of North America, with the goal of funding the revolution (Calomiris 2000: 43–4). A few years later, as a result of political opposition, the Bank of North America lost its national charter; given a new state charter, the Bank resettled in Delaware and moved later to Pennsylvania. In 1791, responding to Alexander Hamilton's initiative, Congress chartered a national bank, the Bank of the United States, to help fund the federal government (Johnson 1999: 7–10). In 1816, five years after the bank charter's expiration, Madison's government reinstated it as the Second Bank of the United States. But political opposition contributed to the demise of the national bank, following Jackson's presidential veto of the bank's re-chartering in 1832.

State-chartered banks began to flourish, in part, as an unintended consequence of the Constitution of 1788 (Sylla et al. 1987: 391–3). The Constitution deprived states of the power to issue money. This created a serious financial problem for state governments, which had gotten used to creating currency to finance state operations. States found a solution in banks. The Constitution did not prevent states from chartering state banks, which could then issue bank notes. According to Sylla et al. (1987: 393), state-chartered banks became key pillars of state public finance from 1790 to 1860. States obtained bank-derived revenues by acquiring bank shares or by taxing banking institutions. As a source of public finance, banks had a political advantage over general property taxes: "the incidence of taxation seemingly was shifted from persons and property in general to privileged, monied institutions" (Sylla et al. 1987: 402).

As we saw in chapter 2, state-chartered banks suffered a strong decline with the adoption of the National Banking Act of 1863, which sought to establish a national banking system (Johnson 1999: 11–12). National banks were allowed to issue bank notes backed by government bonds. To further strengthen national banks, Congress taxed bank notes issued by state-chartered banks. The Act also established minimum capital and reserve requirements for national banks, limited their ability to make real estate loans (White 1982: 34), and was interpreted by regulators as prohibiting bank branching (Calomiris 2000: 47). As White (1982) points out, this new institutional framework created a challenge for state governments, as it shifted money-issuing powers from state banks to national banks. At the same time, the capital requirements and loan restrictions included in the Act "prevented the supply of banking services from keeping pace with the demand as the country grew and expanded westward" (White 1982: 34).

Following the Banking Act of 1863, federal and state regulators engaged in a contest to fill the gap in banking services and shape the structure of the banking system (White 1982: 34–5). In the late 1880s and 1890s, states started to pass "free banking laws" aimed at improving the position of state-chartered banks *vis-à-vis* national banks. "Free banking laws" lowered entry barriers for state-incorporated banks by eliminating the need to get a special charter from state legislatures. Furthermore, compared to national bank regulations, state rules were more lenient regarding minimum capital and reserve requirements, and loan provisions (White 1982: 34–5). This coexistence of competing regulatory systems worked in favor of state-chartered banks, whose number increased very rapidly from 1890 to 1900 (White 1982: 35–7). In an effort to boost incentives for national banks, federal regulators also loosened rules on capital and reserve requirements, and reduced loan restrictions. By contrast, limitations on branch banking remained in place.

As Roe (1994: 57) points out, branching limitations shored up a banking industry based on many small, local banks, which in turn became a strong political force in support of the status quo. Even when, in the 1890s, high failure rates spurred a movement in favor of branch banking and consolidation, the influential small, local bankers were largely successful in opposing a relaxation of branching limitations (Calomiris 2000: 52). In their fight against branch banking, small unit bankers were not alone. They often had the support of the general public, anxious to have "more bank offices," and state regulators, who favored ease of entry as a way to expand banking services (White 1982: 35). By contrast, no broad coalition emerged in support of branch banking (White 1982: 38–9). New regulations in the early twentieth century did not go far in loosening restrictions: the McFadden Act of 1927 permitted branch banking at the city or town level; a new Act in 1933 allowed banks to branch at the state level subject to state laws (Roe 1994: 94–5).

Branching limitations were compounded by restrictions on the ownership of corporate stock. The National Bank Act of 1863 did not explicitly authorize banks to hold corporate equity and the Supreme Court interpreted this as an outright ban (Roe 1994: 55). During the New Deal period, Congress passed the Glass–Steagall Act, which, as we saw in chapter 2, further restricted commercial banks' ability to hold corporate equity. In the nineteenth century, commercial banks had circumvented the regulatory framework by operating through bank affiliates which dealt in corporate stocks and bonds. The Glass–Steagall Act of 1933 dictated a strict separation between commercial banks and their bank affiliates, which then became investment banks (Morrison and Wilhelm 2007: 209; Roe 1994: 95–6). In 1956, Congress dealt another blow to commercial banks' ability to own securities by issuing the Bank Holding Company Act. This Act barred bank holding companies – separate banks reincorporated as subsidiaries and grouped into a holding company – from owning more than 5% of voting stock in non-financial corporations (Roe 1994: 98–9).

Rules limiting bank size and scope have hindered American financial institutions as a source of funds for non-financial companies and prevented U.S. banks from assuming a German-style role in corporate governance (Roe 1994: 21–2). It is not surprising, then, that large corporations in the late nineteenth century would rely primarily on retained earnings and the sale of equity to finance their expansion (Calomiris 2000). According to Calomiris and Ramirez (1996: 57), "regulatory restrictions on the geographic range and scope of activities of intermediaries may have significantly raised the cost of financing for U.S. companies." Furthermore, branching limitations, in particular, made American financial institutions more vulnerable to bank panics, as shown by the contrast between the U.S. and Canada in the 1920s and 1930s (White 1981: 556).

The American banking system remained an agglomeration of "geographically isolated banks, with circumscribed activities" for most of the twentieth century (Calomiris 2000: 334). However, the banking industry began to experience profound changes in the early 1980s. Since the mid-1970s and even earlier – depending on which measure is considered – "traditional banking" had become less profitable and banks had started to lose market share. With the emergence of money market mutual funds, the expansion of commercial paper and junk bond markets, and the development of securitization, banks lost their "competitive advantage" in attracting funds and supplying credit (Edwards and Mishkin 1995: 31–2). Widespread bank failures and mergers during the 1980s, and onerous interest-rate caps, prompted U.S. regulators to deregulate the banking industry, in an effort to make banks more competitive in the new financial environment (Davis 2009: 116–21). As deregulation progressed, some American banks grew into "large, nationwide" institutions and banking itself got redefined through a new emphasis on "rich, complex bank–client relationships" and new products such as securitizations, loan sales, and underwriting (Calomiris 2000: 334–5). As part of these changes, banks assumed greater risks "by pursuing riskier strategies in their traditional business lines or by seeking out new and riskier activities" (Edwards and Mishkin 1995: 40).

Has financial deregulation produced convergence between the United States and credit-based financial systems like the German? Is the distinction between credit-based and market-based financial systems still meaningful? And what does deregulation mean for the relationship between banks and non-financial firms? As Edwards and Mishkin (1995: 32–5) indicate, the "decline in traditional banking" and the diversification of banking activities was not confined to the U.S., but occurred throughout the world (see also Sinclair 2005: 54–7). Nevertheless, cross-national differences remain significant. For example, the U.S. banking system is still much less concentrated than that in France or Germany (Allen and Gale 2000: 232). Furthermore, it is not clear whether this partial convergence in the banking industry extends to corporate governance. Calomiris (2000: 344) suggests that American banks have gained greater influence on non-financial firms and "have become much more like their banking colleagues in Europe and Japan." Roe (1994: 101), by contrast, argues that recent changes notwithstanding, the institutional scaffold that shaped the American banking industry in the past continues to condition corporate structures and practices; this is because, in his words, "previously built organizations adapt slowly." If Roe is right, we should still find evidence of corporate governance problems which hark back to regulations limiting the role of financial institutions in non-financial firms.

In the next section, we will examine in more detail issues of corporate governance. Before doing so, however, it is important to acknowledge an analysis that counters arguments about U.S. banks' limited power *vis-à-vis* non-financial firms. Mintz and Schwartz

(1985) argue that banks' control over capital enables them to exercise *financial hegemony* over non-financial corporations. The concept of hegemony refers to a kind of "noninterventionist leadership," which operates without the need of "overt coercion" by determining "the viable options available" to non-financial corporations (Mintz and Schwartz 1985: xii). As the authors explain, "decision making over capital flows regularly confers upon financial institutions this hegemonic leverage" over non-financial corporations (Mintz and Schwartz 1985: 39–40). By exercising control over capital flows and thus affecting investment choices, banks are able to create or eliminate options, and thus shape the environment in which non-financial firms operate. Typically, this type of leverage expresses itself in different ways such as "a veto power over proposed projects," conditions attached to loans, and investment initiatives that mobilize non-financial firms through the availability of funds (Mintz and Schwartz 1985: 40).

Mintz and Schwartz (1985) base their theory of financial hegemony on a quantitative study of interlocking directorates for all major firms listed in *Fortune* magazine (the so-called "Fortune 500") for the period 1962–73. An interlock, in the organizational literature, refers to the presence of a representative of a particular firm on another firm's board of directors. An interlock can connect two non-financial firms, a financial institution to a non-financial corporation, or vice versa. Like others, Mintz and Schwartz face the question of how to interpret interlocks. Take, for example, the presence of a bank representative on an industrial firm's board of directors. What does this interlock mean? Is this a sign of bank "cooptation" by the industrial firm, or that the industrial firm has been infiltrated by its lender in an effort to closely monitor its activities (Mizruchi and Stearns 1988: 195)? Or is this just a vehicle for elite cohesion, a mechanism by which corporate elite members bridge their differences and pursue their "shared political interests" (Mintz and Schwartz 1985: 135)?

Mintz and Schwartz's longitudinal study of interlocks shows that "commercial banks send and receive interlocks more frequently than other types of corporations" (Mintz and Schwartz 1985: 146). Furthermore, money market banks and insurance companies occupied the center of the interlock networks through the 1960s. In their view, these findings indicate that banks rely on interlocks, mainly, to gather information on investment opportunities in the corporate world. In that sense, banks are particularly interested in inviting industrial leaders to their boards, as these leaders may become sources of information about lending opportunities. Interlocks, therefore, reflect "patterns of capital flows" and are instrumental to financial hegemony because they "facilitate decisions relating to the allocation of loan capital by supplying investment information to the financial world" (Mintz and Schwartz 1985: 145).

Corporate Governance

By focusing on banks' influence on corporate choices, Mintz and Schwartz distinguish themselves from a long tradition of studies emphasizing the weakness of restraints on managerial power in publicly held corporations. After recent corporate scandals, however, it is worth revisiting discussions of dispersed ownership, investor vulnerability, and corporate governance. Berle and Means initiated this tradition in the 1930s with their seminal analysis of the "separation of ownership and control" in the publicly held corporation. According to them, in the late nineteenth century, American capitalism went through a change as consequential as the previous shift from independent worker-owners to wage workers who "surrendered" control of their labor to a factory owner. A comparable type of surrender occurred later on – Berle and Means claimed – with the emergence of the public corporation, as large numbers of dispersed investors relinquished control of their wealth to corporate managers. In the authors' words, this change amounted to "the dissolution of the old atom of ownership into its component parts;" control of physical assets and the right to receive profits from their use would now fall into different hands (Berle and Means 1968: 8).

In Berle and Means' view, the separation of ownership and control would seriously alter "the ends for which the modern corporation can or will be run" (Berle and Means 1968: 9). As long as the owners were in control – the authors contended – we could safely assume that profit-seeking would steer the corporation into an "effective use" of industrial property. However, with the multiplication of owners and their detachment from corporate control, this assumption might no longer be valid. In particular, Berle and Means were concerned with the division between owners and managers. Self-interested managers would gain more money by diverting profits into their own pockets than by running the corporation effectively. If managers were primarily motivated by other goals, such as pride or prestige, they might shy away from risk and pursue non-economic ends. In both cases, shareholders' interests would be hurt, since they would get reduced profits from their stakes in the corporation.

Berle and Means' propositions became a customary starting point for the analysis of corporate governance in the American context. Roe (2004a: 1), for example, considers the separation of ownership and control "the core fissure in American corporate governance." Roe acknowledges the benefits of this pattern of economic organization. Dispersed ownership can be a good strategy for new companies to secure finance and for existing corporations to raise capital on a very large scale. Furthermore, dispersed ownership offers investors a relatively low-cost exit strategy and the opportunity to diversify their stakes. At the same time, dispersed ownership goes hand in hand with the separation of ownership and control, a situation which may lead to less-than-optimal performance. Either because managers appropriate corporate funds or because they may not be competent enough, the separation of ownership and control creates what analysts have called an "agency problem": Will "agents," in this case corporate managers, look after the interests of small, distant shareholders? Or will they pursue their own agenda? Furthermore, will managers have the necessary skills and vision to focus on "maximizing shareholder value" (Roe 2004b: 3)?

Agency theorists have advocated using compensation as a mechanism for "aligning" managers' interests with those of shareholders (Jensen and Meckling 1976). In fact, agency theory explanations are often used by corporations as a rationale for introducing incentive compensation plans, in the form of bonuses, stocks, and stock options, designed to link executive compensation to firm performance (Zajac and Westphal 1995). The idea behind these forms of compensation is to create incentives for management to "maximize shareholder wealth" (Zajac and Westphal 1995: 285). With the right incentives in place, managers would give priority to shareholders' interests and avoid "shirking behaviors" or pursuing a self-serving agenda. As Roe (2004b) warns, though, this type of incentive compensation may not be efficacious for motivating managers who are already very wealthy. Moreover, incentive compensation plans have had their own unintended consequences, as different scholars have reported.

Frydman and Saks (2007) analyze long-term trends and changes in the structure of executive compensation for the period 1936–2005. Looking at total executive compensation – including salaries, bonuses, long-term incentive payments, and stock options – the authors distinguish three periods in the evolution of executive pay. From 1936 to the early 1950s, executive compensation dwindled. During the next twenty-five years, executive compensation grew, albeit at a slow pace (an average of 0.8% yearly). Starting in the mid-1970s, the growth rate has accelerated, although with a brief fall from 2001 to 2003. Frydman and Saks also note significant changes in the structure of executive compensation. From 1936 to the mid-1950s, executives were paid mainly through salaries and current bonuses. In later years, long-term bonuses and stock option grants have become a larger share of executive pay.

Many have welcomed the increased use of stocks and stock option grants in executive compensation packages. To the extent that they increase executives' pay sensitivity to firm performance, they may help to alleviate the agency problem. In practice, however, compensation arrangements fall short in aligning executives' and shareholders' interests. As some scholars point out, some aspects of these arrangements have actually become "*part* of the agency problem itself" (Bebchuk and Fried 2003: 72, authors' emphasis). Owing to managers' influence in setting their own pay, compensation arrangements have often turned into opportunities for "managerial rent-seeking" (Davis 2009: 96–9)

Management compensation is set through negotiation between top executives and the board. The board, however, rarely achieves complete independence from the CEO. Instead, the CEO has a say in "renominating directors to the board" and in setting directors' compensation and perks (Bebchuk and Fried 2003: 73). As a result, board directors tend to agree to managers' compensation increases, unless such increases provoke an outcry from outsiders. In fact, research shows that the weaker is the board *vis-à-vis* the CEO, the higher is executive compensation (Bebchuk and Fried 2003: 77; Core et al. 1999).

Furthermore, some aspects of compensation packages are designed not to maximize shareholder value but to "camouflage" managers' extraction of rent. This is the case, for example, with in-kind retirement perks and guaranteed post-retirement consulting fees. As Bebchuk and Fried point out, these benefits are hardly justifiable on "efficiency grounds" but they "make pay less salient" to outsiders (Bebchuk and Fried 2003: 79–80). Another example discussed by the authors is the use of executive loans – lending money to executives at favorable interest rates – which used to be widely embraced by firms as a form of "stealth compensation," until the Sarbanes–Oxley Act prohibited them in 2002. As these examples show, managers' influence in setting their own pay may result in "suboptimal pay structures" that raise costs for shareholders.

Besides the "excess compensation" that executives may get, "suboptimal pay structures" may create the wrong incentives for top management. In particular, the fact that managers are largely free to dispose of their options and shares may give them "incentives to misreport corporate performance and suppress bad news" (Bebchuk and Fried 2003: 89; see also Bar-Gill and Bebchuk 2002). Another factor that may distort managers' incentives is rapid CEO turnover. In combination, soaring executive pay, incentive compensation, and rapid managerial turnover have resulted in a recurring cycle of unrealistic expectations and misleading financial reporting. As Langevoort (2003) explains, in order to get hired, candidates for top management positions have incentives to promise more than they can deliver. Once on the job, top managers are set to make extraordinary amounts of money, but they are unlikely to keep their position for too long. In this scenario, hiding real returns for some time when they lag behind investors' expectations becomes a rational strategy to extend the job's rewards just a bit longer. It is not surprising, then, that embellishing financial performance has become a rather common practice in the corporate world, even though it has not always reached the extremes of the most publicized corporate scandals.

Conflicts of Interest and Regulatory Weakness

How extensive is the manipulation of financial reports? In an attempt to assess the extent of financial manipulation on a national scale, Lev reviews two sources of evidence. First, there is the "direct, case-specific evidence," which includes corporate earnings restatements, securities fraud lawsuits, and Securities and Exchange Commission (SEC) enforcement releases. Earnings manipulations detected through these sources are not numerous: "there are roughly 100–150 litigated or SEC-enforced cases per year" (Lev 2003: 42). It is important to point out, though, that these instances have increased in recent years and that, more and more, they involve top firms in their sectors. Second, there is "indirect, cross-sectional evidence," including the pattern of declared earnings during or close to specific circumstances like a stock offering, which might encourage managers to engage in "creative accounting." In light of this type of evidence, the author concludes that "a large number of managers regularly fine-tune their reported evidence to meet external targets" (Lev 2003: 42). In other words, manipulation of earnings is not an isolated phenomenon.

Widespread as it is, the manipulation of financial reports entails significant social costs (Lev 2003). By inflating investors' expectations, the manipulation of earnings has fueled market bubbles and aggravated their subsequent collapse; furthermore, manipulation has prevented investors from becoming aware of corporate investment in unprofitable business ventures. In Lev's view, a problem that may invite manipulation is that financial reports are not just based on past facts; inevitably, they include estimates of future earnings or expenses, things that are not yet known at the time the report is published. It is hard for investors or regulators to tell the difference between an intentional exaggeration and a *bona fide* mistake.

When discussing corporate reports and the manipulation of earnings, it is necessary to recognize the role of auditors and regulators. Auditors and regulators are part of a system of safeguards intended to protect investors from corporate managers' misconduct. For auditors to fulfill this role, though, they need to remain independent from the firms they audit. Thus, for example, auditors are banned from owning shares in their corporate clients (Demski 2003: 57). However, accounting firms not only perform auditing work, but they also provide tax and consulting services. In fact, as a result of recent changes in the auditing industry, audit revenues declined and accounting firms have compensated by expanding their consulting services. Furthermore, auditors have sought to build long-term relationships with their corporate clients, which often translated into opportunities for auditors to transfer to the audited firm. For some, a fluid relationship between the auditor and its client, which improves the auditor's knowledge of its client's business, may enhance the quality of audit work (Demski 2003: 57). However, this type of relationship may also play against the auditor's ability to be impartial *vis-à-vis* the client.

The SEC oversees corporate reporting and auditing work by watching over and enforcing mandatory disclosure and accounting rules. Financial reporting standards are set not by the SEC itself, however, but by the Financial Accounting Standards Board (FASB), a seven-member organization in the private sector, supported by a staff of about sixty-eight professionals with diverse backgrounds, including government, public accounting, academia, and the corporate world (Financial Accounting

Standards Board 2007: 6). The FASB in turn consults with other bodies, including the Emerging Issues Task Force. Comprised of representatives of public accounting firms, large corporations, and users of financial statements, this interpretative body offers guidance on financial reporting and intermediates between the FASB and reporting practice (Demski 2003: 62; Financial Accounting Standards Board 2007: 7). As Demski suggests, this regulatory structure may not be adequately insulated from the auditing industry and its clients. Symptoms of this lack of independence are the FASB's slow pace and its propensity to issue extremely detailed, exception-ridden reporting standards. These two characteristics reflect auditors and reporting firms' considerable influence on regulatory decision-making (Demski 2003: 63).

Regulators' vulnerability to private interests is not limited to the area of financial reporting standards but affects corporate governance regulation more generally. As Roe (2004a) points out, the decentralized and fragmented character of the American regulatory system provides a platform for the regulated to reach and influence regulators. The United States does not have an all-powerful, centralized agency in charge of regulating corporate governance. Instead, this task is divided among an array of institutions and actors with different jurisdictions and responsibilities. At the federal level, the SEC affects corporate governance by enforcing financial reporting standards and by regulating trade in financial markets. At the state level, governments set standards for corporate charters. In addition, courts have a say in corporate governance through their interpretation of federal laws regulating corporate policy. Finally, there is also self-regulation through private codes of conduct and autonomous bodies such as the New York Stock Exchange (Roe 2004a). Such a fragmented regulatory system leaves ample room for the regulated – especially corporate managers, but also accountants, lawyers, and credit rating agencies – to lobby regulators and block more stringent regulation. Congress and the courts, in particular, have often become veto points for the regulated to neutralize or weaken any attempt to strengthen regulation.

Financial Innovation, Corporate Fraud, and the "Financialization" of the Economy

Regulatory problems have worsened in the last two decades with the wide diffusion of new financial instruments, which made it easier for companies to hide risk from investors. Financial innovation multiplied the holes in the regulatory framework; regulators either lagged behind the creation of new financial instruments or left them completely outside of their purview. This was especially true with derivatives, which are so named because their "value is derived from other assets," such as stocks, currencies, commodities, and so on (Partnoy 2003: 5). A common type of derivative is the currency option. As Partnoy (2003: 11–12) explains, when buying a currency option, the buyer acquires the right to buy or sell a certain amount of foreign currency at a later point in time and at a fixed rate. By purchasing the option, buyers are insuring themselves against future currency fluctuations that could affect their businesses. In the 1980s, only very basic forms of derivatives like this were traded, derivatives trading represented a very small proportion of trading in financial markets, and it took place in regulated markets. This changed in the following decade, however, when new and more sophisticated derivatives were invented, in many cases to escape existing regulations (Partnoy 2003: 4–6).

In the 1990s, derivatives trading became widespread, derivatives started to be traded in largely unregulated "over-the-counter deals," between private parties,[4] and companies began to use specially created firms, partnerships, or trusts called "special-purpose entities" in order to make derivative deals and avoid full disclosure of risk to investors or regulators (Partnoy 2003). The growth in this market was such that the notional value of all over-the-counter derivatives at the end of 2008 was $592 *trillion* (Bank for International Settlements 2009: 1). In 1991, the SEC accepted that, as long as an outside investor controlled at least 3% of the special-purpose entity, derivative deals could be treated as off-balance-sheet operations regardless of the amount of money involved (Partnoy 2003: 80–1). Throughout the decade, government officials and legislators repeatedly refused to regulate derivatives, and legal changes in the mid-1990s restricted investors' chances of filing securities' lawsuits against corporate managers (Partnoy 2003: 172–3; see also Goodman 2008). As Partnoy points out, regulatory changes created a *laissez-faire* environment for corporate governance: financial reports became more and more fictitious, investors and outside board members had increasing trouble monitoring top management, and even top managers were at pains controlling aggressive employees involved in financial transactions (Partnoy 2003: 187, 296–7). Not surprisingly, a wave of corporate scandals marked the 1990s and 2000s.

The importance of financial innovation and the regulatory vacuum in which it has unfolded are important factors in the analysis of corporate fraud because, in contemporary capitalism, not only financial firms but also non-financial companies are actively engaged in profit-seeking through financial activities. As Krippner (2005: 182) has detailed in her study of "financialization," the analysis of the sources of income for non-financial firms shows since the 1970s "the growing importance of 'portfolio income' (income from interest payments, dividends and capital gains on investments) relative to revenue generated by productive activities." Assessing the savings-and-loans crisis – which preceded the recent wave of corporate scandals – Calavita, Pontell, and Tillman (1997: 171) argue that "collective embezzlement" may be characteristic of "finance capitalism." As they explain: "Unrestrained by investments in infrastructure and with little of their own capital at stake, those who handle other people's money" face fewer restraints to engaging in fraudulent behavior (Calavita, Pontell, and Tillman 1997: 172).

One of the most publicized episodes in the rather long list of corporate scandals was Enron's collapse in October 2001.[5] Enron was established in 1985 from the merger of two pipeline companies, Houston Natural Gas and Internorth of Nebraska. Soon after its creation, though, the company began to shift from building pipelines and selling energy to trading energy as a commodity. Over time, Enron's incursion into commodity trading would expand to energy contracts and derivatives linked to energy prices and to an ever-growing spectrum of commodities (including pulp, steel, advertising time on television, and even high-speed data and internet capacity). At the same time, Enron never completely abandoned the business of building energy infrastructure, which it carried out in different countries around the world.

Before the company's financial troubles began to unfold, Enron had over 20,000 workers and its reported profits exceeded $100 billion. Enron was an extremely successful player in energy derivatives trading. In fact, Enron's success as a trader continued until the very end, when its credit was cut short by credit agencies' downgrading of its debt (Partnoy 2003: 307). However, Enron's other venues were unprofitable, and the huge investments the company made to set up an e-commerce platform, to fund start-up technology companies, and to trade new products outside of its area of expertise in the energy markets brought little or no profits. At the same time, Enron's executives set up various partnerships, the infamous special-purpose entities, which became vehicles for concealing assets and debts from investors (Partnoy 2003).

The immediate trigger behind Enron's downfall was the California energy crisis, which prompted some financial analysts to look into the company's special-purpose entities (Partnoy 2003: 331). In the fall of 2001, the auditors – who had long overlooked the company's extensive manipulation of its reported profits and losses – finally asked Enron to treat some of the partnerships as part of itself. The move resulted in an immediate evaporation of a substantial portion of shareholders' equity, accompanied by the growth of Enron's debt. An SEC inquiry, related to self-dealing between the company and its special-purpose entities, accelerated Enron's downward spiral (Partnoy 2003: 332). Pressed by dwindling profits and escalating debt, Enron enlisted JPMorgan Chase and Citigroup's assistance to engage in derivative deals that would make its financial statements look healthier. When the information was disclosed, credit rating agencies reacted by downgrading the company's debt, thus putting an end to the company's profitable derivatives trading. The firm filed for bankruptcy in December 2002 (Partnoy 2003: 338).

Enron's story illustrates many of the elements which we have discussed in our outline of corporate governance problems in the U.S. context, starting with the separation of ownership and control. As Partnoy (2003: 297) points out, "Enron's shareholders lost control of the firm's managers, who in turn lost control of employees, especially financial officers and traders." The fact that, over time, Enron's board of directors recruited an increasing proportion of international members, fitting into the company's global reach, probably did not enhance its ability to closely check the company's top management. But far more important for investors' ability to monitor or even understand what was going on within the company was the flurry of innovative, sophisticated financial instruments, which company managers and employees used and abused in order to incur additional debts without recording them on the company's balance sheets. Company insiders themselves were probably not fully aware of Enron's real assets, profits, and liabilities (Partnoy 2003: 344).

What happened with Enron may have been top managers' direct responsibility, but it occurred in a regulatory environment which posed few restraints. This was especially true in the area of energy derivatives, which Bush Administration officials and Congress had kept deregulated, in response to Enron's own aggressive lobbying. Thanks to Enron's political pressure, the Federal Energy Regulatory Commission and the Commodity Futures Trading Commission, two regulatory agencies which could have monitored the firm's activities, lost jurisdiction over trading in energy contracts (Stevenson and Gerth 2002). Finally, it is important to stress auditors' complacency and lack of scrutiny in the face of "creative accounting" in the company's books. On this point, it is worth noting auditors' conflict of interests with the company: auditor functions included not only traditional auditing of the company's books but also lucrative consulting services. Like Enron, auditors succeeded in lobbying regulators, in this case the SEC, to prevent rules limiting such conflicting roles (Stevenson and Gerth 2002).

In 2002, as a response to public outcry about Enron and other corporate scandals, Congress passed the Sarbanes–Oxley Act. The Act introduced new federal criminal offenses in relation to fraud against shareholders of publicly traded companies, destruction, alteration, mutilation, or concealment of evidence, public account-ants' early disposal of review and audit records, and CEOs and CFOs' certification of financial reports which do not comply with the 1934 Securities Exchange Act and do not "fairly" present the issuer's financial situation and performance (*Harvard Law Review* 2002).[6] In addition, the Act mandated stronger penalties for exist-ing federal criminal offenses and required review and amendment of existing federal sentencing guidelines. According to some legal experts, the new criminal offenses do not alter much the regula-tory framework because they duplicate the offenses that already existed without "lowering the existing standards for indictment and prosecution" (*Harvard Law Review* 2002: 732–3). However, prosecutors may gain "discretion and power" with the rise in maximum penalties and the improvement of federal sentencing guidelines. As the *Harvard Law Review*'s editors put it, these changes may give prosecutors greater room of maneuver to "charge bargain" with prospective defendants and "further expedite set-tlements" (*Harvard Law Review* 2002: 734). These legal changes notwithstanding, some argue that the Sarbanes–Oxley Act does not address the problems related to private sector players' strong involvement in the design and interpretation of financial regula-tions (Demski 2003).

Small Business Finance

Now, we shift from big corporate finance to focus on small busi-ness' financial practices. Although big business receives most of the attention, small firms have always been a critical source of economic activity and employment. Most small businesses do not rely on stocks and bonds to raise money. Instead, they use credit from suppliers, bank loans, family funds, and may even exploit an owner's credit cards to finance their operations. On account of their size, it is hard for creditors to assess small firms' credit-worthiness or profitability. For large businesses, creditors can use audited financial statements, SEC filings, rating agencies, analysts' reports, and even the business press in order to evaluate a firm's assets, credit history, or expected profits (Jackson and Mishra 2007: 2). These sources, however, do not exist for small businesses, which are unlikely to produce public, certified, or readily available financial information.

In figure 5.1, we show the evolution of total debt for companies organized as partnerships or proprietorships, the vast majority of which are small businesses (with 500 employees or fewer).[7] Throughout the 1992–2006 period, mortgage loans were, by far, the main component of total debt of partnerships and proprietorships. Uncollateralized bank loans were a distant second, followed by the residual category "other loans." From the late 1990s to 2006, total debt of partnerships and proprietorships increased sharply; most of this rise can be explained by the growth in mortgage loans. Bank loans also increased, though much more slowly, whereas "other loans" remained fairly constant (see figure 5.1).

Much of the scholarly work on small business finance examines the problem of creditors' uncertainty about borrowers' solvency and profitability. Economists argue that the "asymmetries of

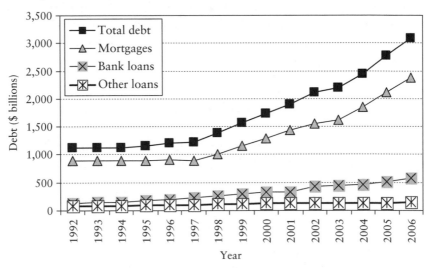

Data source: Board of Governors of the Federal Reserve System. Report to the Congress on the Availability of Credit to Small Businesses, 1997, 2002 and 2007

Figure 5.1   Total debt of partnerships and proprietorships, 1992–2006

information" between small businesses and potential lenders may be so serious that they lead to credit rationing (Stiglitz and Weiss 1981). Potential creditors may prefer to restrict financing rather than lend money at higher interest, even if borrowers are willing to pay. The problem is that, without reliable information on small firms' performance, creditors remain very uncertain about borrowers' ability to repay their loans. And raising interest rates may actually increase lenders' risk because higher interest rates attract only high-risk borrowers (so-called "adverse selection"). Furthermore, when taking loans at higher interest rates, borrowers may choose riskier business projects to compensate for higher financial costs (so-called "moral hazard"). As Craig et al. (2007: 119) point out: "As a result of these two effects, a bank's expected return may increase less rapidly than the interest rate; and, beyond a point may actually decrease. Clearly, under these conditions, it is conceivable that the demand for credit may exceed the supply of credit in equilibrium."

In the United States, as well as in other industrialized countries, policymakers have made it a top priority to promote the small business sector (Craig et al. 2007). Policymakers and the popular press regularly portray small businesses as a cradle for innovation and as an engine for economic growth and job creation. Such perceptions have produced a wide array of policies to support the small business sector, including tax breaks, subsidies, and programs to ensure credit availability for small firms. In 1953, legislation was passed to create the Small Business Administration (SBA), and the agency soon offered direct loans to small business and guaranteed bank loans to small firms. Since the mid-1980s, the agency has focused on programs to guarantee private bank loans to small businesses. Craig et al. (2007: 117) characterize the SBA as the "largest single financial backer of small businesses in the United States." The authors point out – based on SBA 2004 data – that "over the period 1991 to 2000, the SBA assisted almost 435,000 small businesses in obtaining more than $94.6 billion in loans." Furthermore, Craig et al. find evidence of a positive, moderate relationship between SBA-guaranteed lending and local economic growth.

Although the macro-institutional framework is important, there are also micro-level processes that can improve credit conditions for small businesses. A growing literature has explored the role of relationships in solving the asymmetries of information between banks and small firms. Petersen and Rajan (1994: 5), for example, examine the idea that "through close and continued interaction, a firm may provide a lender with sufficient information about, and a voice in, the firm's affairs so as to lower the cost and increase the availability of credit." The authors test this idea with data from the National Survey of Small Business Finances. They use three indicators to measure the strength of a relationship between a bank and a firm: the length of the relationship, the number of financial services sold by the bank to the firm, and the concentration of the firm's borrowing with the lender. Their evidence does not clearly support the hypothesis that strong relationships with banks reduce the cost of finance for small firms. But, according to them, strong relationships with banks do increase the availability of credit for small businesses.

Uzzi (1999) explores in more detail how social relationships and networks affect small businesses' cost of finance and access to capital. His study focuses on what he calls the "mid-market," including firms with fewer than 500 workers or less than $500 million in annual sales. He contends that banks and mid-market firms experience mutual "ambiguity" when evaluating each other. Bank personnel face difficulties evaluating mid-market firms' performance, first, because these firms "are not debt rated or certified." Second, among these firms there is no clear separation between the business and the private lives of managers, which heightens the bank's concern about the firm's performance. Mid-market firms, in turn, experience ambiguity about the bank's integrity, because "they lack sophisticated financial expertise" and are not powerful enough to be sure they will not be taken advantage of.

Uzzi (1999) argues that embedding commercial transactions in "social attachments" allows banks and mid-market firms to overcome their mutually experienced ambiguity. Banks' relationship managers (RMs) and entrepreneurs invest in close, personal relationships with each other, including frequent interaction with each other's families in social settings. Through these personal, extended ties, banks' RMs and entrepreneurs develop trust and a deeper knowledge of each other's character and business dealings. As Uzzi (1999: 488) explains: "RMs and entrepreneurs form direct relations with third persons, such as spouses and children, which entrepreneurs and RMs confidentially rely on for perceptions of character and trustworthiness in their business dealings with others." The private information shared in the context of these "social attachments" can then be used by the bank's RM to form a more accurate picture of the firm's performance and future prospects. Based on such information, the bank's RM may leverage his or her influence within the bank on the firm's behalf so that the firm can get credit. Moreover, the bank's RM and the entrepreneur may design "contingent loan agreements," tailored to the firm's specific needs, with a "tiered price structure" that reduces the cost of borrowing over time according to the firm's performance.

Economic sociologists have shown that social networks are crucial not just for individual firms but also for promoting development in whole regions. This has been the case for the high-technology industry in Silicon Valley since the late 1950s. Castilla's (2003) study suggests that Silicon Valley's economic success has not just been the product of a high concentration of skills and technology. Other regions with similar concentrations of skills and technology, like Route 128 outside Boston, have yet to achieve comparable success. What, then, makes Silicon Valley unique? The response, according to Castilla, lies in the social network of venture capitalists that sustain entrepreneurial efforts in the high-technology sector.

Venture capitalists are management firms that finance other companies; the money comes from individual and corporate investors who pool resources into a fund (Castilla 2003: 115). Venture capitalists, however, do much more than simply provide start-ups with capital; they supply "management, recruiting, accounting and legal advice and other consulting services which are just as important to the success of the new venture as is the funding" (Castilla 2003: 115). Silicon Valley stands out among other technology-oriented regions for the high degree of collaboration and cohesiveness among venture capital firms, and their tendency to invest a higher percentage of their money locally. It is this underlying social network – and its active support for start-up companies – that helps to explain the success of new firms and the long-term economic development of the region.

Building on this literature, Wang (2008) considers the precise mechanism by which networks increase finance for start-up companies. How does network membership improve access to credit? Wang's research is focused on the venture capital market in China, where he interviewed representatives of internet and telecom start-up firms, venture capitalists, government officials, and science park managers, and looked at venture capitalists' decision-making processes. Venture capitalists decide which start-up applicants to fund in two stages, "awareness" and "evaluation." First, venture capitalists become "aware" of investment opportunities. Once they have selected a subset of potential beneficiaries, they proceed to evaluate those firms to decide which ones to fund. For a start-up entrepreneur, belonging to the venture capitalist's network becomes a key advantage during the "awareness" stage; a connected entrepreneur has better chances to be considered as a potential beneficiary. However, being part of the network becomes secondary during the "evaluation" stage; venture capitalists do not rely on network ties but resort to other methods to gather information and decide whom to fund.

Outside of a minority of firms in telecommunications, software, and other high-tech industries, small businesses are largely dependent on banks for external credit (Berger and Udell 2002: F33). But not all banks are equally amenable to financing small entrepreneurs. Small private banks, with smaller bureaucracies, are better suited to finance small businesses than large, publicly held banking institutions (Berger and Udell 2002: F48–9). This has to do with the importance of social ties between bank representatives and small entrepreneurs. Close, enduring relations between banking representatives and small entrepreneurs are more likely to emerge when the banking partner is small, private, and locally based. Indeed, small banks allocate a higher share of their assets to finance small business compared to large banks (Berger and Udell 2002: F49).

If small banks are so important for small business finance, what has happened, then, with the move towards greater banking consolidation in the U.S. since the 1990s? Are small businesses worse off as a result of recent merger and acquisition activity? The evidence is not conclusive (Frame et al. 2001). Berger and Udell (2002: F49) report that loans to small businesses decrease with "mergers and acquisitions involving large banking organizations." At the same time, they point to compensatory "external effects" of banking consolidation: "relationship loans that are dropped by consolidating banks may be picked up by other existing banks in the local market or by de novo banks that start operations after consolidation in these markets" (Berger and Udell 2002: F49). Frame et al. (2001), on the other hand, find that increasing use of credit-scoring techniques reduces information asymmetries and boosts large banks' funding of small businesses.

As in the case of consumer credit, there exist significant gender and racial disparities in credit conditions for small businesses. Coleman (2000) shows that women-owned businesses are less likely to rely on external financing than male-owned businesses, but does not attribute this to gender discrimination by financial institutions. Instead, consistent with previous research, the study suggests that women find themselves at a disadvantage in credit markets because their firms tend to be smaller. The length of the relationship with a financial institution, though, can help offset the size disadvantage for women entrepreneurs.

Robb and Fairly (2007), in turn, find that African American-owned firms have lower access to start-up capital when compared to white-owned firms. These differences appear to be "the most important explanatory factor" in accounting for the gap in business outcomes between white-owned businesses and African American-owned firms (Robb and Fairly 2007: 63). Both wealth disparities and lending discrimination may be at work behind African American businesses' lower access to external credit. Citing Cavalluzzo et al. (2002), Robb and Fairly (2007) point out that even after controlling for different variables associated with creditworthiness, African Americans applying for loans have worse chances. The authors conclude that "lending discrimination may have a direct effect on business outcomes because it limits access to loans that can help a business 'weather a storm' or limits the ability of firms to expand or diversify into new products or markets" (Robb and Fairly 2007: 66).

Financial Globalization

The sociological study of credit in the corporate economy blends into broader themes of public policy, institutional arrangements, and economic development. In this section, we revisit these topics, in connection with debates about financial globalization and the international mobility of capital. Globally, capital mobility has been on the rise since the collapse of the Bretton Woods system in the early 1970s (see chapter 2). Thus, to give an example, daily currency exchange turnover went from 0.7% of world GDP in 1980 to 6.8% of world GDP in 1998 (Guillén 2001: 239). International banking assets, in turn, reached over $120 trillion in 2007, up from just below $20 trillion in 1989 (see figure 5.2).

Another indicator of increased capital mobility is foreign direct investment (FDI). Both measured in absolute figures and as a percentage of global GDP, in-flow FDI for the world as a whole grew from the early 1990s to the year 2000, then it fell abruptly, and resumed growth during the 2003–7 period (see figures 5.3 and 5.4). In-flow FDI for the developed economies followed closely in-flow foreign direct investment for the world as a whole. Yet, it is important to note that the picture changes when considering FDI for the developed economies *as a percentage of total FDI*; measured in this way, in-flow FDI for the developed world did not rise, but showed instead an irregular, slightly downward pattern from 1980 to 2007 (see figure 5.4).

In-flow FDI for *developing* economies also rose in absolute figures and as a percentage of global GDP from the early 1990s to the year 2000 and from 2003 to 2007, but it did so more slowly. By contrast, in-flow FDI for what UNCTAD calls "economies

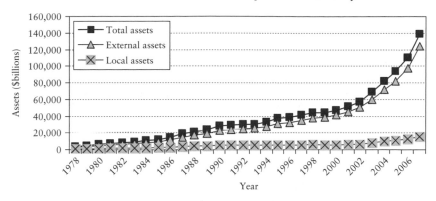

Data source: Bank for International Settlements, Locational Banking Statistics

Figure 5.2 International banking assets, 1978–2007

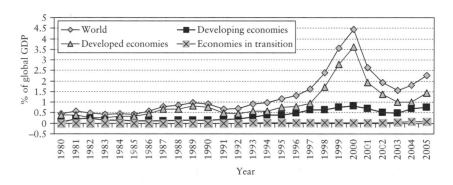

Data source: UNCTAD FDI table 1980 to 2007 & IMF. World Economic Outlook
Database

Figure 5.3 In-flow of world foreign direct investment, 1980–2005

in transition" – which include the Russian Federation and other
republics that belonged to the former Soviet Union or to its sphere
of influence – remained fairly stagnant throughout the period
when considered in absolute figures. However, this indicator did
rise slightly during the last decade when measured as a percentage
of global GDP.

Technological advances, economic processes, ideological forces,

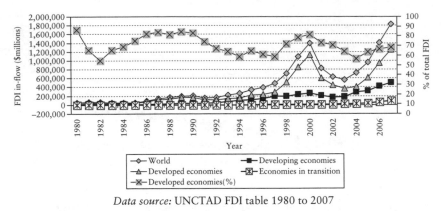

Data source: UNCTAD FDI table 1980 to 2007

Figure 5.4 In-flow of world foreign direct investment, 1980–2007

and political decisions have reinforced each other to encourage the growth of international capital flows (Carruthers and Babb 2000). Andrews (1994: 198) points to three different types of factors strengthening the capacity of capital to move across borders. First, technological changes have made it easier and faster to transfer financial assets from one country to another. Second, financial firms have capitalized on these technological advances and invented new financial instruments suitable for transferring capital across borders. And third, governments themselves have facilitated international capital mobility, by eliminating capital controls restricting in-flows and out-flows.

One issue under debate is to what extent increased capital mobility has limited the freedom of national governments to pursue independent policy goals. Even if national governments' own decisions opened the door to greater capital mobility, governmental authorities may now face serious obstacles to undoing this process. Goodman and Pauly (1993), for example, acknowledge that governments could reinstate capital controls – and they have done so occasionally. However, governments have found these controls increasingly ineffective because multinational corporations can easily work around them (see also Edwards 2002). The expansion of international capital markets gives multinational corporations the opportunity to "evade" capital controls by relying on their subsidiaries abroad to borrow or lend money. Furthermore, corporations can resort to "exit" strategies: for example, they can transfer their operations elsewhere to avoid financial regulations. In the authors' words, "pressures for capital decontrol are now deeply embedded in firm structure and strategy" (Goodman and Pauly 1993: 81).

In the same vein, Andrews (1994: 202) argues that international capital mobility has become "a structural feature of international politics: a constraining condition" that limits state autonomy. Once "unleashed," international capital mobility has become a force of its own, setting off a new dynamics of "competition for capital" among national states. Faced with the prospect of losing investors to their neighbors, states have been pressed to "court" capital and further liberalize domestic financial markets. This competitive environment has discouraged authorities from reintroducing financial regulations at the national level and complicated collective action for regulatory action at the international level.

The discussion about capital controls has further implications for state autonomy because it relates to governments' ability to pursue expansionary monetary and fiscal policies. Within a world of limited international capital mobility, expansionary monetary policy, based on low interest rates, has been a traditional policy tool to encourage domestic investment, economic growth, and job creation (Goodman and Pauly 1993: 58). However, in a context of unfettered international capital mobility, an expansionary monetary policy may fail to produce economic expansion; instead, low interest rates may lead to capital out-flows, as domestic savings get attracted by higher interest rates abroad. For some scholars, governments' reduced ability to manage capital flows clearly constrains their macroeconomic options (Andrews 1994).

Other scholars, however, challenge these claims about the loss of state autonomy. Garrett and Lange (1991), for example, acknowledge that heightened international capital mobility can thwart governments' efforts to promote domestic investment and job creation through expansionary monetary and fiscal policies. Nevertheless, they refuse to take this as an indicator of reduced government capacity to pursue independent economic policies (see also Frieden 1991; Mosley 2003: 2–3). Governments on the political right and left may converge in their macroeconomic management, but they can still adopt different "supply-side policies" regarding "industrial innovation, investment, and labor markets" (Garrett and Lange 1991: 541). Where rightist governments face weak labor movements, they are more likely to give market forces a stronger role in shaping economic adjustment to the new international environment. In contrast, where leftist parties can count on strong labor movements ("corporatist" countries), they are more likely to carry out adjustment through interventionist policies. These policies include, in addition to the redistribution of wealth, "retraining and relocation programs," "subsidies and public investment," and the "manipulation of corporate taxation structures" to ease labor and capital's adaptation to changing business conditions (Garrett and Lange 1991: 545–7). Garrett and Lange test their argument with a sample of fifteen developed democracies for the period 1960–87. Their findings reveal continuing divergence in supply-side policies between "weak labor" and "corporatist" countries, before and after changes in the international economic environment.

A subsidiary debate has to do with the welfare state's chances of survival within a world of greater financial integration and heightened capital mobility (Guillén 2001; Krippner 2005; Ó Riain 2000). Summing up the extensive literature on the topic, Stryker (1998: 5) recounts that welfare states flourished after World War II, bolstered by "centralized labor movements and strong 'traditional' class voting – voting for left parties by members of a relatively large working class." Within relatively closed domestic economies, left-oriented governments succeeded at redistributing wealth without sacrificing economic performance. This equilibrium rested on a "social accord" between capital and labor, which awarded workers full employment and an array of social protections, while benefiting capital with labor's compliance and economic growth (Silver 2003; Stryker 1998). However, this multi-layered arrangement began to crumble in the 1970s, with increased international economic interdependence in trade, the organization of production, and financial flows.

Financial globalization, in particular, may have contributed to the welfare state's withdrawal through "the *perceived* risk or *credibility* of risk of capital flight, when business views domestic tax and expenditure policies as unfavorable to short-term profitability, and perceives the availability of more favorable conditions elsewhere" (Stryker 1998: 7, the author's emphasis). Reinforcing fears of capital flight, a strong ideological movement in favor of reduced government spending, deregulation, and privatization has, with varying degrees across the world, engulfed policymakers, multilateral institutions, and gatekeepers such as credit rating agencies (Sinclair 2005).

Yet, there is still considerable dispute on the extent of welfare state retreat and the causal connections between financial globalization and welfare state transformation. Swank (2002), for example, argues that political institutions in each country mediate the effect of capital mobility on the welfare state. Garrett and Mitchell (2001), for their part, questioned the idea that the welfare state is too costly from the point of view of mobile capital. The authors analyzed data for eighteen OECD countries, covering the period 1961–3. They found, first, that total government spending did fall with greater international financial openness; however, financial openness did not affect those dimensions of public spending directly associated with the welfare state, for example consumption expenditures and social security transfers. Neither did greater financial integration produce significant changes in the tax structure. The authors conclude that, contrary to the classical capital flight thesis, countries with welfare states may offer investors substantial "collective goods," which are absent from countries with less interventionist state structures. Welfare states may still attract investors not only because of their greater "human capital accumulation, physical infrastructure and research and development" but also because of their stronger "social stability and support for the open international economy itself" (Garrett and Mitchell 2001: 175).

Conclusions

In this chapter, three general themes bring together the research on credit in the modern corporate economy: the embeddedness of economic action, the problem of trust, and the diversity of institutional arrangements. The embeddedness of economic action in culture, social structure, and institutions is at the core of the sociological study of capital markets: economic practices in these markets do not only respond to profit-seeking but are guided also by social governance mechanisms and cultural expectations. The idea of embeddedness is also central for the study of small business finance. A large part of the literature on this topic converges around the problem of trust, and how it can be managed through social embeddedness. Social embeddedness can result in better credit conditions for small firms and can also provide the foundation for regional economic development.

Problems of trust come up again in the study of credit in large, publicly traded corporations and in the discussion of corporate governance. The dispersion of ownership in publicly owned corporations has allowed managers to privilege their own interests at the expense of shareholders. Agency theorists have proposed incentive-based compensation as a solution to corporate governance problems. However, continuous corporate scandals have shown the persistence of investors' vulnerability. The very structure of executive compensation, conflicts of interests between auditing firms and audited companies, a decentralized and poorly isolated regulatory apparatus, and the processes by which profits are created contribute to systemic breakdowns in corporate governance.

Finally, the diversity of institutional arrangements figures prominently in work on the origins and evolution of market-based and bank-based financial systems. Research on these topics treats financial systems as historical products – resulting from the confluence of political decisions, ideological forces, the structure of the political system, and the geopolitical situation – and as historical forces shaping government action, banks' power over non-financial institutions, and corporate governance. The diversity of institutional arrangements reappears in the debate on the internationalization of capital flows and its consequences for state power: for some, increased capital mobility leads to a progressive erosion of institutional diversity, whereas for others such diversity is resilient in the face of financial integration.

Credit and the Modern Corporate Economy

Discussion Questions

1 A bankrupt firm is a firm that can't repay its debts. Corporate bankruptcy law generally allows for two outcomes: liquidation and reorganization. In a liquidation, the firm's assets are seized and used to repay creditors, and the firm is shut down: factories and stores close, employees lose their jobs, shareholders lose their money. In a reorganization, the firm's debts are restructured and its operations modified in order to make the firm profitable again: loans are refinanced, costs cut, wages reduced, and so on. Should bankruptcy laws favor one alternative over the other? Should laws be "tough" and simply shut failed firms down, or should they give a troubled firm a "second chance"?

2 Imagine you're a venture capitalist and a start-up company approaches you with a proposal to launch a new gadget. The gadget seems very marketable, at least on paper, but the company does not have a long track record. How would you decide whether to invest your money in this proposal? What would you do in order to evaluate the entrepreneur's creditworthiness? And if you decided to go along with the proposal, what steps would you take to monitor the start-up company?

3 Credit rating agencies like Moody's play a key role in today's capital markets. Credit raters traditionally rate bonds issued by big corporations, giving their highest ratings to the bonds they deemed to be the safest and most secure investments. Recently, they earned a lot of money rating exotic financial instruments like mortgage-backed securities and collateralized debt obligations. In the financial crisis of 2008, it turned out that the high ratings they gave to these exotic instruments were misleading, and that the rating agencies substantially overestimated their quality. What kinds of consequences, if any, should the rating agencies suffer from their mistakes? How can they be encouraged not to make similar mistakes in the future?

4 In light of the numerous financial scandals of the last two decades, what else, if anything, should be done to prevent a new wave of financial fraud? Should a new regulatory agency with broad powers be created at the federal level? Should countries set common regulatory guidelines at the international level? How would these guidelines be enforced? Should the curriculum at business schools be changed to promote a "healthier" business culture? Should ordinary citizens reduce their investments in financial markets?

6

Conclusion

In the midst of the current financial crisis, economic value – if not money *per se* – and credit have revealed themselves as rather evanescent entities, much more ephemeral, in any case, than what consumers, business people, and policymakers would have ever liked to see. As Nobel Prize-winning economist Paul Krugman (2009a) commented: "until very recently, Americans believed that they were getting richer, because they received statements saying that their houses and stock portfolios were appreciating in value faster than their debts were increasing." Krugman went on to say that "The surge in asset values had been an illusion – but the surge in debt had been all too real." As people come to terms with devalued assets and trimmed budgets, consumer demand drops, worsening the already serious contractionary effects of the near-collapse of the financial system. In his weekly columns for the *New York Times*, Krugman has clamored for strong state intervention – including a temporary public takeover of troubled banks and a far more ambitious stimulus package than the one approved by Congress. Without such intervention, Krugman warns, it will take years until credit and consumer demand pick up again, and economic growth resumes (see also Krugman 2009b).

In current times, it has become more common to hear public demands for active government intervention in the economy to salvage economic value, prop up credit, and stimulate economic growth. Reversing the trend of the 1980s and 1990s, those who advocate for unfettered markets, free from political and social regulatory mechanisms, seem to have become a minority. As economic sociologists have shown, though, state and social intervention are not just a temporary remedy to economic crisis, but part and parcel of economic life. Throughout the book, we have sought to highlight the political and social underpinnings that sustain a well-functioning monetary system and a continuous credit supply. Not just in times of crisis when money fails – as happens, for example, during hyperinflationary episodes – or when credit disappears – as occurs, most clearly, during recessionary periods – but also in regular times, political and social arrangements are necessary for money to work and for credit to flow.

Our discussion of money and credit is indebted to Polanyi's landmark conception of the economy as "embedded and enmeshed in institutions, economic and noneconomic" (Polanyi 1957a: 250). It is true that some of Polanyi's writings reinforce the opposition between the "embedded economy" in pre-market societies and the "disembodied" economic sphere in modern, market societies (Krippner and Alvarez 2007). However, his definition of the economy as an "instituted process" suggests that even modern market economies are built upon extra-economic conditions; market exchange occurs within an institutional frame, which allows for what we know as market-oriented behavior.[1] As discussed by Block (2003), Polanyi posits the extra-economic foundations of market exchange in the case of land, labor, and money. Polanyi calls land, labor, and money "fictitious commodities," because they could simply not exist as commodities without political mediation (Polanyi 1957b: 68–76). Land, labor, and money could not be exchanged as commodities in the absence of institutional arrangements that regulated their supply and demand. Thus, turning land into a commodity required, among other things, shielding the rural population from "dramatic income fluctuations that might drive them off the land" (Block 2003: 296). The existence of labor as a commodity, in turn, could not be maintained without an institutional setup to restrain "exploitation" and without "an educational system to provide needed skills." Finally, the production of money as a commodity rested on "the rise of central banks" able to strengthen the banking system and manage the money supply (Block 2003: 296). Extending Polanyi's discussion of "fictitious commodities," we have sought to present money and credit as "social artifacts," grounded in changing institutional, social, and cultural foundations.

The Sociological Study of Money

In chapter 2, we discussed how modern standardized money, valid as legal tender within a national territory, was a significant social achievement, the product of a long history of institutional building and experimentation with different media and varying coordination mechanisms. Over time and in different places, many different objects have been used as money. Even though money has changed considerably in its reach, its media, its association with precious metals, and its convertibility, it has remained intertwined with political sovereignty. Throughout history, rulership has included, as one of its core traits, the right to issue money for use within a given political jurisdiction (Wood 2002: 100). And particular media have become money when they have been required for the payment of taxes. In the case of Western Europe, during the Middle Ages, the money supply consisted of coins made out of precious metals; using precious metals contributed to making money acceptable, but left the money supply vulnerable to unpredictable fluctuations in the availability of gold and silver (Hunt and Murray 1999: 63). Only very slowly, in the context of long-distance trade, did new paper monetary instruments, which "represented" precious metals, come to be used in lieu of coins. And it wasn't until the nineteenth century that governments in Western Europe established their own "territorial currency," a uniform and homogeneous currency that would circulate as legal tender within a given national territory (Helleiner 2003).

The history of money is not a story of steady progress. In the United States, in particular, the process of establishing a uniform "territorial currency" was far from smooth. Up to the early nineteenth century, English, French, and Spanish coins circulated simultaneously, together with dollar bills issued by different state banks – with different values depending on the solvency of the issuing institution. Ensuring that the supply of currency was both stable in value and abundant was a constant challenge for states (Moss and Brennan 2001). A key step in the development of a uniform currency was the National Banking Act of 1863, which created a new system of nationally chartered banks issuing more uniform bank notes. Soon after, a heated political conflict ensued over whether the U.S. should return to the gold standard, a dispute combining political and distributional differences with philosophical discussions about the nature of money itself. The U.S. joined the gold standard with the Gold Standard Act of 1900 and got its first functioning central bank with the creation of the Federal Reserve System in 1913. The collapse of the financial sector during the Depression led to greater state intervention and oversight. As a response to widespread bank failures and credit tightening, new regulations were put in place to insure bank deposits, separate investment from commercial banks, cap interest rates on checking and saving deposits, and monitor capital markets. Institution building did not proceed just within the U.S., but also at the international level, especially after World War II, with the establishment of the Bretton Woods system, the IMF, and the World Bank. The collapse of the Bretton Woods system in the early 1970s ushered in a new era of enhanced international capital mobility, eased by new technological developments and financial innovation. Stronger economic interdependence went hand in hand with a process of financial deregulation, both at the national and the international levels, although part of the regulatory framework built during the New Deal period and after World War II persists until today.

Chapter 2 dealt with the history of money and the development of modern standardized money. Chapter 3 emphasized the unfinished character of this standardization process. Primarily, this is because "money-in-practice" never fully conforms to its narrow legal definition. While the law establishes money as uniform, fungible, divisible, and universally accepted as legal tender within a given territory, people erode these attributes in their monetary practices. As Carruthers (2008: 24) points out, "people attribute meaning and significance to money by undercutting (although not entirely undoing) modern money's fungibility and generality." In everyday life, individuals and organizations create boundaries to money's circulation, introduce distinctions within legally uniform money, and tie different categories of money to specific uses. Through these operations, people endow money with meaning beyond its capacity to convey quantitative value.

Cognitive psychologists have explored the meaning of money in contemporary Western society through experiments and surveys. Psychologists and behavioral economists interested in "mental accounting," for example, have studied how people keep their money in different "mental accounts," which renders their money non-fungible (Thaler 1999). Because of these separate mental accounts, people perceive differently $100 won in an office football pool and $100 received as a tax refund, and these perceptions, in turn, affect how the extra money is spent (O'Curry 1997). As Thaler (1999: 197) points out, "people have a tendency to match the seriousness of the source of some windfall with the use to which it is put."

Anthropologists have also paid attention to how people carve distinctions within uniform money. But if psychologists are concerned with psychological needs such as time-saving and self-control, as the motives behind "mental accounting," anthropologists pay attention to culturally driven classifications. Wilson's (1997) study of monetarization in rural villages near Shanghai, for example, finds that people give money different names "depending on the exchange context." Villagers use the word "cash" to name money applied to purchases in shops and markets, but they refer to money as "sentiment" in the context of gift exchange. Wilson's telling example counters claims that the advance of monetarization inevitably dissolves social relationships and cultural meaning. Like Zelizer's (1989) study of money in turn-of-the-century America, Wilson shows a two-way transformation of money and social relations. In Wilson's Chinese example, money transformed social relations – expanding social interactions and exchanges, and rendering gift exchange more competitive – but its use was in turn shaped by existing traditions and cultural norms (Wilson 1997: 98).

Fostering renewed sociological interest in the study of money, Zelizer's work points to a "growing paradox" (Zelizer 1994: 205): the creation of multiple currencies out of standardized money becomes a more "elaborate" process with the increasing monetization of social life. As Zelizer (1994: 204) explains, people and organizations differentiate homogeneous money into distinct currencies, among other things, because they need to "manage complex social relations that express intimacy but also inequality, love but also power, care but also control, solidarity but also conflict." When money enters different social settings, people seek to modulate its use in line with the particular web of relations and the various social transactions that unfold within these settings. Zelizer (2005) has shown, however, that this process is laden with conflict because participants' wealth, power, freedom, status, and prestige are at stake when carving distinctions within standardized money. Thus, family members may contest the differentiation of money and its allocation rules within the household, workers may disagree among themselves and with their employers over company budgeting and payment systems, and citizens, interest groups, and political parties may fight over how to categorize and what strings to attach to public funds (Zelizer 1994). Conflicts on how to classify and earmark public money can have profound economic and distributional consequences, as can be seen with current debates over "rescue" funds for insolvent banks, "assistance" for indebted homeowners, and the "stimulus" package to reactivate the economy.

The Sociology of Credit

Money cannot simply be taken for granted, and a well-functioning monetary system rests on a multifaceted, history-laden institutional structure. The same applies to credit. As we saw in chapters 4 and 5, credit is troublesome, both for borrowers, because they may not get the credit they need or want, and for lenders, who are uncertain about who can or will repay a loan. Lenders want to know whom they can trust and borrowers want to appear trustworthy. In some instances, debtors and creditors rely on pre-existing social ties to help manage the uncertainties involved in the credit relationship. In addition, a variety of private and public institutions have developed to encourage the expansion of credit for individuals as well as for firms.

Given the scarcity of cash, credit was very important for consumers in early America. Farm families depended on credit to buy seed and equipment and to pay for their living expenses until the fall harvest. Wage earners resorted to credit to deal with unexpected expenses or losses of income. Consumers got credit from suppliers, merchants, country stores, department stores, and friends and family. Credit in local trade networks was governed by an ethos of neighborliness and civility (Clark 1990), but trade and credit relations expanded nationally during the nineteenth century with the development of canals, railroads, and other forms of transportation. In the early twentieth century, sources of credit multiplied further and more people got drawn into the consumer economy; installment lending, pawn shops, loan sharks, small loan lending, credit unions, and bank loans for consumers fueled greater consumption and higher indebtedness for American households. As trade expanded in scale, new techniques to evaluate debtors' creditworthiness replaced the old reputation-based methods associated with local, dense social ties. Starting in the mid-1800s, mercantile agencies collected credit information and supplied credit ratings on small businesses, a practice that extended to individual consumers with the emergence of consumer credit bureaus at the end of the century.

Government policy in the U.S. was crucial for the expansion of consumer credit, especially in the area of homeownership. Already in the early twentieth century, a small number of states had launched programs to encourage mortgage lending to farms. But public support for mortgage lending, which benefited farmers, the construction industry, and homeownership by American families, became a pillar of federal government policy during the New Deal. With the creation of a new web of institutions – including, among others, the Home Owners Loan Corporation, the Federal Housing Administration, and the Federal National Mortgage Corporation

– the federal government helped to channel credit into the housing market and to transform the standards of mortgage lending. The new institutional infrastructure supported longer-term, self-amortizing, and high-loan-to-value mortgages, making it easier for buyers to purchase homes. Fostered by government policy, homeownership expanded to close to two-thirds of the American population by 1997 (see figure 4.2), growth that was marked, though, by strong geographic and racial inequalities.

Consumer credit reached new heights in the post-war era, when America became a mass consumer society. New innovations, in particular the invention and diffusion of credit and debit cards, made credit more flexible by decoupling it from particular purchases. At the same time, new institutions helped creditors handle the asymmetries of information entailed in the credit relationship. Credit scores – summarizing vast amounts of information on borrowers' spending and credit history – have become ubiquitous in the world of consumer credit. The use of collateral – based not just on real estate, but on almost any asset owned by the borrower – has also increased. Finally, lenders have benefited from an expansion of secondary markets for individual debt (known as "securitization"), which allow creditors to recover their capital before the debt is fully repaid.

In chapter 5, we returned to the problems of borrowers' need for credit and creditors' uncertainty about borrowers, but examined them at the level of the modern corporation. The study of credit for business firms raises questions about public policy, institutional design, and economic development. To stimulate economic growth, all capitalist economies need to find mechanisms for "shifting resources from savings to investment" (Zysman 1983: 69). As Zysman explains, how this process is accomplished differs in market-based and credit-based financial systems. In market-based systems, capital markets play a dominant role in transforming savings into investment; business firms issue shares and bonds as a primary external source of funds; and households, insurance companies, pension and trust funds and others purchase these instruments as an investment. In credit-based financial systems, by contrast, financial institutions intermediate between savers and borrowers and provide a larger share of investment funds; firms resort mainly to bank lending as an external source of finance. Some have argued, though, that global financial deregulation has produced a measure of convergence between countries with market-based financial systems and those with credit-based systems (Calomiris 2000: 344). This has partly to do with the greater importance of "capital market funding" throughout the world, coupled with a change in banking as banks have gotten more active in issuing and trading securities (Sinclair 2005: 56–7).

Once savings are channeled into investment, a number of problems can arise in the use of those funds. One problem – which was common in the prototypical examples of credit-based financial systems – is what economists call "moral hazard" (Loriaux 1991: 11). Economists use this term to refer to situations where the users of capital bear "only a portion, or none, of the consequences" of their decisions (Stiglitz 1997: 134–5).[2] Loriaux (1991: 61) studies this problem in the French economy, where the state's control over finance ensured that credit was cheap and abundant, giving "industry little cause to concern itself over money." In the case of South Korea, subsidized credit resulted in an economy populated by oversized and highly leveraged industrial firms; whenever these firms approached bankruptcy, the state was inclined to bail them out to avoid greater economic and social costs. These firms were "too big to fail" (Woo 1991: 12–13). Because of the continuous flow of subsidized credit and the strong likelihood of a state rescue, big firms had little incentive to control their costs or be appropriately risk-averse. Situations of "moral hazard," however, are not unique to credit-based financial systems. One could argue that in the United States – with an archetypal market-based financial system – some episodes of financial deregulation have proliferated "moral hazard." This was clear in the case of the savings-and-loans crisis of the 1980s, when extensive deregulation of the industry was coupled with measures to increase the federal insurance of deposits. Backed by federal insurance, depositors and other constituents did little to prevent savings-and-loans executives from financing extremely risky investments (Calavita, Pontell, and Tillman 1997: 11–15).

Conclusion

Beyond the more general problem of moral hazard, the dispersion of ownership in market-based financial systems raises issues of corporate governance. Ever since Berle and Means' (1968) analysis of the "separation of ownership and control," first published in 1932, scholars have been preoccupied with the rift between managers and shareholders' interests. Agency theorists endorsed incentive compensation systems to encourage managers to "maximize shareholder value" (Jensen and Meckling 1976; Zajac and Westphal 1995), and as Frydman and Saks (2007) show, incentive compensation has become a larger portion of executive pay since the 1950s. The widespread diffusion of incentive compensation packages, however, has produced unforeseen consequences which, in some cases, aggravated shareholder vulnerability. Managers' influence over the board of directors may result in "excess compensation" and "suboptimal pay structures" (Bebchuk and Fried 2003). Furthermore, for some scholars, there is an association between the rise in incentive compensation systems and managers' greater proclivity to inflate earnings and hide losses and liabilities through various accounting tricks (Bebchuk and Fried 2003; Langevoort 2003). Bebchuk and Fried (2003) conclude that the manipulation of financial reports is a fairly common corporate practice, which widely exceeds the limited number of cases litigated or enforced by the SEC each year.

As we saw in chapter 5, corporate governance doesn't just involve managers, boards of directors, and investors, but also outside players, including auditors, regulators, and policymakers. The recent wave of corporate scandals has brought to light serious conflicts of interest at different organizational and institutional levels. Changes in the auditing industry have expanded the range of services provided by accounting firms, which now complement their traditional auditing role with lucrative tax and consulting services that threaten to diminish their impartiality as auditors (Demski 2003). Furthermore, the regulatory structure that monitors auditing work is poorly shielded from auditors and reporting firms' influence. The SEC has largely delegated the task of setting financial reporting standards to private sector organizations, which tend to produce excessively detailed, exception-ridden reporting standards (Demski 2003). In addition, legislators and the courts have sometimes yielded to interest group lobbying efforts from auditors, lawyers, credit rating agencies, and reporting firms (Roe 2004a). U.S. policymakers responded to the most publicized breakdowns in corporate governance with the Sarbanes–Oxley Act of 2002, which strengthened penalties and changed federal sentencing guidelines (*Harvard Law Review* 2002).

The dispersion of ownership and the opposition between managers and shareholders' interests are less salient issues in the case of small businesses because, in almost all cases, owners are also managers. Bank loans, the owners' personal savings, friends and family, and credit card financing are the primary sources of funds for small firms. Small business finance has its own challenges, though, given the serious "asymmetries of information" between small firms and their creditors. In the absence of credible information about small firms' assets and credit history, creditors may be wary of supplying funds. In the United States, policymakers have tried to address this problem by creating the Small Business Administration, whose programs guarantee bank loans to small firms (Craig et al. 2007). Besides government intervention, business firms and their creditors have relied on social relationships to alleviate the asymmetries of information that threaten the credit relationship (Petersen and Rajan 1994). Close social ties improve credit conditions for small business by facilitating the transfer of private, first-hand information between borrowers and creditors (Uzzi 1999). Social networks are especially important in the case of start-up firms; venture capital networks help to make investors "aware" of opportunities in such firms (Wang 2008) and contribute to "nurturing" them by channeling management, accounting, and legal expertise, in addition to funding (Castilla 2003).

A Final Note on Networks and Institutions

Throughout the chapters, our discussion underscored the salience of networks and institutions in the development of money and credit. For quite some time, sociologists have paid attention to individuals and organizations' embeddedness in multiple networks, studied variations in network patterns, and distinguished different types of network ties. They have analyzed the consequences of social networks for people's identities, resources, choices, and opportunities, and explored how networks are formed and change. As part of this effort, research has drawn attention to how networks influence credit conditions for individuals and organizations, and channel credit at the regional, national, and international levels.

Recently, economists have also discovered the importance of networks, and why they matter for financial systems. Drawing on work in physics and computer science, they have focused on the structural components of networks and how they affect the stability of the system. Nier et al., for example, are concerned with reducing systemic risk within a national banking system, and look at "how the *structure* of a banking network may affect its susceptibility to systemic breakdown." (Nier et al. 2008: 5, authors' emphasis). The authors conceptualize the network as formed by connections through "interbank exposures." Banking networks may be more or less resistant to "contagious defaults," depending on certain key features: banks' capitalization, the size of interbank liabilities, the number of banks comprised in the network, and the number of links among these banks. The authors model how variations in these features affect the banking network's capacity to absorb, rather than propagate, bank defaults.

While Nier et al. (2008) used an abstract model, other researchers conducted empirical studies of existing interbank networks (see Boss et al. 2004). Lublóy (2006), for instance, used payment data from the Hungarian banking system to identify which institutions were most likely to provoke contagious defaults. Using a set of "centrality measures" that took into account the financial weight of a bank's linkages to other institutions and the average distance – in number of linkages – separating a bank from others, the author identified those institutions in the network whose liquidity problems "could cause the most serious contagion effects" (Lublóy 2006: 33). They were not the biggest Hungarian banks – classified by assets – but those banks with intense participation in the currency swap markets.

As economists themselves acknowledge, their analyses of financial networks are still very preliminary and exclude behavioral aspects which could be relevant for explaining financial outcomes (Boss et al. 2004: 683). In particular, economists' simulations and empirical analyses seem to be restricted to the topology of networks and its effects, without paying attention to the type of action or the content of the interaction that unfolds within networks. This point sets apart their treatment of networks from sociological approaches, which are often informed by empirical observation of market participants and how they behave and interact with their network partners. Thus, Baker's analysis of financial markets, for example, stresses market participants' "bounded rationality," which means that market participants tend to limit their trade to "those in proximity" and large trading crowds get segmented into smaller "cliques" (Baker 1984: 783).[3] Another example is Uzzi's (1999) study of mid-market firms, which offers a detailed description of social interaction in the context of embedded ties. Uzzi underscores the importance of "expectations of trust" and "reciprocity" in social exchanges between banks' relationship managers and entrepreneurs (Uzzi 1999: 485–90).

Economists' analyses and sociological studies on networks differ in other significant ways. In economists' analyses, organizations are analyzed as if they belonged to just one network: in the studies on financial stability referenced here, for example, banks are considered "nodes" in the interbank network formed by interbank exposures. By contrast, sociologists are sensitive to organizations' embeddedness in *multiple* networks. Thus, from a sociological perspective, banks can belong to the interbank network traced by interbank exposures, but also to other networks, such as those formed by interlocking directorates (Mintz and Schwartz 1985).

Furthermore, sociological analyses are more attentive to the dynamic aspects of networks. Economists tend to provide "snapshot analyses": for example, to offer a picture of the network structure at a certain point in time in order to determine its effects on the stability of the system. Instead, sociologists have also examined how networks are formed and how they change. Mizruchi and Stearns (1988), for example, provide evidence on the formation of networks through a longitudinal study on interlock ties between large industrial companies and financial institutions in the U.S. from 1956 to 1983. The study shows that non-financial firms tend to include banks' representatives in their boards when they are experiencing financial difficulties, but also when there is a rise in overall demand for capital. In addition, the authors find that "during recessions, when firms are more likely to be financially unstable, the effect of aggregate demand on financial appointments is highest" (Mizruchi and Stearns 1988: 204). By using a longitudinal approach, the authors show that not only the financial situation of firms themselves but also environmental conditions drive the formation of interlock ties.

Sociologists have contributed to the study of money and credit by drawing on their understanding of networks and by building upon the accumulated knowledge on institutional persistence and change. In previous chapters, the significance of institutions appeared time and again. As we saw, the law confers "legal tender" status on money and a reliable legal system upholds credit relations. A web of financial institutions organizes the world of consumer credit, improving credit conditions for some groups, while putting others at a disadvantage. Furthermore, a broad, complex institutional framework defines available sources of finance for non-financial firms, shapes banks' influence on non-financial corporations, and structures relations between managers and shareholders. And institutional arrangements can be affected but also have an effect on how changes in the global environment impinge on economic adjustment (and social welfare) within each country.

In today's financial crisis, some of the institutions populating the world of consumer credit and corporate finance have been discredited and lost some of their legitimacy. The current crisis is likely to stimulate new policy debates on how to encourage savings, channel savings into investment, curb moral hazard problems, improve corporate governance, promote small business finance, and manage consumer credit. Like previous crises, current events in financial markets may create opportunities for institutional building and experimentation. But we shouldn't assume a simple or straightforward relationship between the financial crisis and the likelihood of institutional change. As Skowronek (1995: 92) points out, the prevailing association of institutions with the production of order and stability has often translated into the view that "change comes from elsewhere and is likely to be a transition between relatively stable institutional orderings." In this view, a stable institutional system would guide economic action along predictable paths, until crisis struck and spurred the creation of new institutional arrangements (see Krasner 1984). Historical institutionalists in political science and political sociologists, however, have pointed to several flaws in this conception of institutional evolution (Clemens and Cook 1999; Thelen 1999).

To begin, it is important to reconsider the characterization of institutions themselves. Institutions have alternatively been defined as coordinating mechanisms embodying solutions to recurrent collective action problems, as historical products of past struggles, and as internalized cognitive "scripts" (Clemens and Cook 1999: 444–5; Thelen 1999: 382). Regardless of which definition is adopted, Skowronek (1995) suggests that attention to institutions' history and durability should go hand in hand with awareness of institutional arrangements' uneven temporalities. This means that "change in one institution is unlikely to run parallel to changes that all other institutions undergo" (Skowronek 1995: 94). What we find in "any complex society," then, is not a mutually consistent set of institutions, but an array of multiple, conflicting institutional arrangements, with distinctive, often contradictory, logics and histories. This "messiness" also characterizes the assemblage of institutions that govern money and credit. Think, for example, of the "dual banking system" that developed in the U.S. with the adoption of the National Banking Act of 1863. As we saw in chapter 5, states responded to efforts to establish a national banking system by passing "free banking laws," which lowered barriers to entry for state-chartered banks. Ensuing competition between federal and state regulators weakened regulations for both national and state banks (White 1982: 35–7). As Skowronek (1995: 95) points out, the "juxtaposition" of different institutional logics can often be a source of institutional change (see also Orren and Skowronek 1994).

Conclusion

Like Skowronek, Clemens and Cook (1999) are skeptical of the common association between institutions and permanence. Countering this image, they think of institutions in terms of "schemas and resources," with an eye on the contradictions and the diversity of institutional arrangements (Clemens and Cook 1999: 443). Furthermore, they advocate replacing the one-sided focus on institutional permanence with a broader attention to "processes of reproduction, disruption, and response to disruption." This is necessary to grasp the variety of mechanisms of institutional change.

Through this conceptual shift, scholars have become more sensitive to how institutions may change not only during crises but also during "normal" times, through processes of "learning" and "diffusion" (Clemens and Cook 1999). Borrowing from organizational theory (Heclo 1974; Levitt and March 1988; March 1991), Clemens and Cook (1999: 451–2) point out that actors can alter the content of institutions as they engage in problem-solving, resort to "trial-and-error experimentation," and work out responses to changes in the environment. The evolution of institutions that fostered the growth in consumer spending in the late nineteenth century and early twentieth century – which we traced in chapter 4 – exemplifies these processes of "problem-solving" and "trial-and-error." Institutions can also get transformed when they are "transposed" to new settings (Sewell 1992). Adoption by new social groups or organizations doesn't happen in an institutional vacuum, but occurs in a world already shaped by "existing practices, resources, and competing schemas" (Clemens and Cook 1999: 452; see also Campbell 1998). As Clemens and Cook explain, change and innovation may result from actors' attempt to reconcile new institutional frames with preexisting institutional schemas.

Following Orren and Skowronek (1994), Thelen (1999) puts forward an alternative set of ideas to overcome the stark opposition between institutional stability and change. Thelen brings together two different streams within the historical institutionalist approach. The first, which she puts in the category of "critical junctures," focuses on how institutions emerge and pays attention to the "timing" and "sequencing" of different political processes in order to explain cross-national variations in institutional outcomes. A second group of studies, which she labels as "feedback effects," considers how institutions get reproduced over time, by paying attention to the "coordination effects" and "distributional biases" of institutional arrangements. Combining these two streams, she argues that "institutions rest on a set of ideational and material foundations that, if shaken, open possibilities for change" (Thelen 1999: 397). Explaining institutional change requires, as a precondition, identifying the particular foundations of a given institution and "specifying" the mechanisms by which it gets reproduced (Thelen 1999: 400).

Only time will tell what the effects of the current financial crisis on existing institutional arrangements will be. But these ideas suggest how to analyze the effects. It would make sense, following Clemens and Cook (1999), to break the general problem into more nuanced, specific questions. Which financial institutions, within each country, are more likely to get "disrupted"? Is the crisis exacerbating preexisting contradictions between (and within) different institutional logics (see Skowronek 1995)? Furthermore, using Thelen's (1999) language, how has the "sequencing" and "timing" of the financial crisis, in relation to other political and economic processes, influenced government responses? And, applying her framework, where and how is the crisis interfering with the concrete mechanisms of reproduction of particular institutional arrangements? These are challenging questions that won't be answerable for a time, but they can help frame an agenda for future work in the sociology of money and credit.

Notes

Chapter 1 Introduction

1 A FICO score is named after the Fair Isaac Corporation, which uses credit histories and other information to calculate a score measuring the creditworthiness of an individual.
2 FDI consists of foreign investment in domestic factories, structures, equipment, and organizations.

Chapter 2 A Brief History of Money

1 A promissory note is simply a written promise to pay a sum of money. Bills of exchange were traditionally used to make long-distance payments, and were a written document instructing one person to pay a sum of money to another.
2 It is one of the ironies of confidence that being sure you can do something means you won't actually do it.
3 A "call loan" was a loan repayable on demand at any time.
4 A classic bank run occurs when most or all depositors of a bank try to withdraw their money all at once.

Chapter 3 The Social Meaning of Money

1 Dialogue from *Schindler's List,* released in 1993; Steven Zaillian wrote the screenplay, based on the novel by Thomas Keneally (1982).
2 It is important to note that the monetary function which economists list as "deferred payment" differs from what Polanyists call "payment." For the latter, the term applies to unilateral payments "discharging of obligations," such as the payment of a fine or tribute (Polanyi 1968: 192).
3 Of course, the influences have gone both ways, as recent anthropological and

psychological studies on the meaning of money have also drawn on Zelizer's ideas. See Maurer (2006) for a review of anthropology's treatment of money and Lea et al. (1987) for a summary of psychological studies on the same topic.

4 Tober (2002) reports that extra financial incentives are offered to East Indian and Asian women, whose eggs are in high demand.

Chapter 4 Credit and the Modern Consumer Society

1 As one commentator put it: "No other kind of property is as proof against destruction by the elements, and no other kind of property is affected so little by legislation, panics or upheavals of any kind" (White 1909: 592).

2 A modern mortgage is self-amortizing in that the monthly payment covers both principal and interest and stays constant over the term of the loan.

3 In particular, the new appraisal rules were biased against racially integrated or minority-dominated neighborhoods, and in general emphasized racial composition as a determinant of home value (see Crossney and Bartelt 2005; Jackson 1985: 201; Mason 2004: 114; Massey and Denton 1993: 51; Stuart 2003: 46).

4 They also cut their transaction fees, so that today they charge merchants 1–2% of the transaction amount (Mann 2006: 26).

5 Remedial loan societies and other charitable lenders are obvious exceptions to this rule.

6 Over the long run, the cost may be much higher. Mason (2004: 260) puts it in the ball park of $500 billion (see also Calavita, Pontell, and Tillman 1997: 1).

Chapter 5 Credit and the Modern Corporate Economy

1 Commercial paper consists of unsecured (i.e., no collateral) promissory notes with a maturity of less than 270 days.

2 As we will explain in more detail below, options are derivative instruments whose value depends on an underlying financial asset. There are different types of options; stock options' value is tied to the underlying corporate stock.

3 Zysman (1983: 70–2) distinguishes between two types of credit-based financial systems. State influence on the allocation of finance is paramount in credit-based systems with government-administered prices, such as in France in the mid-1970s, but not in credit-based systems that are bank-dominated, such as the one existing in Germany.

4 Over-the-counter derivatives are traded privately, not on an organized exchange.

5 Our summary of Enron's story relies on Eichenwald (2002) and Partnoy (2003).

6 Sarbanes–Oxley Act § 802(a) (codified at 18 U.S.C. § 1519 (LEXIS through August 20, 2002)); Sarbanes–Oxley Act § 802(a) (codified at 18 U.S.C. § 1520); Sarbanes–Oxley Act § 807(a) (codified at 18 U.S.C. § 1348); and Sarbanes–Oxley Act § 906(a) (codified at 18 U.S.C. § 1350).

7 Board of Governors of the Federal Reserve System, Report to the Congress on the Availability of Credit to Small Businesses (2007: 10–12).

Chapter 6 Conclusion

1 Although we acknowledge, following Krippner and Alvarez (2007), that Polanyi's writings have invited conflicting interpretations, we side with Block's (2003) exegesis of Polanyi on modern market society.

2 The concept of moral hazard is commonly used in the context of insurance, and draws attention to the fact that those who purchase insurance have less incentive to take preventive measures to protect their assets than the uninsured, because the insured expect to receive compensation in case their property is damaged (Stiglitz 1997: 134–5). Another example would be if a car owner drove less carefully because his or her car was insured.

3 See Simon (1982) for a discussion of "bounded rationality."

References

Allen, Franklin and Douglas Gale. 2000. *Comparing Financial Systems*. Cambridge, MA: MIT Press.

Anderson, Elisabeth. 2008. "Experts, Ideas, and Policy Change: The Russell Sage Foundation and Small Loan Reform, 1909–1941," *Theory and Society* 37: 271–310.

Anderson, Elizabeth. 1993. *Value in Ethics and Economics*. Cambridge, MA: Harvard University Press.

Andrews, David M. 1994. "Capital Mobility and State Autonomy: Toward a Structural Theory of International Monetary Relations," *International Studies Quarterly* 38(2): 193–218.

Aristotle. 1984. *The Complete Works of Aristotle*. Jonathan Barnes ed. Princeton: Princeton University Press.

Babb, Sarah and Bruce G. Carruthers. 2008. "Conditionality: Forms, Function, and History," *Annual Review of Law and Social Science* 4: 13–29.

Bailyn, Bernard. 1955. *The New England Merchants in the Seventeenth Century*. Cambridge, MA: Harvard University Press.

Baker, Tom. 2001. "Blood Money, New Money, and the Moral Economy of Tort Law in Action," *Law and Society Review* 35(2): 275–319.

Baker, Wayne E. 1984. "The Social Structure of a National Securities Market," *The American Journal of Sociology* 89(4): 775–811.

Baldwin, Carliss Y. and Kim B. Clark. 1994. "Capital-Budgeting Systems and Capabilities Investments in U.S. Companies after the Second World War," *Business History Review* 68: 73–109.

Balleisen, Edward J. 2001. *Navigating Failure: Bankruptcy and Commercial Society in Antebellum America*. Chapel Hill: University of North Carolina Press.

Balleisen, Edward J. 2004. "Bankruptcy and the Entrepreneurial Ethos in Antebellum American Law," *Australian Journal of Legal History* 8: 61–82.

Bandelj, Nina. 2008. *From Communists to Foreign Capitalists: The Social*

Foundations of Foreign Direct Investment in Postsocialist Europe. Princeton: Princeton University Press.

Bank for International Settlements. 2009. *OTC Derivatives Market Activity in the Second Half of 2008*. Basel: BIS.

Bar-Gill, Oren and Lucian Bebchuk. 2002. "Misreporting Corporate Performance," Working Paper No. 400, Harvard Olin Center for Law, Economics, and Business, Cambridge, MA.

Bebchuk, Lucian and Jesse Fried. 2003. "Executive Compensation as an Agency Problem," *The Journal of Economic Perspectives* 17(3): 71–92.

Bebchuk, Lucian and Jesse Fried. 2004. *Pay without Performance: The Unfulfilled Promise of Executive Compensation*. Cambridge, MA: Harvard University Press.

Belk, Russell W. and Melanie Wallendorf. 1990. "The Sacred Meanings of Money," *Journal of Economic Psychology* 11: 35–67.

Benería, Lourdes and Martha Roldán. 1992. *Las encrucijadas de clase y género*. Fondo de cultura económica ed. México: El colegio de México.

Bensel, Richard Franklin. 1990. *Yankee Leviathan: The Origins of Central State Authority in America, 1859–1877*. Cambridge: Cambridge University Press.

Bergengren, Roy F. 1937. "Cooperative Credit," *Annals of the American Academy of Political and Social Science* 191: 144–8.

Berger, Allen N. and Gregory F. Udell. 2002. "Small Business Credit Availability and Relationship Lending: The Importance of Bank Organisational Structure," *The Economic Journal* 112(477): F32–F53.

Berle, Adolf A. and Gardiner C. Means. 1968. *The Modern Corporation and Private Property*. New York: Harcourt, Brace & World.

Biggart, Nicole Woolsey. 2001. "Banking on Each Other: The Situation Logic of Rotating Savings and Credit Associations," *Advances in Qualitative Organization Research* 3: 129–53.

Billings, Dwight B. and Kathleen M. Blee. 2000. *The Road to Poverty: The Making of Wealth and Hardship in Appalachia*. Cambridge: Cambridge University Press.

Bird, Edward J., Paul A. Hagstrom, and Robert Wild. 1999. "Credit Card Debts of the Poor: High and Rising," *Journal of Policy Analysis and Management* 18(1): 125–33.

Bloch, Maurice. 1989. "The Symbolism of Money in Imerina," pp. 165–90 in *Money and the Morality of Exchange*, Jonathan Parry and Maurice Bloch eds. Cambridge: Cambridge University Press.

Bloch, Maurice and Jonathan Parry. 1989. "Introduction: Money and the Morality of Exchange," pp. 1–32 in *Money and the Morality of Exchange*, Jonathan Parry and Maurice Bloch eds. Cambridge: Cambridge University Press.

Block, Fred. 2003. "Karl Polanyi and the Writing of *The Great Transformation*," *Theory and Society* 32(3): 275–306.

References

Bloomfield, Arthur. 1959. *Monetary Policy under the International Gold Standard: 1880–1914*. New York: Federal Reserve Bank of New York.

Bodenhorn, Howard. 2000. *A History of Banking in Antebellum America: Financial Markets and Economic Development in an Era of Nation-Building*. Cambridge: Cambridge University Press.

Bodenhorn, Howard. 2003. *State Banking in Early America: A New Economic History*. New York: Oxford University Press.

Bogue, Allan G. 1955. *Money at Interest: The Farm Mortgage on the Middle Border*. Ithaca, NY: Cornell University Press.

Bohannan, Paul. 1955. "Some Principles of Exchange and Investment among the Tiv," *American Antropologist* (New Series) 57(1): 60–70.

Bohannan, Paul. 1959. "The Impact of Money on an African Subsistence Economy," *The Journal of Economic History* 19(4): 491–503.

Boss, Michael, Helmut Elsinger, Martin Summer, and Stefan Thurner. 2004. "Network Topology of the Interbank Market," *Quantitative Finance* 4: 677–84.

Braudel, Fernand. 1979. *The Structures of Everyday Life*. Siân Reynolds tr. New York: Harper & Row.

Breen, T.H. 1985. *Tobacco Culture: The Mentality of the Great Tidewater Planters on the Eve of Revolution*. Princeton: Princeton University Press.

Brewer, H. Peers. 1976. "Eastern Money and Western Mortgages in the 1870s," *Business History Review* 50(3): 356–80.

Bruegel, Martin. 2002. *Farm, Shop, Landing: The Rise of Market Society in the Hudson Valley, 1780–1860*. Durham, NC: Duke University Press.

Bucks, Brian K., Arthur B. Kennickell, and Kevin B. Moore. 2006. "Recent Changes in U.S. Family Finances: Evidence from the 2001 and 2004 Survey of Consumer Finances," *Federal Reserve Bulletin* 2006: A1–A38.

Calavita, Kitty, Henry N. Pontell, and Robert H. Tillman. 1997. *Big Money Crime: Fraud and Politics in the Savings and Loan Crisis*. Berkeley: University of California Press.

Calavita, Kitty, Robert Tillman, and Henry Pontell. 1997. "The Savings and Loan Debacle, Financial Crime, and the State," *Annual Review of Sociology* 23: 19–38.

Calder, Bobby J. and Barry M. Staw. 1975. "Self-Perception of Intrinsic and Extrinsic Motivation," *Journal of Personality and Social Psychology* 31(4): 599–605.

Calder, Lendol. 1999. *Financing the American Dream: A Cultural History of Consumer Credit*. Princeton: Princeton University Press.

Callon, Michel. 1998. "Introduction: The Embeddedness of Economic Markets in Economics," pp. 1–57 in *The Laws of the Markets*, Michel Callon ed. Oxford: Blackwell.

Calomiris, Charles W. 2000. *U.S. Bank Deregulation in Historical Perspective*. Cambridge: Cambridge University Press.

References

Calomiris, Charles W. and Carlos D. Ramirez. 1996. "The Role of Financial Relationships in the History of American Corporate Finance," *Journal of Applied Corporate Finance* 9: 52–73.

Campbell, John L. 1998. "Institutional Analysis and the Role of Ideas in Political Economy," *Theory and Society* 27(3): 377–409.

Campbell, John L. 2004. *Institutional Change and Globalization*. Princeton: Princeton University Press.

Carruthers, Bruce G. 1996. *City of Capital: Politics and Markets in the English Financial Revolution*. Princeton: Princeton University Press.

Carruthers, Bruce G. 2005. "The Sociology of Money and Credit," pp. 355–78 in *The Handbook of Economic Sociology*, 2nd edn, Neil J. Smelser and Richard Swedberg eds. Princeton: Princeton University Press and Russell Sage Foundation.

Carruthers, Bruce G. 2008. "Money and Society: Towards a Sociological Perspective." Unpublished paper, Evanston: Northwestern University.

Carruthers, Bruce G. and Sarah Babb. 1996. "The Color of Money and the Nature of Value: Greenbacks and Gold in Postbellum America," *American Journal of Sociology* 101(6): 1556–91.

Carruthers, Bruce G. and Sarah L. Babb. 2000. *Economy/Society: Markets, Meanings, and Social Structure*. Thousand Oaks, CA: Pine Forge Press.

Carruthers, Bruce G. and Wendy Nelson Espeland. 1998. "Money, Meaning, and Morality (Changing Forms of Payment)," *American Behavioral Scientist* 41(10): 1384–408.

Carruthers, Bruce G. and Arthur L. Stinchcombe. 2001. "The Social Structure of Liquidity: Flexibility in Markets, States, and Organizations," pp. 100–39 in *When Formality Works: Authority and Abstraction in Law and Organizations*, Arthur L. Stinchcombe. Chicago: University of Chicago Press.

Carsten, Janet. 1989. "Cooking Money: Gender and the Symbolic Transformation of Means of Exchange in a Malay Fishing Community," pp. 117–41 in *Money and the Morality of Exchange*, Jonathan Parry and Maurice Bloch eds. Cambridge: Cambridge University Press.

Caskey, John P. 1991. "Pawnbroking in America: The Economics of a Forgotten Credit Market," *Journal of Money, Credit and Banking* 23(1): 85–99.

Castilla, Emilio J. 2003. "Networks of Venture Capital Firms in Silicon Valley," *International Journal of Technology Management* 25(1/2): 113–32.

Cavalluzzo Ken, Linda Cavalluzzo, and John Wolken. 2002. "Competition, Small Business Financing, and Discrimination: Evidence from a New Survey," *Journal of Business* 75(4): 641–79.

Cellarius, Barbara A. 2000. "You Can Buy Almost Anything with Potatoes: An Examination of Barter during Economic Crisis in Bulgaria," *Ethnology* 39(1): 73–92.

Chandler, Lester V. 1971. *American Monetary Policy 1928–1941*. New York: Harper & Row.

References

Clark, Christopher. 1990. *The Roots of Rural Capitalism: Western Massachusetts, 1780–1860*. Ithaca, NY: Cornell University Press.

Clark, Evans. 1930. *Financing the Consumer*. New York: Harper & Bros.

Clarke, Sally H. 1994. *Regulation and the Revolution in United States Farm Productivity*. New York: Cambridge University Press.

Clarke, Sally H. 2007. *Trust and Power: Consumers, the Modern Corporation, and the Making of the United States Automobile Market*. New York: Cambridge University Press.

Clemens, Elisabeth S. and James M. Cook. 1999. "Politics and Institutionalism: Explaining Durability and Change," *Annual Review of Sociology* 25: 441–66.

Cohen, Jane Maslow. 1987. "Posnerism, Pluralism, Pessimism," *Boston University Law Review* 67: 105–75.

Cohen, Lizabeth. 2002. *A Consumers' Republic: The Politics of Mass Consumption in Postwar America*. New York: Knopf.

Coleman, Susan. 2000. "Access to Capital and Terms of Credit: A Comparison of Men- and Women-Owned Small Businesses," *Journal of Small Business Management* 38(3): 37–52.

Core, John E., Robert W. Holthausen, and David F. Larcker. 1999. "Corporate Governance, Chief Executive Compensation, and Firm Performance," *Journal of Financial Economics* 51(3): 371–406.

Craig, Ben R., William E. Jackson III, and James B. Thomson. 2007. "Small Firm Finance, Credit Rationing, and the Impact of SBA-Guaranteed Lending on Local Economic Growth," *Journal of Small Business Management* 45(1): 116–132.

Cross, Gary. 1993. *Time and Money: The Making of Consumer Culture*. London: Routledge.

Crossney, Kristen B. and David W. Bartelt. 2005. "The Legacy of the Home Owners' Loan Corporation," *Housing Policy Debate* 16(3/4): 547–74.

Crowther, David, Anne-Marie Greene, and Dian Marie Hosking. 2002. "Local Economic Trading Schemes and Their Implications for Marketing Assumptions, Concepts and Practices," *Management Decision* 40(4): 354–62.

Davis, Gerald F. 1991. "Agents without Principles? The Spread of the Poison Pill through the Intercorporate Network," *Administrative Science Quarterly* 36: 583–613.

Davis, Gerald F. 2009. *Managed by the Markets: How Finance Re-Shaped America*. New York: Oxford University Press.

Davis, Lance E. and Robert J. Cull. 1994. *International Capital Markets and American Economic Growth, 1820–1914*. Cambridge: Cambridge University Press.

Demski, Joel S. 2003. "Corporate Conflicts of Interest," *The Journal of Economic Perspectives* 17(2): 51–72.

Dickenson, Donna. 1997. *Property, Women and Politics: Subjects or Objects?* New Brunswick, NJ: Rutgers University Press.

References

Dominguez, Virginia R. 1990. "Representing Value and the Value of Representation: A Different Look at Money," *Cultural Anthropology* 5(1): 16–44.

Dynan, Karen E. and Donald L. Kohn. 2007. "The Rise in U.S. Household Indebtedness: Causes and Consequences," Federal Reserve Board Finance and Economics Discussion Series Working Paper 2007-37, Federal Reserve Board, Washington, D.C.

Earle, Peter. 1989. *The Making of the English Middle Class: Business, Society and Family Life in London, 1660–1730*. Berkeley: University of California Press.

Edwards, Franklin R. and Frederic S. Mishkin. 1995. "The Decline of Traditional Banking: Implications for Financial Stability and and Regulatory Policy," *Economic Policy Review* 1(2): 27–45.

Edwards, Sebastian. 2002. "Capital Mobility, Capital Controls, and Globalization in the Twenty-First Century," *Annals of the American Academy of Political and Social Science* 579: 261–70.

Eichengreen, Barry. 1984. "Mortgage Interest Rates in the Populist Era," *American Economic Review* 74(5): 995–1015.

Eichengreen, Barry. 1996. *Globalizing Capital: A History of the International Monetary System*. Princeton: Princeton University Press.

Eichenwald, Kurt. 2002. "Enron's Collapse: Audacious Climb to Success Ended in a Dizzying Plunge," *NYTimes.com*, January 13, 2002, http://www.nytimes.com/2002/01/13/us/enron-s-collapse-audacious-climb-to-success-ended-in-a-dizzying-plunge.html?scp=1&sq=ENRON%27S%20COLLAPSE:%20Audacious%20Climb&st=cse, accessed on September 16, 2009.

Einzig, Paul. 1966. *Primitive Money*. Oxford: Pergamon.

El Qorchi, Mohammed, Samuel Munzele Maimbo, and John F. Wilson. 2003. *Informal Funds Transfer Systems: An Analysis of the Informal Hawala System*. Washington, D.C.: International Monetary Fund and World Bank.

Espeland, Wendy Nelson. 1998. *The Struggle for Water: Politics, Rationality, and Identity in the American Southwest*. Chicago: University of Chicago Press.

Espeland, Wendy Nelson and Mitchell Stevens. 1998. "Commensuration as a Social Process," *Annual Review of Sociology* 24: 313–43.

Etzion, Dror and Gerald F. Davis. 2008. "Revolving Doors? A Network Analysis of Corporate Officers and U.S. Government Officials," *Journal of Management Inquiry* 17(3): 157–61.

Evans, David S. and Richard Schmalensee. 2005. *Paying with Plastic: The Digital Revolution in Buying and Borrowing*, 2nd edn. Cambridge, MA: MIT Press.

Falola, Toyin. 1995. "Money and Informal Credit Institutions in Colonial Western Nigeria," pp. 162–87 in *Money Matters: Instability, Values and Social Payments in the Modern History of West African Communities*, Jane I. Guyer ed. Portsmouth, N.H.: Heinemann.

References

Federal Reserve Board. 1992. "Changes in Family Finances from 1983 to 1989," *Federal Reserve Bulletin*, January.

Federal Reserve Board. 2005. "Recent Developments in the Credit Card Market and the Financial Obligations Ratio," *Federal Reserve Bulletin*, Autumn.

Federal Reserve Board. 2006. "Recent Changes in U.S. Family Finances: Evidence from the 2001 and 2004 Survey of Consumer Finances," *Federal Reserve Bulletin*, March.

Ferguson, Niall. 2001. *The Cash Nexus: Money and Power in the Modern World*. New York: Basic Books.

Financial Accounting Standards Board. 2007. *FACTSaboutFASB*. http://www.fasb.org/facts/facts_about_fasb.pdf, accessed on September 16, 2009.

Finn, Margot C. 2003. *The Character of Credit: Personal Debt in English Culture, 1740–1914*. Cambridge: Cambridge University Press.

Firth, Raymond. 1967. "Themes in Economic Anthropology: A General Comment," pp. 1–28 in *Themes in Economic Anthropology*, Raymond Firth ed. London: Tavistock, ASA Monograph 6.

Foster, William Trufant. 1941. "The Personal Finance Business under Regulation," *Law and Contemporary Problems* 8(1): 154–72.

Frame, W. Scott, Aruna Srinivasan, and Lynn Woosley. 2001. "The Effect of Credit Scoring on Small-Business Lending," *Journal of Money, Credit and Banking* 33(3): 813–25.

Frederiksen, D.M. 1894. "Mortgage Banking in America," *Journal of Political Economy* 2(2): 203–34.

French, David M. 1941. "The Contest for a National System of Home-Mortgage Finance," *American Political Science Review* 35(1): 53–69.

Frieden, Jeffry A. 1991. "The Politics of National Policies in a World of Global Finance," *International Organization* 45(4): 425–51.

Friedman, Milton and Anna Jacobson Schwartz. 1963. *A Monetary History of the United States, 1867–1960*. Princeton: Princeton University Press.

Froman, Lewis A. 1935. "Credit Unions," *Journal of Business* 8(3): 284–96.

Frydman, Carola and Raven E. Saks. 2007. "Executive Compensation: A New View from a Long-Term Perspective, 1936–2005," Federal Reserve Board Finance and Economics Discussion Series Working Paper 2007-35, Federal Reserve Board, Washington, D.C.

Furnham, Adrian and Michael Argyle. 1998. *The Psychology of Money*. London: Routledge.

Furnham, Adrian and Alan Lewis. 1986. *The Economic Mind: The Social Psychology of Economic Behavior*. New York: St. Martin's Press.

Garrett, Geoffrey and Peter Lange. 1991. "Political Responses to Interdependence : What's 'Left' for the Left?," *International Organization* 45(4): 539–64.

Garrett, Geoffrey and Deborah Mitchell. 2001. "Globalization, Government Spending and Taxation in the OECD," *European Journal of Political Research* 39: 145–77.

References

Gelpi, Rosa-Maria and François Julien-Labruyère. 2000. *The History of Consumer Credit: Doctrines and Practices*, Mn Liam Gavin tr. London: Macmillan Press.

Gilpin, Robert. 2000. *The Challenge of Global Capitalism: The World Economy in the 21st Century*. Princeton: Princeton University Press.

Glasberg, Davita Silfen and Dan Skidmore. 1997. "The Dialectics of State Economic Intervention: Bank Deregulation and the Savings and Loan Bailout," *Sociological Quarterly* 38(1): 67–93.

Good, Barbara A. 1998. "Private Money: Everything Old is New Again," *Federal Reserve Bank of Cleveland: Economic Commentary* April 1, 1998: 1–4.

Goodman, John B. and Louis W. Pauly. 1993. "The Obsolescence of Capital Controls? Economic Management in an Age of Global Markets," *World Politics* 46(1): 50–82.

Goodman, Paul. 1993. "The Emergence of Homestead Exemptions in the United States: Accommodation and Resistance to the Market Revolution, 1840–1880," *Journal of American History* 80(2): 470–98.

Goodman, Peter S. 2008. "The Reckoning: Taking Hard New Look at a Greenspan Legacy," *NYTimes.com*, October 9, 2008, http://www.nytimes.com/2008/10/09/business/economy/09greenspan.html, accessed on September 16, 2009.

Goody, Jack. 2004. *Capitalism and Modernity: The Great Debate*. Cambridge: Polity Press.

Gowa, Joanne S. 1983. *Closing the Gold Window: Domestic Politics and the End of Bretton Woods*. Ithaca, N.Y.: Cornell University Press.

Granovetter, Mark. 1992. "Economic Action and Social Structure: The Problem of Embeddedness," pp. 53–81 in *The Sociology of Economic Life*, Mark Granovetter and Richard Swedberg eds. Boulder, CO: Westview Press.

Green, Richard K. and Susan M. Wachter. 2005. "The American Mortgage in Historical and International Context," *Journal of Economic Perspectives* 19(4): 93–114.

Grimes, William A. 1926. *Financing Automobile Sales by the Time-Payment Plan*. Chicago: A.W. Shaw.

Guillén, Mauro F. 2001. "Is Globalization Civilizing, Destructive or Feeble? A Critique of Five Key Debates in the Social Science Literature," *Annual Review of Sociology* 27: 235–60.

Gulati, Ranjay. 1998. "Alliances and Networks," *Strategic Management Journal* 19(4): 293–317.

Guseva, Alya. 2008. *Into the Red: The Birth of the Credit Card Market in Postcommunist Russia*. Stanford: Stanford University Press.

Guyer, Jane I. 1995. "Introduction," pp. 1–33 in *Money Matters: Instability, Values and Social Payments in the Modern History of West African Communities*, Jane I. Guyer ed. Portsmouth, N.H.: Heinemann.

Guyer, Jane I. 2004. *Marginal Gains: Monetary Transactions in Atlantic Africa*. Chicago: University of Chicago Press.

References

Haller, Mark H. and John V. Alviti. 1977. "Loansharking in American Cities: Historical Analysis of a Marginal Enterprise," *American Journal of Legal History* 21(2): 125–56.

Ham, Arthur H. 1912. "Remedial Loans: A Constructive Program," *Proceedings of the Academy of Political Science in the City of New York* 2(2): 109–17.

Ham, Arthur H. and Leonard G. Robinson. 1923. *A Credit Union Primer*, rev. edn. New York: Russell Sage Foundation.

Hancock, David. 1995. *Citizens of the World: London Merchants and the Integration of the British Atlantic Community, 1735–1785*. Cambridge: Cambridge University Press.

Hansen, Bradley A. and Mary Eschelbach Hansen. 2005. "The Role of Path Dependence in the Development of U.S. Bankruptcy Law, 1880–1938," *Journal of Institutional Economics* 3(2): 203–25.

Harvard Law Review. 2002. "Corporate Law: Congress Passes Corporate and Accounting Fraud Legislation. Sarbanes–Oxley Act of 2002," *Harvard Law Review* 116(2): 728–34.

Healy, Kieran. 2006. *Last Best Gifts: Altruism and the Market for Human Blood and Organs*. Chicago: University of Chicago Press.

Heath, Chip and Jack B. Soll. 1996. "Mental Budgeting and Consumer Decisions," *The Journal of Consumer Research* 23(1): 40–52.

Heclo, Hugh. 1974. *Modern Social Politics in Britain and Sweden: From Relief to Income Maintenance*. New Haven: Yale University Press.

Helleiner, Eric. 2003. *The Making of National Money: Territorial Currencies in Historical Perspective*. Ithaca, N.Y.: Cornell University Press.

Hert, Arthur H. 1938. "Charge Accounts of Retail Merchants," *Annals of the American Academy of Political and Social Science* 196: 111–20.

Hoagland, Edward. 2002. *Notes from the Century Before: A Journal from British Columbia*. New York: Modern Library.

Hodson, Clarence. 1919. *Anti-Loan Shark License Laws and Economics of the Small-Loan Business*. New York: Legal Reform Bureau.

Hoigard, Cecilie and Liv Finstad. 1992. *Backstreets: Prostitution, Money and Love*. Cambridge: Polity Press.

Howard, Christopher. 1997. *The Hidden Welfare State: Tax Expenditures and Social Policy in the United States*. Princeton: Princeton University Press.

Howgego, Christopher. 1992. "The Supply and Use of Money in the Roman World 200 B.C. to 300 A.D.," *Journal of Roman Studies* 82: 1–31.

Hunt, Edwin S. and James M. Murray. 1999. *A History of Business in Medieval Europe, 1200–1550*. Cambridge: Cambridge University Press.

Hunt, Robert M. 2005. "A Century of Consumer Credit Reporting in America," Federal Reserve Bank of Philadelphia Working Paper 05-13, Federal Reserve Bank of Philadelphia, Philadelphia.

Hurst, James Willard. 1973. *A Legal History of Money in the United States, 1774–1970*. Lincoln: University of Nebraska Press.

References

Ingham, Geoffrey. 2004. *The Nature of Money*. Cambridge: Polity Press.

Ingham, Geoffrey. 2008. *Capitalism*. Cambridge: Polity Press.

Jackson, Kenneth T. 1985. *Crabgrass Frontier: The Suburbanization of the United States*. New York: Oxford University Press.

Jackson, William E. and Chandra S. Mishra. 2007. "Small Enterprise Finance, Governance, and Imperfect Capital Markets: An Introduction to the Inaugural Office Depot Forum Special Issue," *Journal of Small Business Management* 45(1): 1–4.

Jacobs, Meg. 2005. *Pocketbook Politics: Economic Citizenship in Twentieth-Century America*. Princeton: Princeton University Press.

James, Harold. 2001. *The End of Globalization: Lessons from the Great Depression*. Cambridge, MA: Harvard University Press.

James, John A. 1978. *Money and Capital Markets in Postbellum America*. Princeton: Princeton University Press.

Jensen, Michael C. and William H. Meckling. 1976. "Theory of the Firm: Managerial Behavior, Agency Costs, and Ownership Structure," *Journal of Financial Economics* 3: 305–60.

Johnson, Juliet. 2000. *A Fistful of Rubles: The Rise and Fall of the Russian Banking System*. Ithaca, N.Y.: Cornell University Press.

Johnson, Roger T. 1999. *Historical Beginnings . . . The Federal Reserve*. Boston: Federal Reserve Bank of Boston.

Jones, Fred Mitchell. 1936. "Retail Stores in the United States, 1800–1860," *Journal of Marketing* 1(2): 134–42.

Kaye, Joel. 1998. *Economy and Nature in the Fourteenth Century: Money, Market Exchange, and the Emergence of Scientific Thought*. New York: Cambridge University Press.

Keehn, Richard H. and Gene Smiley. 1977. "Mortgage Lending by National Banks," *Business History Review* 51(4): 474–91.

Keister, Lisa A. 2002. "Financial Markets, Money, and Banking," *Annual Review of Sociology* 28: 39–61.

Keller, Morton. 1963. *The Life Insurance Enterprise, 1885–1910*. Cambridge, MA: Harvard University Press.

Keneally, Thomas. 1982. *Schindler's Ark*. London: Hodder & Stoughton.

Kerr, W.G. 1963. "Scotland and the Texas Mortgage Business," *Economic History Review* 16(1): 91–103.

Klassen, Henry C. 1992. "T.C. Power & Bro.: The Rise of a Small Western Department Store, 1870–1902," *Business History Review* 66(4): 671–722.

Knorr Cetina, Karin and Urs Bruegger. 2002. "Global Microstructures: The Virtual Societies of Financial Markets," *The American Journal of Sociology* 107(4): 905–50.

Konig, David Thomas. 1979. *Law and Society in Puritan Massachusetts, Essex County 1629–1692*. Chapel Hill: University of North Carolina Press.

Krasner, Stephen D. 1984. "Approaches to the State: Alternative Conceptions and Historical Dynamics," *Comparative Politics* 16(2): 223–46.

Krippner, Greta R. 2005. "The Financialization of the American Economy," *Socio-Economic Review* 3: 173–208.

Krippner, Greta R. and Anthony Alvarez. 2007. "Embeddedness and the Intellectual Projects of Economic Sociology,"*Annual Review of Sociology* 33: 219–40.

Krugman, Paul. 2009a. "Decade at Bernie's," *NYTimes.com*, February 16, 2009, http://www.nytimes.com/2009/02/16/opinion/16krugman.html, accessed on September 16, 2009.

Krugman, Paul. 2009b. "Who'll Stop the Pain?" *NYTimes.com*, February 20, 2009, http://www.nytimes.com/2009/02/20/opinion/20krugman.html, accessed on September 16, 2009.

Kulikoff, Allan. 1993. "Households and Markets: Toward a New Synthesis of American Agrarian History," *William and Mary Quarterly* 50(2): 342–55.

Kuran, Timur. 2004. *Islam and Mammon: The Economic Predicaments of Islamism*. Princeton: Princeton University Press.

Lamoreaux, Naomi. 1994. *Insider Lending: Banks, Personal Connections, and Economic Development in New England*. Cambridge: Cambridge University Press.

Langevoort, Donald C. 2003. "Managing the 'Expectations Gap' in Investor Protection: the SEC and the Post-Enron Reform Agenda," *Villanova Law Review* 48(4): 1139–65.

Le Goff, Jacques. 1988. *Your Money or Your Life: Economy and Religion in the Middle Ages*. New York: Zone Books.

Lea, Stephen E.G., Roger M. Tarpy, and Paul Webley. 1987. *The Individual in the Economy. A Survey of Economic Psychology*. Cambridge: Cambridge University Press.

Lev, Baruch. 2003. "Corporate Earnings: Facts and Fiction," *The Journal of Economic Perspectives* 17(2): 27–50.

Levitt, Barbara and James G. March. 1988. "Organizational Learning," *Annual Review of Sociology* 14: 319–40.

Lewis, Edward M. 1994. *An Introduction to Credit Scoring*, San Rafael: Athena Press.

Light, Ivan and Edna Bonacich. 1988. *Immigrant Entrepreneurs: Koreans in Los Angeles, 1965–1982*. Berkeley: University of California Press.

Light, Ivan. 1977. "Numbers Gambling among Blacks: A Financial Institution," *American Sociological Review* 42: 892–904.

Loriaux, Michael. 1991. *France after Hegemony: International Change and Financial Reform*. Ithaca, N.Y.: Cornell University Press.

Lublóy, Ágnes. 2006. "Topology of the Hungarian Large-Value Transfer System," Magyar Nemzeti Bank Occasional Papers 57, Magyar Nemzeti Bank, Budapest.

References

Lynd, Robert S. and Helen Merrell Lynd. 1929. *Middletown: A Study in Modern American Culture*. New York: Harcourt, Brace & Co.

Lynn, Robert A. 1957. "Installment Credit before 1870," *Business History Review* 31(4): 414–24.

McCormick, Michael. 2001. *Origins of the European Economy: Communications and Commerce, A.D. 300–900*. Cambridge: Cambridge University Press.

McFarlane, Larry A. 1983. "British Investment and the Land: Nebraska, 1877–1946," *Business History Review* 57(2): 258–72.

McGraw, A. Peter and Philip E. Tetlock. 2005. "Taboo Trade-Offs, Relational Framing, and the Acceptability of Exchanges," *Journal of Consumer Psychology* 15(1): 2–15.

MacKenzie, Donald. 2006. *An Engine, Not a Camera: How Financial Models Shape Markets*. Cambridge, MA: MIT Press.

MacKenzie, Donald and Yuval Millo. 2003. "Constructing a Market, Performing Theory: The Historical Sociology of a Financial Derivatives Exchange," *American Journal of Sociology* 109(1): 107–45.

Mann, Bruce H. 1987. *Neighbors and Strangers: Law and Community in Early Connecticut*. Chapel Hill: University of North Carolina Press.

Mann, Bruce H. 2002. *Republic of Debtors: Bankruptcy in the Age of American Independence*. Cambridge, MA: Harvard University Press.

Mann, Ronald J. 2006. *Charging Ahead: The Growth and Regulation of Payment Card Systems*. New York: Cambridge University Press.

March, James G. 1991. "Exploration and Exploitation in Organizational Learning," *Organization Science* 2(1): 71–87.

Martin, David. 1977. "The Changing Role of Foreign Money in the United States, 1782–1857," *Journal of Economic History* 37: 1009–27.

Marx, Karl. 1978. *The Marx–Engels Reader*, 2nd edn, Robert C. Tucker ed. New York: Norton.

Mason, David L. 2004. *From Buildings and Loans to Bail-Outs: A History of the American Savings and Loan Industry, 1831–1995*. Cambridge: Cambridge University Press.

Massey, Douglas S. and Nancy A. Denton. 1993. *American Apartheid: Segregation and the Making of the Underclass*. Cambridge, MA: Harvard University Press.

Maurer, Bill. 2006. "The Anthropology of Money," *Annual Review of Anthropology* 35: 15–36.

Melitz, Jacques. 1970. "The Polanyi School of Anthropology on Money: An Economist's View," *American Anthropologist* 72(5): 1020–40.

Mickel, Amy E. and Lisa A. Barron. 2008. "Getting 'More Bang for the Buck': Symbolic Value of Monetary Rewards in Organizations," *Journal of Management Inquiry* 17(4): 329–38.

Mihm, Stephen. 2007. *A Nation of Counterfeiters: Capitalists, Con Men, and the Making of the United States*. Cambridge, MA: Harvard University Press.

References

Miller, Margaret J. 2003. "Introduction," pp. 1–21 in *Credit Reporting Systems and the International Economy*, Margaret J. Miller ed. Cambridge, MA: MIT Press.

Mints, Lloyd W. 1945. *A History of Banking Theory in Great Britain and the United States*. Chicago: University of Chicago Press.

Mintz, Beth and Michael Schwartz. 1985. *The Power Structure of American Business*. Chicago: University of Chicago Press.

Mizruchi, Mark. 1996. "What Do Interlocks Do? An Analysis, Critique, and Assessment of Research on Interlocking Directorates," *Annual Review of Sociology* 22: 271–98.

Mizruchi, Mark S. and Linda Brewster Stearns. 1988. "A Longitudinal Study of the Formation of Interlocking Directorates," *Administrative Science Quarterly* 33(2): 194–210.

Moggridge, D.E. 1969. *The Return to Gold, 1925*. London: Cambridge University Press.

Moore, William H. 1949. "State Experiments in Mortgage Lending," *Journal of Business* 22(3): 169–77.

Morrison, Alan D. and William J. Wilhelm, Jr. 2007. *Investment Banking: Institutions, Politics, and Law*. Oxford: Oxford University Press.

Mosley, Layna. 2003. *Global Capital Markets and National Governments*. Cambridge: Cambridge University Press.

Moss, David A. and Sarah Brennan. 2001. "Managing Money Risk in Antebellum New York: From Chartered Banking to Free Banking and Beyond," *Studies in American Political Development* 15: 138–62.

Muldrew, Craig. 1998. *The Economy of Obligation: The Culture of Credit and Social Relations in Early Modern England*. New York: St. Martin's Press.

Muldrew, Craig. 2001. "'Hard Food for Midas': Cash and Its Social Value in Early Modern England," *Past and Present* 170: 78–120.

Munnell, Alicia H., Geoffrey M.B. Tootell, Lynn E. Browne, and James McEneaney. 1996. "Mortgage Lending in Boston: Interpreting HMDA Data," *American Economic Review* 86(1): 25–53.

Myers, Margaret G. 1970. *A Financial History of the United States*. New York: Columbia University Press.

Neifeld, M.R. 1931. "Credit Unions in the United States," *Journal of Business* 4(4): 320–45.

Nier, Erlend, Jing Yang, Tanju Yorulmazer, and Amadeo Alentorn. 2008. "Network Models and Financial Stability," Bank of England Working Paper 346, Bank of England, London.

Nightingale, Pamela. 1990. "Monetary Contraction and Mercantile Credit in Later Medieval England," *Economic History Review* 43: 560–75.

Nussbaum, Arthur. 1950. *Money in the Law: National and International*. Brooklyn, N.Y.: Foundation Press.

References

O'Curry, Suzanne. 1997. "Income source effects." Unpublished working paper, DePaul University, Chicago.

Ó Riain, Sean. 2000. "States and Markets in An Era of Globalization," *Annual Review of Sociology* 26: 187–213.

Obstfeld, Maurice and Alan M. Taylor. 2004. *Global Capital Markets: Integration, Crisis, and Growth*. Cambridge: Cambridge University Press.

Olegario, Rowena. 2003. "Credit Reporting Agencies: A Historical Perspective," pp. 115–60 in *Credit Reporting Systems and the International Economy*, Margaret J. Miller ed. Cambridge, MA: MIT Press.

Olmstead, Alan L. 1976. *New York City Mutual Savings Banks, 1819–1861*. Chapel Hill: University of North Carolina Press.

Olney, Martha L. 1989. "Credit as a Production-Smoothing Device: The Case of Automobiles, 1913–1938," *Journal of Economic History* 49(2): 377–91.

Olney, Martha L. 1999. "Avoiding Default: The Role of Credit in the Consumption Collapse of 1930," *Quarterly Journal of Economics* 114(1): 319–35.

Orren, Karen and Stephen Skowronek. 1994. "Beyond the Iconography of Order: Notes for a 'New' Institutionalism," pp. 311–32 in *The Dymanics of American Politics: Approaches and Interpretations,* Lawrence C. Dodd and Calvin Jillson eds. Boulder, CO: Westview Press.

Paddi, John B. 1938. "The Personal Loan Department of a Large Commercial Bank," *Annals of the American Academy of Political and Social Science* 196: 135–41.

Parker, Geoffrey. 1973. *The Emergence of Modern Finance in Europe, 1500–1730*. London: Fontana.

Parry, Jonathan. 1989. "On the Moral Perils of Exchange," pp. 64–93 in *Money and the Morality of Exchange,* Jonathan Parry and Maurice Bloch eds. Cambridge: Cambridge University Press.

Partnoy, Frank. 2003. *Infectious Greed: How Deceit and Risk Corrupted the Financial Markets*. New York: Holt.

Petersen, Mitchell A. and Raghuram G. Rajan. 1994. "The Benefits of Lending Relationships: Evidence from Small Business Data," *The Journal of Finance* 49(1): 3–37.

Polanyi, Karl. 1957a. "The Economy as Instituted Process," pp. 243–270 in *Trade and Market in the Early Empires*, Karl Polanyi, Conrad M. Arensberg, and Harry W. Pearson eds. Glencoe, IL: Free Press.

Polanyi, Karl. 1957b. *The Great Transformation: The Political and Economic Origins of Our Time*. Boston: Beacon Press.

Polanyi, Karl. 1968. "The Semantics of Money-Uses," pp. 175–203 in *Primitive, Archaic, and Modern Economies: Essays of Karl Polanyi*, George Dalton ed. Boston: Beacon Press.

Porter, Theodore M. 1995. *Trust in Numbers: The Pursuit of Objectivity in Science and Public Life*. Princeton: Princeton University Press.

References

Powell, Marvin A. 1996. "Money in Mesopotamia," *Journal of the Economic and Social History of the Orient* 39(3): 224–42.

Priest, Claire. 2001. "Currency Policies and Legal Development in Colonial New England," *Yale Law Journal* 110(8): 1303–405.

Reddy, William. 1984. *The Rise of Market Culture: The Textile Industry and French Society, 1750–1900*. Cambridge: Cambridge University Press.

Riesenfeld, Stefan A. 1973. "Enforcement of Money Judgments in Early American History," *Michigan Law Review* 71: 691–728.

Ritter, Gretchen. 1997. *Goldbugs and Greenbacks: The Antimonopoly Tradition and the Politics of Finance in America, 1865–1896*. Cambridge: Cambridge University Press.

Robb, Alicia M. and Robert W. Fairly. 2007. "Access to Financial Capital among U.S. Businesses: The Case of African American Firms," *The Annals of the American Academy of Political and Social Science* 613: 47–72.

Roe, Mark J. 1994. *The Political Roots of American Corporate Finance*. Princeton: Princeton University Press.

Roe, Mark J. 2004a. "The Inevitable Instability of American Corporate Governance," The Harvard John M. Olin Discussion Paper Series, Discussion Paper 493, Harvard John M. Olin Center for Law, Economics, and Business, Cambridge, MA.

Roe, Mark J. 2004b. "The Institutions of Corporate Governance," The Harvard John M. Olin Discussion Paper Series, Discussion Paper 488, Harvard John M. Olin Center for Law, Economics, and Business, Cambridge, MA.

Rogers, Douglas. 2005. "Moonshine, Money, and the Politics of Liquidity in Rural Russia," *American Ethnologist* 32(1): 63–81.

Rozman, David. 1927. "Land Credit in the Town of Newton, Manitowoc County, Wisconsin, 1848–1926," *Journal of Land and Public Utility Economics* 3(4): 371–84.

Ryan, Franklin W. 1930. "Family Finance in the United States," *Journal of Business* 3(4): 402–23.

Sandage, Scott A. 2005. *Born Losers: A History of Failure in America*. Cambridge, MA: Harvard University Press.

Sassen, Saskia. 2005. "The Embeddedness of Electronic Markets: The Case of Global Capital Markets," pp. 17–37 in *The Sociology of Financial Markets*, Karin Knorr Cetina and Alex Preda eds. Oxford: Oxford University Press.

Scheper-Hughes, Nancy. 2002a. "Commodity Fetishism in Organs Trafficking," pp. 31–62 in *Commodifying Bodies*, Nancy Scheper-Hughes and Loïc Wacquant eds. London: Sage.

Scheper-Hughes, Nancy. 2002b. "Bodies for Sale – Whole or in Parts," pp. 1–8 in *Commodifying Bodies*, Nancy Scheper-Hughes and Loïc Wacquant eds. London: Sage.

Scheper-Hughes, Nancy. 2004. "Parts Unknown. Undercover Ethnography of the Organs-Trafficking Underworld," *Ethnography* 5(1): 29–73.

References

Sellers, Charles. 1991. *The Market Revolution: Jacksonian America, 1815–1846.* New York: Oxford University Press.

Severson, Robert F., James F. Niss, and Richard D. Winkelman. 1966. "Mortgage Borrowing as a Frontier Developed: A Study of Mortgages in Champaign County, Illinois, 1836–1895," *Journal of Economic History* 26(2): 147–68.

Sewell, William H. Jr. 1992. "A Theory of Structure: Duality, Agency, and Transformation," *American Journal of Sociology* 98(1): 1–29.

Shammas, Carole. 1982. "Consumer Behavior in Colonial America," *Social Science History* 6(1): 67–86.

Shanley, Mary Lyndon. 2002. "Collaboration and Commodification in Assisted Procreation: Reflections on an Open Market and Anonymous Donation in Human Sperm and Eggs," *Law and Society Review* 36(2): 257–83.

Sharkey, Robert P. 1959. *Money, Class, and Party: An Economic Study of Civil War and Reconstruction.* Baltimore, MD: Johns Hopkins University Press.

Shih, Victor. 2004. "Dealing with Non-Performing Loans: Political Constraints and Financial Policies in China," *The China Quarterly* 180: 922–44.

Shipton, Parker. 1989. *Bitter Money: Cultural Economy and Some African Meanings of Forbidden Commodities.* Washington, D.C.: American Ethnological Society, Monograph Series, Number 1.

Silver, Beverly J. 2003. *Forces of Labor: Workers' Movements and Globalization since 1870.* Cambridge: Cambridge University Press.

Simmel, Georg. 1978. *The Philosophy of Money.* Tom Bottomore and David Frisby trs. London: Routledge & Kegan Paul.

Simon, Herbert A. 1982. *Models of Bounded Rationality: Behavioral Economics and Business Organization.* Cambridge, MA: MIT Press.

Simpson, A.W. Brian. 1986. *A History of the Land Law*, 2nd edn. Oxford: Oxford University Press.

Sinclair, Timothy J. 2005. *The New Masters of Capital: American Bond Rating Agencies and the Politics of Creditworthiness.* Ithaca, N.Y.: Cornell University Press.

Skeel, David A. Jr. 2001. *Debt's Dominion: A History of Bankruptcy Law in America.* Princeton: Princeton University Press.

Skowronek, Stephen. 1995. "Order and Change," *Polity* 28 (1): 91–6.

Smelser, Neil J. and Richard Swedberg. 1994. "The Sociological Perspective on the Economy," pp. 3–26 in *The Handbook of Economic Sociology*, Neil J. Smelser and Richard Swedberg eds. Princenton: Princeton University Press and Russell Sage Foundation.

Smith, Adam. 1976. *The Wealth of Nations.* Chicago: University of Chicago Press.

Snelders, H.M.J.J., Gönül Hussein, Stephen E.G. Lea, and Paul Webley. 1992. "The Polymorphous Concept of Money," *Journal of Economic Psychology* 13: 71–92.

References

Snowden, Kenneth A. 1988. "Mortgage Lending and American Urbanization, 1880–1890," *Journal of Economic History* 48(2): 273–85.

Spruyt, Hendrik. 1994. *The Sovereign State and Its Competitors.* Princeton: Princeton University Press.

Spufford, Peter. 1988. *Money and Its Use in Medieval Europe.* Cambridge: Cambridge University Press.

Spufford, Peter. 2003. *Power and Profit: The Merchant in Medieval Europe.* London: Thames & Hudson.

Stevenson, Richard W. and Jeff Gerth. 2002. "Enron's Collapse: The System; Web of Safeguards Failed as Enron Fell," *NYTimes.com*, January 20, 2002, http://www.nytimes.com/2002/01/20/us/enron-s-collapse-the-system-web-of-safeguards-failed-as-enron-fell.html?scp=1&sq=%E2%80%9CENRON%E2%80%99S%20COLLAPSE:%20THE%20SYSTEM&st=cse, accessed on September 16, 2009.

Stiglitz, Joseph. 1997. *Economics.* New York: R.S. Means Company.

Stiglitz, Joseph. 2000. "The Contributions of the Economics of Information to Twentieth-Century Economics," *Quarterly Journal of Economics* 115(4): 1441–78.

Stiglitz, Joseph and Andrew Weiss. 1981. "Credit Rationing in Markets with Imperfect Information," *American Economic Review* 71(3): 393–410.

Stinchcombe, Arthur L. 1990. *Information and Organizations.* Berkeley: University of California Press.

Stryker, Robin. 1998. "Globalization and the Welfare State," *The International Journal of Sociology and Social Policy* 18(2–4): 1–49.

Stuart, Guy. 2003. *Discriminating Risk: The U.S. Mortgage Lending Industry in the Twentieth Century.* Ithaca, N.Y.: Cornell University Press.

Sullivan, Teresa A., Elizabeth Warren, and Jay Lawrence Westbrook. 2000. *The Fragile Middle Class: Americans in Debt.* New Haven: Yale University Press.

Swank, Duane. 2002. *Global Capital, Political Institutions, and Policy Change in Developed Welfare States.* Cambridge: Cambridge University Press.

Swedberg, Richard and Mark Granovetter. 1992. "Introduction," pp. 1–26 in *The Sociology of Economic Life*, Mark Granovetter and Richard Swedberg, eds. Boulder, CO: Westview Press.

Sylla, Richard, John B. Legler, and John J. Wallis. 1987. "Banks and State Public Finance in the New Republic: The United States, 1790–1860," *Journal of Economic History* 74(2): 391–403.

Thaler, Richard H. 1985. "Mental Accounting and Consumer Choice," *Marketing Science* 4(3): 199–214.

Thaler, Richard H. 1999. "Mental Accounting Matters," *Journal of Behavioral Decision Making* 12: 183–206.

Thaler, Richard H. and H.M. Shefrin. 1981. "An Economic Theory of Self-Control," *The Journal of Political Economy* 89(2): 392–406.

References

Thelen, Kathleen. 1999. "Historical Institutionalism in Comparative Politics," *Annual Review of Political Science* 2: 369–404.

Thorp, Daniel B. 1991. "Doing Business in the Back-Country: Retail Trade in Colonial Rowan County, North Carolina," *William and Mary Quarterly* 48(3): 387–408.

Tober, Diane M. 2002. "Semen as Gift, Semen as Goods: Reproductive Workers and the Market in Altruism," pp. 137–60 in *Commodifying Bodies*, Nancy Scheper-Hughes and Loïc Wacquant eds. London: Sage.

Unger, Irwin. 1964. *The Greenback Era*. Princeton: Princeton University Press.

Uzzi, Brian. 1999. "Embeddedness in the Making of Financial Capital: How Social Relations and Networks Benefit Firms Seeking Financing," *American Sociological Review* 64(4): 481–505.

Valenze, Deborah. 2006. *The Social Life of Money in the English Past*. Cambridge: Cambridge University Press.

Verhulst, Adriaan. 2002. *The Carolingian Economy*. Cambridge: Cambridge University Press.

Vilar, Pierre. 1976. *A History of Gold and Money, 1450–1920*. London: Verso.

Vogel, Hans Ulrich and Sabine Hieronymus. 1993. "Cowry Trade and Its Role in the Economy of Yünnan: From the Ninth to the Mid-Seventeenth Century. Part I," *Journal of the Economic and Social History of the Orient* 36(3): 211–52.

Wang, Yanbo. 2008. "Evaluation or Attention: How Do Social Ties Matter in Venture Financing?" Unpublished paper presented at the MIT–Harvard Economic Sociology Seminar, December 11.

Warde, Ibrahim. 2000. *Islamic Finance in the Global Economy*. Edinburgh: Edinburgh University Press.

Wasserman, Stanley and Katherine Faust. 1994. *Social Network Analysis: Methods and Applications*. Cambridge: Cambridge University Press.

Watts, Duncan J. 1999. *Small Worlds: The Dynamics of Networks between Order and Randomness*. Princeton: Princeton University Press.

Weber, Max. 1978. *Economy and Society*, Guenther Roth and Claus Wittich eds. Berkeley: University of California Press.

Webley, Paul and Stephen E.G. Lea. 1993. "The Partial Unacceptability of Money in Repayment for Neighborly Help," *Human Relations* 46: 65–76.

Webley, Paul, Stephen E.G. Lea and R. Portalska. 1983. "The Unacceptability of Money as a Gift," *Journal of Economic Psychology*. 4: 223–38.

White, Edward. 1909. "Farm Lands as Security for Investment," *Bankers' Magazine* 79(4): 592–4.

White, Eugene Nelson. 1981."State-Sponsored Insurance of Bank Deposits in the United States, 1907–1929," *Journal of Economic History* 41(3): 537–57.

White, Eugene Nelson. 1982."The Political Economy of Banking Regulation, 1864–1933," *Journal of Economic History* 42(1): 33–40.

References

Wilson, Scott. 1997. "The Cash Nexus and Social Networks: Mutual Aid and Gifts in Contemporary Shanghai Villages," *The China Journal* 37: 91–112.

Witt, Susan and Christopher Lindstrom. 2004. "Local Currencies in the 21st Century," *In Business* July/August 2004: 24–7.

Wittgenstein, Ludwig. 1958. *Philosophical Investigations*. Oxford: Blackwell.

Woloson, Wendy A. 2007. "In Hock: Pawning in Early America," *Journal of the Early Republic* 27: 35–81.

Woo, Jung-en. 1991. *Race to the Swift: State and Finance in Korean Industrialization*. New York: Studies of the East Asian Institute, Columbia University Press.

Wood, Diana. 2002. *Medieval Economic Thought*. Cambridge: Cambridge University Press.

Woodman, Harold D. 1995. *New South – New Law: The Legal Foundations of Credit and Labor Relations in the Postbellum Agricultural South*. Baton Rouge: Louisiana State University Press.

Woodruff, David. 1999. *Money Unmade: Barter and the Fate of Russian Capitalism*. Ithaca, NY: Cornell University Press.

Wray, L. Randall. 1998. *Understanding Modern Money: The Key to Full Employment and Price Stability*. Cheltenham, UK: Edward Elgar.

Yinger, John. 1995. *Closed Doors, Opportunities Lost: The Continuing Costs of Housing Discrimination*. New York: Russell Sage Foundation.

Zajac, Edward J. and James D. Westphal. 1995. "Accounting for the Explanations of CEO Compensation: Substance and Symbolism," *Administrative Science Quarterly* 40(2): 283–308.

Zelizer, Viviana A. 1989. "The Social Meaning of Money: 'Special Monies,'" *The American Journal of Sociology* 95(2): 342–77.

Zelizer, Viviana A. 1994. *The Social Meaning of Money: Pin Money, Paychecks, Poor Relief and Other Currencies*. New York: Basic Books.

Zelizer, Viviana A. 1996. "Payments and Social Ties," *Sociological Forum* 11(3): 481–95.

Zelizer, Viviana A. 2005. *The Purchase of Intimacy*. Princeton and Oxford: Princeton University Press.

Zysman, John. 1983. *Governments, Markets, and Growth: Financial Systems and the Politics of Industrial Change*. Ithaca, N.Y.: Cornell University Press.

Index

Index

Index

Index

Index

Index

Index

Index

Index

quantification 13, 69

R.G. Dun 111
racial inequality 67, 105–6, 155–6, 172, 183
Rajan, Raghuram, G. 152, 175
Ramirez, Carlos D, 135
rationality/rationalization 13, 15, 110
"real bills" 37–8
real estate 90, 91, 94, 133, 166, 183
Reddy, William 68–9
regulation
    financial and monetary regulation 10–11, 41, 142–4
    financial regulatory agencies 17, 102, 130, 143–4, 148, 174–5
    regulatory interventions 87–8, 93, 145–6, 160, 162, 168
Regulation Q 40
relationships 69–76
    credit 99, 171, 172
    employment 68–70, 73, 170
    social 8–9, 23, 66–74, 75, 102, 124–8, 152–4, 169–70, 175
religion 5–6, 12, 25, 63–4
reproduction 183
reputation-based method (for assessing creditworthiness) 97, 171
reserve requirements 133, 134
retirement perks 141
"revolving credit" 108
Rhode Island 100
Riesenfeld, Stefan A. 91
risk 61–2, 117, 136, 151, 176
Ritter, Gretchen 34
Robb, Alicia M. 155–6
Robinson, Leonard G. 100
Roe, Mark J. 123, 132, 134, 135, 136, 139, 140, 144, 175
Rogers, Douglas 54–6
Roldán, Martha 61
Roosevelt, Franklin Delano 39, 102, 107
rotating credit associations 113–14
Route 128 153
Royal Bank of Scotland 1
Russell Sage Foundation 99, 100
Russia 10, 20, 47, 54–5, 112–13, 157
Ryan, Franklin W. 100

Sacs, Raven E. 140, 174
salt 13, 23, 89
Sandage, Scott A. 110

Sarbanes–Oxley Act of 2002 141, 148–9, 175, 184
Sassen, Saskia 18
sausages 47
savings 20–1, 84, 159, 168, 172, 173, 175, 178
savings accounts 40, 54
savings-and-loans 11, 103–4
    savings-and-loans crisis 3, 40, 119–20, 146, 173, 183
Scheper-Hughes, Nancy 74–6
Schindler's List 51
Schmalensee, Richard 108, 109, 110, 112
Schwartz, Anna Jacobson 31, 37, 38, 39
Schwartz, Michael 19, 129, 136–8, 177
Second Bank of the United States 132
securities 17–18, 39, 122, 129, 135, 173
Securities and Exchange Commission (SEC) 11, 40, 142, 143, 144, 145, 147, 148, 174
Securities Exchange Act of 1934 149
securitization 2, 18, 93, 118, 135, 136, 172
Sellers, Charles 86, 93
September 11th 47–8
Sepych, Russia 55
Severson, Robert F. 92
Sewell, William H., Jr. 180
Shammas, Carole 87
Shanley, Mary Lyndon 67
shareholders 3, 139, 140, 141, 143, 148, 162, 174, 175, 178
Sharkey, Robert P. 31, 33
shells 7, 13, 23, 53
Shih, Victor 131
Shipton, Parker 15, 63, 65
Silicon Valley 153–4
silver 5, 7, 26, 35–6, 167
Silver, Beverly J. 160
Simmel, Georg 15, 52, 69, 71, 76, 80
Simpson, A.W. Brian 90
Sinclair, Timothy J. 161, 173
Skeel, David A., Jr. 115, 116
Skidmore, Dan 40
Skowronek, Stephen 179, 180
slaves 26, 53, 93
Small Business Administration (SBA) 151, 175
small businesses 21, 112, 122, 123, 149–56, 162, 175, 178

213

Index

Index

United Kingdom 1, 25, 33, 56, 58–9, 129
United States
  banks 1, 9, 28, 30–3, 36–7, 39–40, 87, 132–8, 179
  corporate governance 123, 138–42, 144, 147–8, 174–5
  foreign lending 38–9, 130
  history of money 25, 28–41, 43, 167–8
  see also credit; mortgages
United States household saving rate 20–1
usury 11, 15, 99, 109–10
  Church's prohibition of 5–6, 12, 25
Uzzi, Brian 9, 123, 152–3, 175, 177

Valenze, Deborah 25
value 6, 7, 13, 28–9, 70–1
  "intrinsic value" 25, 35, 77–9, 81, 103, 106
  "maximum shareholder value" 121, 174
  monetary values 3–4, 6, 12–13, 25, 34
  pricelessness 3, 14, 66–7, 77–8, 1
  quantitative values 13, 52, 169
  social 20, 52, 170
  symbolic as well as material value 5, 20, 52, 53–4, 170
venture capitalism 153–4, 175
Verhulst, Adriaan 24, 27
Veterans' Administration (VA) 103
Vilar, Pierre 27
virtual money 49
Visa 109, 113, 118
Vogel, Hans Ulrich 23

Wachter, Susan M. 104
wages see CEO compensation; compensation; earnings
Wall Street Journal 1

Wallendorf, Melanie 52, 53, 56, 62, 65, 66
Wang, Yanbo 154, 175
Warde, Ibrahim 25
warfare 26
Wasserman, Stanley 18
Watts, Duncan J. 19
wealth 90, 140, 160, 170
Weber, Max 13, 124
Webley, Paul 56, 66, 68
Weiss, Andrew 151
welfare state 123, 160–1, 178
Western Union 114
Westphal, James D. 140, 174
White, Eugene Nelson 133, 134, 179
White, Harry Dexter 41
Wilhelm, William J. 129, 135
Wilson, Scott 169
winnings 5
Witt, Susan 47
Wittgenstein, Ludwig 58
Woloson, Wendy A. 98
women 5, 55–6, 59, 60–1, 65–6, 110, 155
Woo, Jung-en 130–1, 173
Wood, Diana 24, 25, 26, 167
Woodman, Harold D. 93–4
Woodruff, David 47
World Bank 17, 20, 41–2, 43, 168
World Trade Organization (WTO) 42
World War II 95
Wray, L. Randall 13

Yavapai tribe 77–8
Yinger, John 105
Yugoslavia 6

Zajac, Edward J. 140, 174
Zelizer, Viviana A. 16, 51, 59–62, 68, 72–3, 80, 169–70
Zhu Rongji 131
Zimbabwe 6
Zysman, John 129, 130, 172, 183